34951342

Seeing in the Dark

Seeing

Yale University Press · New Haven and London

Bert O. States

in the Dark

Reflections on Dreams and Dreaming

Earlier version of parts of this
book appeared as the following:
"Authorship in Dreams and Fictions,"
Dreaming 4, no. 4 (December 1994),
237–253; "Dreaming 'Accidentally' of
Harold Pinter: The Interplay of
Metaphor and Metonymy in Dreams,"
Dreaming 5, no. 4 (December 1995),
229–245 (© 1994, Association for the
Study of Dreams); "The Death of the
Finch," *Hudson Review* (Spring 1996),
30–42. I thank the editors of these
journals for permission to reprint the
essays here in revised form.
"The Death of a Toad," from
Ceremony and Other Poems, © 1950
and renewed 1978 by Richard Wilbur
is reprinted by permission of
Harcourt Brace and Company.

Designed by Sonia L. Scanlon.
Set in Simoncini Garamond type by
Tseng Information Systems, Inc.,
Durham, North Carolina.
Printed in the United States of
America by Vail-Ballou Press,
Binghamton, New York.

Library of Congress
Cataloging-in-Publication Data
States, Bert O., 1929–
Seeing in the dark : reflections on
dreams and dreaming / Bert O. States.
p. cm.
Includes bibliographical references
and index.
ISBN 0-300-06910-3
1. Dreams.   I. Title.
BF1078.S675   1997
154.6'3—dc20   96-20997
                                        CIP

10 9 8 7 6 5 4 3 2 1

For Paul Hernadi

'Tis strange! I saw the Skies;
I saw the Hills before mine Eys;
The Sparrow fly;
The lands that did about me ly;
The real Sun, *that* hev'nly Ey!
Can closed Eys ev'n in the darkest Night
See throu their Lids, and be informed with Sight?

—Thomas Traherne, "Dreams"

Contents

Contents

The evidentiary problem in writing about dreams is notorious. There is no artifact that can be shared, no direct means of examination, and no way to prove a hypothesis—including the claim that we actually experience our dreams. (I examine this problem in chapters 3 and 9.) In short, the object of inquiry does not exist. The only hope is that the memory of having dreamed will serve as a verifier of the experience and that intuitive agreement might be achieved by the study of sample dreams that can be reflected against the reader's own experience. As a consequence, the "argument" of my book does not proceed in interlocking stages, each chapter building on the previous one, to a summarizing conclusion. Indeed, the book closes with a chapter that is as close to memoir as it is to theory or hypothesis. I take some comfort in the precedent that a good deal of phenomenological description flirts with autobiography; that is, it relies on firsthand intuitive experience as the source of its evidence, and in doing so it engages in what Maurice Natanson calls "methodological solipsism" (1974, 243). My perspective, in the main, is phenomenological, in the loose sense that poetry can be considered a species of phenomenology. The business of poetry, as Shelley puts it in the *Defense,* is to compel us "to feel that which we perceive, and to imagine that which we know." The poet "purges from our inward sight the film of familiarity which obscures from us the wonder of our being" (1890, 42). This passage may seem dated, but it is effectively what Victor Shklovsky was saying about art in his famous essay of 1917 on "defamiliarization" (1965). To put it another way, phenomenology, as Bruce Wilshire says, is "the systematic attempt to unmask the obvious" (1982, 11), and I think much the same thing could be said about poetry, if not all art.

Few human experiences are, in one sense, as "obvious" as the dream; unmasking the dream in objective scientific language may be possible, but I doubt that the result would be of much interest to dreamers. I find myself continually resorting to the figural and analogical techniques of poetry as a means of clarifying the experience of dreaming to the extent that I can for readers who may have wondered about the same questions respecting their own dream life. Though the chapters could probably be read in almost any order without serious confusion, they build on each other in complementary ways. Thus by the word *reflections* in the subtitle I refer not only to my own thoughts on each subject but also to the reciprocal way I hope they reflect on and enlarge each other. I think of the book as being cubistic in design, as if one were looking into a room through various windows and seeing the same interior from different points of view.

Two close friends and colleagues have been particularly influential in the thinking and planning that have gone into the book: Dan McCall of Cornell University and Paul Hernadi of the University of California at Santa Barbara.

Seeing in the Dark

Introduction

This book is concerned primarily with the transit of waking experience into dreams and secondarily with the relation between dreams and fictions written in the light of day. But one of my assumptions is that whatever fictions do with our experience was done first in the dream. By this I mean simply that the dream and art, in all its varieties, are manifestations of the same biological need to convert experience into structure and that dreaming, in all likelihood, preceded art-making in historical priority. If the structures produced are different, in either case, the differences have to do mainly with the conditions of creation. These chiefly involve the physiological differences between sleep and the waking state and the personal versus social ends served by dream and art, respectively. In any case, the need to produce both dreams and art seems to me biologically based.

This is a notion I hold with some deference to biologists because I am a literary theorist by trade, albeit one with a lifelong interest in science. But all my reading suggests that we have kept biology and literature apart for an unnecessarily long time and that there is much to be gained by seeing what biological theory may have in common with aesthetic and literary theory. The best, or at least most enduring, explanation that literary people have made for the purpose of art is that it is "useful and pleasing," *utile et dulce,* a doctrine that originates mainly with Horace and can probably still be considered the ongoing received theory. Usefulness, when it is defined at all, normally implies a more or less educational function whereby we learn to be better persons through our experience with art; pleasure usually implies that we enjoy being moved by the images of art and, in the worst versions of the idea, that art is a kind of sugar-coating that makes the lesson of the pill easier to swallow.

Yet the world does not seem to have gotten any better over the centuries, and one can't even claim that people who are exposed to a great deal of art are morally or ethically or in any other way better than people who aren't. They may be more sensitive to the nuances of experience, but it would be hard to defend even that assertion. A few years ago the Center for the Neurobiology of Learning and Memory at the University of California at Irvine announced "that twenty minutes of listening to a Mozart sonata raised the measurable IQ of college students by up to nine points" (*Los Angeles Times,* Oct. 14, 1993). This is good news for Mozart lovers, and eventually it may have deeper implications for art at large. Unfortunately, the boost in IQ lasted only ten minutes, so the jury is still out on the usefulness of art, at least in the measurable sense.

I don't think the *utile et dulce* theory is wrong as much as its basis has been insufficiently examined, and this is where biology seems to enter the picture as a helpful corrective. I take the position that art and dreaming are, in principle, the same activity in that they involve the same or highly similar mental processes (the production of images and narratives based on human experience) and that making art is no more elective, or voluntary, for the human being than dreaming. By this I certainly don't mean that everyone is biologically compelled to paint pictures, write stories, or compose music, but that we are all drawn, to one degree or another, into using our imaginations, creating symmetries and designs, or in various ways refining our world beyond the needs of pure utility. If nothing else, we all daydream and draw doodles on napkins, and these are forms of storymaking that must be doing something for us at a fairly unconscious level. So we all have some innate stake in "the beautiful," and in this we are apparently different from other species. Maybe.

But to come back to the point: dreaming is plainly a biological activity because it is virtually universal, among mammals at least, and it occurs at a distinct level of consciousness with distinct physical characteristics. Like animals, humans are complex adaptive systems that process the information of daily experience, converting it into memory that can be used to ensure suitable behavior for our survival. Memory, as neuroscientist Steven Rose tells us, "is not only about learning, but also about subsequently recalling that memory, retrieving it" (1993, 316). And "each time we remember, we in some sense do work on and transform our memories; they are not simply being called up from store and, once consulted, replaced unmodified" (91). Memory, in short, is a dynamic process of updating what we already have in mind, not simply a storagehouse for what has already happened. My hunch is that dreams may be our clearest window into this whole process of ongoing conversion of experience into patterns that help to maintain order in the system; that the dream does its work without the least awareness that we, as dreamers, are looking in on it all; and that the dream is finally beneath our understanding in any more than the self-evident sense in which dreams reflect our concerns, fears, and needs. Beyond this it is anyone's guess as to what is going on in dreams or why such a mechanism is biologically necessary; but for various reasons I assert that the purpose of dreams has little to do with keeping us self-informed, as if dreamwork were an interior alter ego, whispering messages and giving progress reports to the dreamer from some mysterious clearinghouse. I invite the reader, rather, to think of the dream as a part of consciousness that, owing to the peculiar conditions of sleep, has the astonishing property of appearing to us as if it had originated as an exterior reality. To some extent this is also true of daydreams and other forms of memory recall in which we can momentarily become "lost to the world." But in the dream, where the influence of external stimuli is minimized almost to zero and there is no inside-outside division, we experience the revision of memory itself as if it were taking place a first and only time. I think of the dream as a process which we, as dreamers, can observe from only one limited point of view—its veridical quality as experience—and not as the natural processing mechanism that it is.

In any event, there is a good possibility that dreams and art may be serving common purposes, whatever these turn out to be, and that they have something to do with our survival, as opposed to our edification and pleasure. What, one wonders, might be the *function* of having pleasure (beyond its pleasurability)? The doctrine that art is useful and pleasing, in short, ends where it should have begun. It is content to take derivatives as causal explanations. All in all, saying that art is useful and pleasing and leaving it at that is rather like explaining mating and childrearing by saying that children are fun to have and that they will eventually do chores around the house.

My present goal, however, is not to explain what dreaming and art-making do for us. That is a book that would be better written by a biologist, a brain scientist, a philosopher, and perhaps an aesthetician, working in collaboration. I am concerned primarily with the mechanisms that underlie each of these imaginative activities, the ways they go about being what they are—what they do *to* us, rather than *for* us. I am particularly interested in the problem of authorship, or how the human mind thinks up things that never happened and presents them (in the case of the dream at least) in the mode of "the real." As I write, interest in consciousness theory and Darwinian evolution has been on the rise, both of which have influenced my own thinking immensely. The view I hold now, as a consequence, is that any comprehensive theory of dreaming or of art must begin at the level of consciousness, prior to the formulation of narrative, theme, and what is commonly referred to as meaning (as in the expression "What does this work or dream mean?"). In other words, we will have to begin well before the cat is out of the cognitive bag.

Another of my assumptions is that if dreams mean anything, the meaning is no different in kind from the meaning that may be given to waking experience. If you want to find out about yourself or what is "on" your mind, you can do just as well by examining what has passed during the day. Curiously, one rarely hears of anyone examining the day—or even a daydream—for its meaning. For the most part, we take each day for granted. Who has ever thought to ask, "What did my vacation in Maine mean?" But a dream *about* the vacation is another matter. We like to believe that dreams "mean something," that the events they depict are deliberately charged with a significance that the real experience (the vacation) did not have.

It is understandable that dreams would be one of the things that bedevil us with questions about meaning. Dreams are, after all, events we make up in our heads without any awareness of doing so or any power to prevent their occurring; they seem to stand at once outside us, beyond our reach, and deep within us in a queer way that endows them with a subversive authority. Like Kafka's fictions, dreams are dry and matter-of-fact in going about their business, however emotionally involved we may get in them. I think, for instance, of Kafka's "In the Penal Colony," in which the prisoner's crimes are written on his body by an ingenious etching machine. So too the dreamwork etches stories of our fears, desires, and social practices on the body of the psyche. So it makes sense, the logic runs, that dreams express things that are secretly on our minds, things we're not supposed to know or didn't know we knew, given the fact that the dream never makes its point clear (as allegories and didactic fictions do). And that makes the dream all the more mysterious because it would seem to take as much cunning to *avoid* making sense as it does to make sense. Hence Freud's famous theory of censorship.

We say dreams express our hidden insecurity or our guilt. But it would be simpler to say that we *are* insecure and guilty creatures, among other things, and that guilt and insecurity (among other things) are on our minds during the day as well as the night, otherwise we wouldn't dream about them; therefore, the meaning of dreams is essentially the same as the meaning of the events of our waking life. So one of my beliefs is that the dream is really doing much the same thing that the mind does during the day, only under different "working" conditions, and it is these conditions that I shall examine here.

Another part of the mystery is that dreams are largely about uneventful things: I am teaching a class (sometimes brilliantly, sometimes poorly), I am trying to unload a refrigerator from the bed of a pick-up truck, I am shopping for a shirt, I am talking to my friend Dan, who is riding a unicycle. These are trivial things in the sense that they don't seem to "go" anywhere; they don't lead to climaxes and they aren't climaxes of something that came before. They are very much like the things that happen in daily life, except that something about the way they appear in dreams is different from the way we perceive them in the waking state. And in this respect dreams have as much in common with art as they have, in another way, with unmediated waking reality. The dream wipes away all the excess of automatic waking behavior and "selects" only what can be charged with affect: if you were bored in a dream, you would be vividly bored, precisely as a painting depicting a bored person (an Edward Hopper, for example) can be thrilling to look at. If you seem to be going on a long walk in a dream, the dream will shorten it, just as the novelist does ("Charles walked through the fields for hours, and finally he arrived at the manor"). We accept this as a natural feature of the dream, as we do of the novel; yet what agency in the dreaming brain has so rapidly abbreviated the plot in order to avoid self-duplication of affect and how did it know where to go *next?* This is a question I approach from several directions.

Dreaming and art-making, then, appear to share a "technique" of purification of waking experience. They are essentializing processes, as aestheticians say. For example, take off your sock and look at your foot. Nothing interesting there. Now look at Michelangelo's sketch of a foot. It's the same foot, more or less—except that his foot is fascinating to look at. What has he *done* to the foot? He has taken it out of the world of anatomy and put it into the world of resemblance. He has caught the foot's *way* of being a foot by slightly enhancing certain footlike features. As Heidegger might say, Michelangelo has "deconcealed" the foot (1975, 39); he has taken the sock of familiarity off the foot. What he has done to the foot is essentially what the dream does to the experiences of your waking life, and it does it without thinking about it.

This is of course what art is all about: it asks you to look at things you haven't been seeing—Cézanne's rocks, Monet's lilies, Hopper's rural gas stations. Cézanne once said that he wanted above all else to paint the "world's instant," a wonderful phrase for what the world becomes when you look at it in the phenomenal, or "thingly" mode. In my view, dreams are also a record of these instants, though highly personalized and undeliberate: they drain things of their inconspicuousness; relentlessly, it seems, the dream ransacks the day, passing (usually) over big events, dramas that advance or undo us, without noticing them, alert only to the small sin, the odd accident of behavior, or the visual event that somehow catches the world committing one of its habits: Mother being perfectly herself, my friend Paul saying something Paul-like, my high school teacher Mr. Sherk nervously bouncing chalk in his hand during a chemistry lecture. During the day you see someone with stained imperfect teeth set off against an otherwise healthy complexion and that night the teeth will show up on someone's face in a dream, a propos of nothing, or at least nothing you know about. The teeth are of no more use or symbolic value than Michelangelo's sketch of the foot (though psychoanalysis will tell you otherwise), but they caught your attention, if only subliminally. And they showed up in the dream as precisely right, perfectly imperfect teeth. So you are a Michelangelo of sorts.

I'm not suggesting that this remarkable power is something the dream does deliberately, in order to give us the pleasure that art gives us. To speak of the dream as being "clever" or "cunning" or as "choosing" (as I will be doing) is strictly a form of metaphorical shorthand: dreams do not have human qualities or drives. The dream does these things to empirical experience because the conditions of dreaming can deal with experience only in that way. You can't ask why the dream does it, unless you put the question at the neurological level. "Why?" is an inappropriate question to ask of the dream because it presupposes a conscious or unconscious motive, a person in there somewhere, and there is no proof that dreams have motives of any kind. Dreamwork is no more a volitional mechanism than is any other function of the body. However, one could ask what possible relations between dream-making and art-making might exist, or whether art-making is necessarily a more deliberate act for the species than is dreaming.

Obviously, not all events in dreams are trivial. Occasionally we are chased by a huge beast and partially eaten, and of course this isn't trivial, though it is usually painless. Or now and then I am teaching a class in my underwear (though no one seems to notice). But this isn't really the main menu of dreams—my dreams anyway. I am much more likely to spend an entire dream trying to perform an impossible task, trying to find something I've lost, or being lost, or trying to get home on my bicycle with night approaching. In short, the matter of daily life raised to the tenth power: getting and spending, being embarrassed, being late, being caught in (or out of) my underwear, being overjoyed, or being overlooked and, most tedious of all, being forced to perform the same mundane task over and over.

On the most obvious level, dreams are a form of time travel, though one never knows this in a dream. For instance, in a dream I go back to the schoolyard of my boyhood, not as a boy but as the self that has simply endured as the center of presence I call my self. I am neither old nor young—I am always the "same" age in dreams—even though everybody else normally appears as I remember them. This is the queer thing about consciousness. It doesn't age, it has no age. The octogenarian is a teenager in thought—one of the great frustrations of life! Experience, maturity, and wisdom have no more effect on consciousness than what you can see through a window affects the window itself. Maybe an aging consciousness forgets more things, or sees things differently, makes fewer mistakes of a certain kind or more of another, but the window itself doesn't change. Consciousness is what is always around, the one thing that is immune to the flux of time—until, of course, it flickers and goes out.

The common factor of all thoughts in and about time, as Saint Augustine says in my favorite discussion of time, is that each "time" takes place in a *present:* the present of things past (which Augustine calls memory), the present of things future (expectation), and the present of things present (sight). This is wonderfully simple, but it is the bottom line of what can be said about time. There is, indeed, nothing else but the present, and of course "it" is always traveling, always coming and going, poised on the knife edge of this specious now that even philosophers cannot grasp or define to our satisfaction. Witness Augustine's frustration with the whole question and, finally, his tossing it all back in God's lap.

Augustine could as easily have used the word *consciousness* instead of time itself. For without consciousness time does not exist. We could think of consciousness, using his terms, as the presence of a present — or, if you will, being present in one (or all) of these three sorts of presents. That is what dreams seem to be: the triumph of consciousness over the various kinds of waking time; thought, as Augustine would say, wandering "amidst times," guided only by the transcendent lure of free association, which is nothing more than the confusion of times caused by threads of resemblance extending through the events of memory. In this, dreams behave like a vacuum. In a vacuum a lead ball and a feather fall at the same speed. So, too, a dream, like a vacuum, is without chronological and spatial "friction." It knows no distinctions in nearness or farness (in time or space) or in weight (importance, size). In dreams all objects (images) fall at the same rate of speed, precisely as any square millimeter of a Cézanne canvas is as important, expressive, or as near or far as any other. The painting does not become more important as it nears the subject it depicts. So, too, all dream objects are drawn into existence by the same gravity of association.

What a great satisfaction it was to come upon a passage in Umberto Eco's *Six Walks in the Fictional Woods* in which Eco explores the mysteries of the imperfect tense in English grammar. It is "a very interesting tense," he says, "because it is both durative and iterative. As a durative, it tells us that something was happening in the past but does not give us any precise time, and the beginning and the end of the action are unknown. As an iterative, it implies that the action has been repeated. But one is never certain when it is iterative, when it is durative, or when it is both." And, he adds, "it is the ambiguity of [the imperfect] tense that makes it the most suitable for recounting dreams or nightmares" (1994, 12–13). One is left to conclude that dreams themselves are the essence of "imperfection" in just this double way of putting us "amidst times," of condensing duration and iteration into one. And it seems reasonable to think that if our grammar needs the imperfect tense as a sort of "et cetera" tense to account for temporal ambiguity, we have been given the dream—though no one knows to what end—as the complementary alternative to unambiguous waking life, in which time is told by the clock. It seems almost as if it were biologically necessary that the body and mind that are pinned down in the strict space and time of daily life should require an instrument by which it could wander without restriction through a world of pure possibility. Maybe that isn't why we dream, but it's an awfully nice dividend.

This fact is entirely lost on the dreamer—another frustration! The poor dreamer misses the uniqueness of dreaming while the dream is going on, and she loses the wonder of dreaming when she wakes up. And here is another deep paradox of dreaming: each moment of a dream co-exists as both a recollection and an original event, as a de-temporalized past reappearing as a never-before-experienced present. At the bottom, then, every dream is a conflation of times. You say at breakfast, "I dreamed of Mother last night," scarcely thinking that Mother is dead and that what you saw and talked to in the dream was a lifetime of mother-memories sharpened into a single image about whose edges, however clear otherwise, there is a faint halo of unreliability. However vivid the dream, Mother was both uniquely actual and imperfect, in Eco's double sense of being a duration and a self-repetition. The frustration is that one becomes so used to the dream world, or so accommodated to the futility of grasping it, that it finally becomes as pedestrian as the space-time of waking reality. Only when you wake up, still within the penumbra of the dream, do you think about it at all: but there is no way to get it back, or to understand what it is or what it means. Finally, you end up saying, "I dreamed of Mother last night," with a slight ironical smile and let it go at that, as though there were no point in telling the dream but that it ought somehow to be said aloud that you dreamed it, before the fact is swallowed in the urgent and unambiguous business of the day.

1

Why We Dream
The Lingering Question

I suspect that Western culture, unlike many others, thinks so casually about dreaming because, like the earlobe or the appendix, it has no obvious purpose. Nontechnological societies find many uses for the dream, and in some places it is regarded as being equal to waking reality and endowed with special powers of soothsaying, communal governance, and direct connection to the world of spirits. Industrial societies, in contrast, find nothing useful in dreaming, except possibly a tool for diagnosing neuroses produced by the society itself. Even literary people have little, if any, professional interest in the dream unless it occurs in fictional form, as in the works of Kafka, Stevenson, or Dostoevsky. Even then it isn't the dream that is of interest but what the dream tells us about the artist or the work. So there again the dream is thought of as a medium for something else, rather as we use the earlobe as a place to hang earrings. This is understandable because, after all, of what other use is the earlobe? As for the dream, it has no real existence, nothing one can really study that fits in the hand, like a book. What can you do or say about your dream? It has no "text," save for the graceless text of your descriptive summary ("I was in this strange room . . ."). You can't show it to anybody or expect sympathy, envy, or surprise from telling it to someone, unless you're paying by the hour. You might as well talk about your arthritis.

So we gradually slip into taking dreams for granted, like a body function, a kind of mental refuse that is better ignored. And indeed, the mind obliges in this process by erasing most of our dreams from memory before we wake. There is even a vein of theory running from W. Robert (1886) to Sir Francis Crick (1986) and Hanna Segal (1992) that dreams are themselves an excretionary process by which the mind flushes undigested or worthless impressions, binding them together, as Robert puts it so evocatively, "into a rounded whole by threads of thought borrowed from the imagination" (cited in Freud, 1900, 4:80). Now and then you have a dream that is interesting enough to stick in the memory, and you usually want to tell it to someone. But no one really wants to hear it because few things are as boring as hearing about something that *didn't* happen to someone else, and, moreover, something that obeys none of the rules governing things that do.

It would be hard to name any form of human behavior that has been studied so vigorously and from so many different points of view yet whose role in our lives we know less about. To complicate matters, the immense bibliography on dreams is further subdivided into special areas of study (neurophysiology, cognitive and experimental psychology, psychoanalysis, ethnography, philosophy, to name a few), each with a highly specialized vocabulary. Understandably, the psychologists have the biggest corner on dream study, and they tend, for good reason, to consider the dream as belonging to them on the grounds of squatter's rights. Unfortunately, as soon as one takes a particular perspective on the dream, a great many other perspectives are automatically excluded, if only because one set of tools can do only certain kinds of investigating. Moreover, a specialist in one area has little time or inclination to read what is going on in the others. This is, of course, the modern problem.

As a result we have various answers to the question of why we dream. Neurologists answer the question with hard neurological facts pertaining to wiring and firing, chemical and electrical discharge, cell organization, and network activation; therapists will claim that dreams tell us useful things about ourselves; psychoanalysts that they try to avoid telling us about ourselves, or do so only when decoded; phenomenologists that the experience of dreaming is all that is important; and so on, a classic instance of the blind men trying to understand the whole elephant from the part each one is touching with his hand.

Still, some eloquent theories have been advanced, but each of them seems inadequate, or in some way challengeable. Freud's achievement was to give the dream a function that proved widely acceptable for almost a century. Briefly, Freud felt the purpose of dreams was to be the guardian of sleep, a fascinating idea in its time, and it still has its adherents or variants.[1] On top of this, dreams were also wish-fulfillments,

1. An example is the more recent idea advanced by Stolorow and Atwood that dreams do not guard sleep but are the "guardians of psychological struc-

and no conceivable dream, in Freud's view, was exempt, though he made exceptions (traumatic dreams) to the idea later in his life. One of Freud's patients once challenged this view by relating a dream to him in which she had spent her holidays with her mother-in-law. "This is a *wish*-fulfillment?" she asked, incredulously. And Freud's answer—what finesse!—was that she had *wanted* to dream a dream that would contradict his claim and her dream showed that wish fulfilled (1900, 4:151).

The wish-fulfillment, of course, is only half of Freud's psychical dream mechanism. The "second agency" is that of the censor, whose function is to distort the expression of the wish. The first agency, the wisher, is "creative" and does all the inventing within the dream; the second, the censor, is "defensive" and "allows nothing to pass without exercising its rights and making such modifications as it thinks fit in the thought which is seeking admission to consciousness" (1900, 4:144). Thus in the woman's dream the idea of spending her holiday with her mother-in-law was a wish to prove Freud wrong; but the censor contrived to provide a distressing dream content based, as Freud goes on to say, on the cause of her illness. So the "non-fulfillment of one wish [her wish to forget certain events] meant the fulfillment of another [that Freud be proven wrong]" (151). I cite this dream to give some flavor of the versatility of Freud's theory which in this reduction, I'm afraid, sounds like a variation of the old Abbott and Costello "Who's on first?" routine. It has always seemed to me that the idea of a censored dream makes an incredible demand on thought processes that are occurring in the sleep state (I shall return to this theme in the next chapter and in chapter 6). For one thing, the activity of censorship presupposes an elaborate mechanism that almost inevitably divides the brain into two, if not three, regions of thought, one of which knows, so to speak, more than the others, though how it knows is never made clear. Basically, censorship is an "editorial" activity and it requires that there be

---

ture": "By reviving during sleep the most basic and emotionally compelling form of knowing—through sensory perception—the dream affirms and solidifies the nuclear organizing structures of the dreamer's subjective life" (1992, 281).

a content, or "text" of some sort to be censored, present in the brain before censorship can come into play—that is to say, before the dream is actually dreamed. How is it, one wonders, that such a complicated watchdog process can operate beneath any level of awareness—sorting this, repressing that, finding symbols for highly charged affects (usually sexual), and generally making the dream acceptable to the conscious dreaming part of the brain? [2] What form does the pre-dream matter take before it is censored and presented to the dreamer? Moreover, if dreams are the guardians of sleep, if the dream is censored in order to prevent disturbing thoughts, why do so many slip through and wake us up? Why is it that dreams more often than not are based on unpleasant materials (Kramer, 1993), even following the presumed censorship? Thus conceived, the mechanism seems either Byzantine or badly designed, and we can be thankful that the heart and the retina don't operate that sloppily.

Freud's theory is more complicated than I'm making it sound. The important thing about Freud is not the theory of suppression or wish-fulfillment. For me, Freud's extensive discussions of metaphorical association and the means by which the mind produces dreams are unsurpassed. It was Freud who elaborated the idea of associational mechanisms through which the dream develops its imagery and narrative. It is worth reading Freud if only to appreciate how intensely genius can devote itself to a complex problem. Freud was a master detective when it came to tracking a dream image back through the patient's history and in the process teaching us a great deal about the capacity of the brain to manipulate the materials of memory. Whatever he may have been to psychiatry, Freud was also one of the great storytellers of the early

2. Sartre poses much the same argument against the censor in *Being and Nothingness:* "If we abandon all the metaphors representing the repression as the impact of blind forces, we are compelled to admit that the censor must choose and in order to choose must be aware of so doing. . . . In a word, how could the censor discern the impulses needing to be repressed without being conscious of discerning them? How can we conceive of a knowledge which is ignorant of itself" (1966, 93).

twentieth century. By this I mean only that the excitement of reading Freud at his very best springs less from a belief that he is right than from his ability to put us in what Coleridge called a state of willing suspension of disbelief. Arthur Conan Doyle could not have given *The Interpretation of Dreams* or "Fragment of an Analysis" more suspense or narrative zing than Freud did. And I have a private, untestable theory that at least some of Freud's readers, professional and otherwise, are so overwhelmed by the way Freud builds a case, often with dazzling motivational leaps, that they accept the theory outright, little bothering that Freud's evidence, in most cases, has the same status as the evidence one finds in a good detective novel—that is, it is mustered and arranged by an author who knows in advance how everything will turn out, though the reading itself is a gradual process of unconcealing the forgone. But above all, in Freud's pages, whether the theory is right or wrong or a little of both, one finds one of the most remarkable descriptions of the complexity of mental processes. Indeed, Patrick Mahony, in his book *Freud as a Writer,* suggests that Freud's distrust of exact definitions "made his prose a particularly appropriate instrument for describing the vitality of mental events." Moreover, his "wonderful ease of expression and his masterfully articulated syntax make his writing appear, at first blush, clear and less ambiguous than it is" (1987, 77).

Despite Freud's immense fascination with the dream process, his perspective was inevitably one that looked directly or cannily through the dream to its hidden significations. So right there, at the beginning of modern psychoanalysis's interest in the dream, the dream's amazing powers were virtually ignored in favor of seeing it as a means to an end. The end result of psychoanalysis getting to the dream before anyone else in this century is that dreams are primarily considered as carriers of neurosis and trauma. Little room is allowed for the possibility that dreams are about our curiosities, fears, and desires (falling, hands-on sex, wealth, poverty, being lost, finding), the beauty of the world, the precariousness of life, the scintillation of dangerous places, the thrill of visual experience, the sublime, the terrifying, the expansive, friendship,

dignity, the pain of grieving, the joy of moving, seeing, swimming, flying, communicating with animals, knowing things, and being alive: in
short, everything that waking life is about at its best and its worst is the
subject of our dreams.

One highly influential theory is that the dream state is where we cor-
relate incoming information for storage in the long-term memory. When
the body is "down" or "off-line," the brain rolls up its sleeves and processes the day's experience, rather like a postal clerk tossing the fresh
mail into various baskets, for delivery to the far-flung outposts of the
brain. Actually, that metaphor is much too modest and technologically
archaic. Imagine the complexity that must be involved in correlating
the experience of a single day in such detail that you can actually recall
where you were standing and what time it was when your friend Edgar
told you he'd just had the oil changed in his car. This is the remarkable
thing about correlation: trivial and important things are processed in
kind, the essential thing being that they all have call (or should we say
recall?) numbers, the principle behind all good libraries.

We have some idea of the subtlety with which the brain perceives
and correlates incoming information from an experiment cited by
Nicholas Humphrey in *A History of the Mind* (1992): if a pattern is
flashed on a screen for one-tenth of a second, the subject will see it and
report some of its details, "but if the same pattern is followed immediately by another longer-lasting pattern he will . . . no longer see the first
pattern at all—as though it never occurred." The stunning finding, however, is that the "unseen" first pattern will have a subliminal influence
on what the subject sees in the second. For example, if the first pattern
is a man either carrying a birthday cake or wielding a knife, and the
second pattern is "a nondescript young man," the subject will describe
the character of the young man in terms appropriate to the *unseen* first
pattern (85): the man will be either friendly or menacing, depending
on the first image. For me, this is an almost paradigmatic example of
how consciousness carries unseen information, or, more correctly, how
seeing and recording, and hence correlating information extends deep

into unconscious thought, influencing the "character" and nature of the dream image. I shall discuss various aspects of this problem beginning with chapter 4.

Of course, as in the pattern experiment, we don't realize that we're correlating when we dream; we think we're just having another experience (as opposed to blending old experiences). Anyway, it is an attractive theory, and I was so taken by it some years ago that I wrote an entire book (1988) about dreams, using it as a point of departure. The theory has all the right virtues: it is scientific; it sounds like what ought to be taking place in the brain (something has to do the job); it is laced into sleep itself, thus in fact accounting for sleep as the time off-line the brain needs in order to render this important service; and it explains one of the most obvious characteristics of dreaming, that it is almost invariably a mixture of fresh experience and long-term memory. So the brain works overtime while, paradoxically, we sleep that sleep, as Maurice Blanchot puts it, "that even as we sleep allows us no sleep" (Leiris, 1987: xxviii).

The difficulty with this theory as an explanation of dreaming is that, like most (if not all) dream theories, it can't be confirmed by hard empirical facts. It isn't easy to see what is being correlated when you are riding a dream tricycle on a busy freeway, meeting a friend from first grade who has lost his upper lip, or standing on the narrow ledge of a tall building playing solitaire. Moreover, one wants to ask: is the sometimes powerful emotional content of dreams a part of the correlation process or a by-product of it? Are things correlated according to the emotion they are associated with, as many people believe, or does the emotion derive from our reaction to the correlation (as in the pattern experiment)? For example, virtually without thinking about it, I can list fifteen things I fear. This must mean that some emotionally based correlation has taken place that enables me to bring such unrelated things as spiders and deep water together in a single category, even though they are all *also* stored in separate neuronal systems that have nothing to do with fear. Despite such questions, however, the correlation theory has much to be said for it. Allan Hobson holds this view and has made a convincing case for dreams as an activity for reinforcing and reorganizing memory. Basically, the relaxed nature and "altered chemistry" of the dream state allow the brain time to reactivate the past day's memory and distribute it to "other networks . . . by linking it in hyperassociative fashion to every network with which it shares formal features [such as axles with long things, hard things, strong things]" (1994, 114–16).

Then there is the theory that dreams are a means of maintaining our vigilance. Vigilance involves the formation and revision of knowledge structures respecting safety, social behavior, and tensions in the waking world. In short, dreams keep us alert to new and old nemeses. I must admit that this is also an attractive theory. But again, there are so many kinds of dreams that don't involve tensions or safety—at any rate, it is hard to see how—that the theory seems too limited to be a full explanation for such an orchestral phenomenon. Still, one interesting contribution along this line is the work of Michel Jouvet on the dreams of cats. Jouvet surgically reversed the muscle atonia of sleeping cats, with the result that they became sleepwalkers during REM sleep; specifically, they began to carry out the natural movements of predation behavior, though in a random fashion (crouching, stalking, tail-wagging, butt-wiggling). So we are led to hypothesize that dreaming may be a way of rehearsing waking behavior after all. Maybe this isn't the right conclusion to draw, but it suggests that if animals practice their hunting rituals in dreams, or dream that they are hunting, perhaps human dreaming serves a purpose that relates to such behavior. Of course, the cats could be simply dreaming about the only things cats really do or care about. So it would be quite natural for them to dream about hunting prey without assuming that they were practicing their skills, and quite unnatural for them to dream about canoeing, partying, or reading a detective novel. In this they're like us: we dream (for the most part) about what we do in the waking world, and much of it consists of predation routines of one kind or another, though our predation routines are a little more cleverly disguised. If our muscle atonia were reversed

in REM sleep, and we could walk around safely, we'd be pushing grocery carts, driving to work, mowing the lawn, lecturing in the nude, or
falling off a cliff, rather than crouching in the grass flicking our tails.
But it would amount to the same thing. In any case, a truly comprehensive theory of why we dream, as Robert Ornstein has pointed out, must
also include a rationale for why all mammals dream (1991, 197), and the
answer can scarcely be limited to the kinds of purposes advanced by
psychoanalysis. It stands to reason that if cats and humans dream about
different things, their dreams perform similar biological functions.

Related to the idea of vigilance is the so-called adaptive dream. I
shall concentrate on a discussion by Joseph Weiss which deals with com-
bat veterans' dreams of being captured by the enemy. These dreams,
Weiss says, may be called "warning" dreams, or "cautionary tales"
through which the ego "orients [the soldier] throughout the night to the
grave danger he is facing, and it thereby prepares him for it." The dream
tells him, "If I am not careful, I will be captured" (1992, 219). Weiss invokes Freud's idea that the dream itself is incapable of representing the
grammatical "if" because it is beneath visualization; therefore the dream
represents the experience of capture flat-out. The ego, Weiss writes, "in
producing a warning dream, is carrying out the same vital function that
it carries out in waking life when it produces an anxiety signal" (220).

The natural question is: why couldn't the motivation behind the
capture dream—not to mention dreams of falling, of drowning, of endangerment of any kind—be just that: outright fear of the danger itself?
Surely a soldier has never gone into battle without such a fear. Or, if a
man scheduled to be executed dreams of mounting the scaffold, must
we assume that his ego is warning him, or adapting him to the idea of
dying? Wouldn't it be more economical to assume that fear of something is likely to produce (waking or sleeping) thoughts and images of
the thing feared, in much the same way that a teenager on the way to
an exciting prom date is likely to conjure images of the event in dreams
or daydreams? Is any further motivation required than that of expectation, of having something of obvious significance "on one's mind"?

My skepticism is not intended to refute the possibility of warning or adaptive dreams, but to illustrate how difficult it is to reach conclusions about the purposes of even certain kinds of dreams, let alone all dreams. R. D. Laing makes a similar claim in saying that "at some point those very dangers most dreaded can themselves be encompassed to forestall their actual occurrence. Thus . . . to play possum, to feign death, becomes a means of preserving one's aliveness" (1970, 51). This idea occurs in the context of defensive dreams of patients prior to the onset of severe schizophrenia; but how far beyond this the principle can be extended, or whether such motives would be attributed to the same dreams had schizophrenia not ensued, we cannot say. The problem-solving or adaptive dream cannot, on the evidence I have read at least, be differentiated structurally or emotionally from the problem-*putting* dream, and there is a world of difference between the two, as I shall suggest in the next chapter. It is irrefutable that some dreams put forth problems (as well as fears, pleasures, and so on) and that dreams sometimes dwell on finding solutions to the problems they raise, albeit with indifferent success. But one can usually tell, structurally and emotionally, when this is the case. Moreover, one can understand how a vivid fear-of-capture dream might make a soldier more alert to the possibility of capture, or even how such a dream might prevent his capture (if this were possible to determine) or bring on his death (if he elected to run rather than surrender). But this doesn't justify the added step of concluding that the purpose of the dream was to produce a vigilant state of mind ("If I am not careful . . ."). This seems a post hoc argument in which the effect is confused with the cause.

Finally, the ego may be better thought of as an *audience* to the dream than as its instigator. That is, on waking, or even in some "lucid" sense during the dream, the dreamer might construe the dream as a warning or a cause to be alert to the danger. In short, the dreamer would become an interpreter of his dream, but however efficacious the result might be, like all interpretations it has nothing to do with why the dream was dreamed.³ To equate the cause of dreams with any possible meanings they may have is, as Allan Hobson might say, to accept a psychological answer to what may well be a physiological question (1988, 286).

It seems to me that there must be room in dreaming for comparatively simple, or at least elementary concerns that might arise as a result of unplanned exigencies occurring in the dream's progress. Let us say I want to go someplace in a dream and decide to take my car, or someone else's. Once I'm in traffic, however, I have trouble keeping the car going where I want it to go. What does this mean? Charles Rycroft has a passage in *The Innocence of Dreams* covering "automobile symbolism," in which he argues that the meanings of an automobile in a dream are almost as countless as the dreamers who dream about them. By way of example, he says that "difficulties with the steering suggest anxiety about [the dreamer's] self-control" (1979, 84). I'm sure he means "*may* suggest" (not "always suggests"). As a frequent victim of out-of-control cars in dreams, I would agree, but I would stretch the point even further (by way of self-defense) by adding that the dream may instead

3. I am thinking here along the lines of Paul Hernadi's discussion of "internalized conversation" in which the thinking person not only speaks silently to himself but also listens inwardly to "silent messages" that occur to him, in the present case as dreams. "Whatever occurs to me (in both the external and the mental senses of 'occur') awaits transformation, through a kind of internal reading, into meaningful messages" (1995, 18). It is not necessary that the "meaningful messages" be messages, in the intentional sense of something designed to communicate, only that they be construed as useful for some purpose (taking care to avoid capture). If we don't insist on this distinction, dreaming soon degenerates into a regressive mechanism driven by a "ghost" (the ego, the id, etc.) toward a particular end. Thus the usefulness of dreams in psychotherapy does not depend, as classical psychoanalysis insisted, on the "meaning of a dream [being] identical to the dream's causal origin" (Stolorow and Atwood, 1992, 276). It is rather a case of the dream being one means, among many, to diagnostic success. As Merleau-Ponty expresses it: "The childhood memory which provides the key to a dream (and which analysis succeeds in laying bare)" is not the *cause* of the dream. It is "the means for the analyst of understanding a present structure or attitude" (1963, 178).

suggest anxieties about the automobile. In other words, one need not be worried about one's self-control in general in order to dream about disobedient cars. The car-machine itself, as we all find out in learning to drive, has a mind of its own, and one of the terrifying things in life is to be victimized by indifferent or malevolent machinery, or to experience a failure in reliable systems of any kind, an ever-present possibility. The automobile is the machine par excellence that poses for the most self-controlled of us a potential hazard. It falls into the category of flimsy bridges over raging waters, narrow paths along cliffs, sloping roofs, caves with unstable walls, rickety ladders, elevators, airplanes: anything on which we are forced to depend for support is apt to be unreliable in a dream. Dreams about such things, unless they become obsessive or repetitive, probably spring from a creatural fear as much as from anxieties about psychical deficiencies and imbalances. Maybe this is pure casuistry on my part, but I think that it is in the spirit of Rycroft's open-minded conception of dreams and his suspicion of specific meanings that may be assigned to any dream image.

The idea would be, then, that dreams are sometimes about "basics" for no other reason than that they are just that, basic to human experience, as opposed, say, to personal neuroses. A better example, which I take up more fully in chapter 6, is that of "body symbolism," or the idea that body processes are meaningful beyond physiological concerns. Again, this is probably uncontestable in certain cases, but I think the manifest-latent model of the dream almost requires a "deeper" meaning than appears on the surface of the dream, and with the infinite resources of symbolism it is rarely difficult to find it. For example, in a Jungian book, Edward Whitmont and Sylvia Perera argue that "Urinary symbolism has to do . . . with the letting go and allowing of emotion, or of its inhibitions, when, for example, one dreams of urgently having to go and holding it back" (1989, 147). Well, that would depend. Surely this would not be true in a case of real urgency in which the dream was signaling what the dreamer's bladder was screaming in its discomforting plenitude. Surely one would have to put questions of symbolism aside in deference to the firmer "motives" of anatomy; and if this is true then we must surely adapt our notions of the functionality of dreams to include more earthy motives.

It is easy to quarrel with theories. My main reservation about most of them is that they are biased by methodological orientation and are hence too restrictive. Because, as Melvin Lansky says, "repression is the cornerstone of psychoanalysis" and dreams a key tool in the associative process, dreams are generally considered (by psychoanalysts) as repressive mechanisms (1992, 479). It is not that all analysts share this belief, or that all analysts would define the dream as a repressive mechanism outside of the diagnostic project. Even so, the prevailing view of dreams is heavily influenced by this thesis: dreams are two-tiered (manifest/latent), coded symbolic structures dealing with repressed materials. Lansky, I must add, makes a strong plea for a wider understanding of the nature of dreams: "If psychoanalytic conclusions [about the dream] do not apply to the entire domain of dreams," he says, "we are faced with the problem of deciding what falls within the psychoanalytic domain of dreams that have hitherto been limited to those seen in the clinical setting" (490). In short, the problem is not *caused* by psychoanalysis; it is caused by the enigmatic nature of the dream itself, whose silence about its own nature is so consternating, so beckoning, and so amenable to interpretation that almost anything can be said about it and defended within the "domain" of a particular set of data. The dream is like a Swiss bank: you can get out of it what you put into it, and it will never reveal the size and number of your account.

I have a hunch that the explanation of dreams, when it comes, will be relatively simple (in the sense of systemic economy). Some day someone will tell us in clear terms that the purpose of the dream is such-and-such, and we will cry out a collective "Of course! Why didn't we see that before?" (as a lot of people did in the early 1900s when Freud's masterpiece was first read). And it may turn out that another century will produce an entirely different theory. But when the right theory arrives it will be a simple parsimonious explanation on the order of our discovery that the heart pumps blood through the system, that the liver processes sugars, that viruses cause flu, and that the earth revolves around the sun, all examples of discoveries that make us seem dumb, in retrospect, for not discovering them earlier.

Perhaps we could approach the matter another way. We might begin by assuming that the mind, along with the brain and body that support it, needs the kind of thinking that the dream does because we can't do that kind of thinking while awake. Then we would have to decide what this special thinking was. It may seem that this approach puts us back with the old set of theories, but I don't think so. The difference between dream thought and waking thought is obviously that the dream almost invariably presents us with experiences in a narrative or story form. Another characteristic is that the thinking is substantially associative in nature: that is, dream thought puts things together according to rather odd laws of association. Unfortunately, waking thought does these same things, though on a much more "coherent" level. For instance, we tell stories and we make metaphors, some of them very wild, while we are awake. But we have to be careful about a word like *coherent* because it has built-in biases: we think of coherence as a good thing for something to have, whereas incoherence is a bad thing. And coherence presupposes only characteristics of systems in waking reality and waking thought about reality. Moreover, you can test for this kind of coherence; you can verify it in a laboratory, and that's the acid test for waking people.

But suppose there are other orders of coherence that have to do with different kinds of mental activity. An intriguing theory of dreaming has been advanced by Ernest Hartmann who, building on other theories of memory correlation (including his own), finds strong similarities between dreams and psychotherapy itself. Most immediately, both are concerned with "making connections in a safe place" (the bed and sleep, the therapist's office) through a relatively free use of memory association. Is it possible, then, that one purpose of dreams, among others, may be to make connections between the contents of central and peripheral thought networks, between those we use actively in waking behavior and those outlying networks that are left relatively unexplored in the heavy traffic of daily life? Focused waking thought, Hartmann says,

involves serial processing, one thing after another in an orderly sequence. It cannot adequately explore or "appreciate" the distributed, massively parallel nature of our memory nets. But dreaming . . . is able to do this due to [a] linked group of properties: hyperconnectivity, including condensation, emotion-guided contextualization, pulling together related contexts; pulling things together into a picture or pictured metaphor. Dreaming is less serial, more parallel. It deals with "lots of things at once" rather than "one thing after another." (1995, 226)

It is possible, then, that dreaming may serve a "quasi-therapeutic role in the sense of integration and healing in resolving trauma, in adaptation to stress, and in dealing with painful or difficult new material" (225), as well as in generally keeping the nervous system in what we might call a state-of-experience condition (226). So, again, what seems from one standpoint to amount to incoherence may from another be seen as a subtle form of coherence. Hartmann does not deal much with the narrative or "serial" quality of dreams, but he would probably argue that dream narratives are not so much interested in going someplace in an orderly manner as in smelling out the roses of resemblance along the way, all in the interest, in his (and Macbeth's) image, of "knit[ting] up the ravell'd sleave of care" (226).

It an attractive idea, primarily because the kind of therapeutic value Hartmann describes does not imply a conscious "psychiatric" role for dreams that depends on the dreamer consciously learning something *from* dreams, or, if I read him correctly, in giving the dream what we might call an *intentional* function in which it sets out to be therapeutic. Such benefit as dreams may provide must occur, if it is serving a biological function, whether dreams are remembered or not, and most of them aren't. There is of course compelling evidence that REM sleep is associated with memory consolidation, though there is less evidence that its deprivation may have a deleterious effect on this function (Hunt [1989] reviews the literature on this point, 27–28, and passim; see also Hobson, 1988, 287–88). So dreams must be doing something for us, even though what they do is not directly assessable and may depend in no way on our being able to translate it into concepts or interpretations, with or without the help of an analyst (as one interprets poetry to mean certain things). Dreams may be like the body's immune system, which quietly detects incoming "strangers" to the body at the molecular level. I intend this strictly as a metaphor, but immune systems, as Gerald Edelman tells us, are really recognition systems based on evolutionary selectionist principles. "Your immune system," he says, "distinguishes foreign molecules (nonself) from the molecules of your body (self) by virtue of their different shapes" (1992, 76). Perhaps dreams are the visual footprints of a similar process—much "deeper" than the dream itself—whereby the brain sorts incoming information from the day according to "shape" and matches it with information already there;[4] it does this not by making antibodies to resist the alien cells, but by "tagging" them for distribution to various categories of memory fortification.[5] Memory, Edelman says

4. I prefer to leave the word *shape* relatively shapeless because I'm not sure what a psychic equivalent of cell shape might be. We have tended to think of the interpretable units of dreams in linguistic terms (symbols, events, attitudes of dream-characters, etc.), but it may be something far less representational. I'm not making the argument that this is the case, but if dreams serve a subrepresentational and subrecognitional purpose of any sort, it would seem that there is no guarantee how they go about doing what they do or that they are not, to one degree or another, epiphenomenal (see note 5 below).

5. My immune-system metaphor gains some palpability from an article that appears in the same issue of *Dreaming* as Hartmann's. In discussing the possibility that Freud's Irma dream might be "a biological response" to his own mouth cancer, Thomas Hersh suggests that some dreams may be considered as part of the immune system. That is, the operation of the immune system may affect the brain by "contribut[ing] to the formation of some 'cancer dreams' " among those who are subliminally feeling the effects of tumors. If this is the case, such dreams "must be considered part of the body's immune response to a cancer and not just as epiphenomenal by-products of the cancer. . . . It is even possible that, in certain cases a dream might actually be an allergic reaction" (1995, 281–82). I had not

elsewhere, is "the ability to recategorize" (1989, 211) and must constantly revise its holdings. How this is done and how the actual dream relates to the underlying correlation process is anybody's guess, but it seems self-evident that the slightest act of association between two things requires the formidable apparatus of the entire memory-making system, stretching from Hartmann's peripheral networks of all-but-forgotten experience to the busy center of ongoing goal-directed behavior.

In general, then, coherence and coherence levels are tricky subjects to which we bring considerable bias as aggressive dream interpreters. I am reminded of Borges's wonderful description of the Chinese encyclopedia that puts things into impossible and self-contradictory categories. Among other things, it divides animals into such bizarre categories as those belonging to the emperor, stray dogs, tame, innumerable, suckling

---

read Hersh's article before I coined my own "immune" metaphor (and would be embarrassed if I had overlooked it, if only because an article of my own appears between Hartmann's and Hersh's in the same issue!). My connection is looser, and for what it is worth as an unprovable hypothesis, it might be expanded along these lines: perhaps dreams serve a cathartic function of the sort that critics as early as the seventeenth century (e.g., Daniel Heinsius in the Netherlands) identified as the function of tragedy. In effect, the cathartic value of tragedy was to "inject" passions into the spectator through the display of terrible and pitiable events on stage; such passions are not bad in themselves until they become deficient or excessive—in a word, cancerous. These vicarious passions in turn would presumably inoculate spectators against passionate excesses in their own lives, help them to regulate passions in general, and enable them "to endure not only great calamities but also the stresses of everyday life" (Carlson, 1984, 87). This is not unlike the claims frequently made for dreams conceived as hypothetical "rehearsals" of events one might expect to suffer in waking life (the vigilance theory again). Whether dreams, or for that matter tragedy, serve such a function with any degree of success is impossible to say. The truth is that you cannot appreciate or assess a regulatory function, or even a skill or a moral virtue, until you are without it, and REM deprivation experiments have not been of much help thus far in solving the mystery. At any rate, in this further sense dreams might be considered as "part of the immune system," though it occurs to me that if you carry the idea of immunity much further you end up having to include education, parental guidance, cultural practice, and a good deal else in the same category—anything that prevents the contamination of the mind by unwanted bodies and ideas.

pigs, fabulous, drawn with a very fine camelhair brush, et cetera, and having just broken the water pitcher. An impossible melange! Michel Foucault cites this encyclopedia at the beginning of *The Order of Things* (a book, incidentally, about the coherence of thought systems) and concludes by saying, "In the wonderment of this taxonomy, the thing we apprehend in one great leap, the thing that, by means of the fable, is demonstrated as the exotic charm of another system of thought, is the limitation of our own, the stark impossibility of thinking *that*" (1973, xv).

Now the dream is, if anything, even more exotic than the Chinese encyclopedia. There are people, among them many notable neuroscientists, who feel that the incoherence of dreams can be traced to such things as the randomness of the firing order of certain cells or to certain chemical reactions. Thus dreams can become as irresponsible as the Chinese encyclopedia, and the mind tries its best to make sense of what has been randomly tossed up. But there is another way to look at the encyclopedia, and perhaps at the dream as well. Suppose an alien spaceship were to visit Earth, which had been rendered organically inert but otherwise perfectly intact following a planetary catastrophe, something on the order of a global "clean bomb" strike. After considerable research the alien scientists are able to bring together all the legal, moral, scientific, doctrinal, and social codes and records and mythologies of all past Earth societies. Would they not have on their hands a veritable Alexandrian library of Chinese encyclopedias? And the only possible explanation for their stark impossibilities, the only way one might begin to detect order in the disorder and confusion of priorities, would be to reconstruct, piece by piece, the evolution of nations from the Neanderthal era to the present. Only then could one know why shellfish are prized in one society and despised in another, why cows are sacred in India and routinely eaten in the United States, why certain religious sects worship snakes and others find them evil, why certain aboriginal peoples of Australia put honey and canoes into the same semantic category, or why something as archaic and dangerous as the right of every citizen to carry weapons should survive in a society as violent as our own. Coherence, then, lies in the infinitesimal tensions that bind peoples together while still keeping them in separate and orderly groups.

Actually, we need look no further than the typical American household to find a micro-example of this orderly disorder. Every home has its own Chinese encyclopedic way of storing its goods and durables. For example, I was looking for the green garden tape one day because I had noticed that our lone tomato plant is finally in need of staking. The tape is supposed to be kept in the top drawer of the sideboard in the dining room where we keep the butane fire igniter, the soil moisture probe, the dinner napkins, the fondue-pot candles, and two boxes of thank-you cards. It isn't there, and the reason is probably that I was the last person to use it and I never understood the logic of putting it there in the first place and must have put it away somewhere else. However, I've forgotten the logic I used when I returned it. I think the tape should be kept in the chest beside the telephone along with the scissors (which you need in order to cut it), the address book, the Scotch tape, assorted papers and receipts, the calculator, and the Lilliput Spanish dictionary. But apparently I didn't put it there, either. Anyway, all these things were put where they are over the years for as many reasons as there are things to put away, and overriding all of these reasons there is probably a factor of efficiency based on the rhythms and cow paths that come to regulate family life and habit—each household, as Tolstoy would say, in its own way.

So the coherence of any system of thought can be determined, as Lévi-Strauss has said, only from the inside out: that is, from an account of what unsystematic and contingent events brought the system about in the first place. As in our pattern experiment, one has no way of knowing what "information" precedes or lies behind the surface of the image that might coherently explain its seeming incoherence. (For example, how can one begin to explain the cultural influences that cause new blue jeans to be prized less than those with holes in the knees?) One may be able to explain the bizarreness of a dream from an electrochemical point of view (this is, after all, the physiological basis of all brain activity), but there is an as yet unexplained reason why we dream *as we dream,* rather than in some other way or not at all, or why we dream of certain things more than others (for instance, unpleasant subjects; and why are bathrooms in dreams always filthy?). Maybe the impossibilities and the incoherence are necessary to the dream's way of thinking, as suckling pigs or animals that have just broken the water pitcher may be necessary (if one had the wit to figure it out) to the Chinese system of thought about the animal kingdom. Dreaming is virtually universal among both higher animals and people, and nature does not indulge in systems that do not perform services to the organism. So there is every reason to believe that dreaming serves some purpose (or purposes) and that the absurd confusions of dreams may be grounded in a logic similar to the one that puts honey and canoes in the same category simply because both are manufactured products. Unless you belonged to the group that created that classification, you would probably find it senseless, a little like classifying centipedes with marching bands. But that is only because you are using one kind of thinking to assess another for which a key motivational connection is missing. In short, maybe this logic is the same sort that allows me to put spiders, caves, high places, and deep water in the same category because all of them scare me stiff, or to put the butane igniter in the same drawer as the dinner napkins because we don't generally use the fireplace in the evening unless we have dinner guests.

My own feeling, based on the crudest evidence, is that minds have to have something to do even while the body sleeps. You can easily say that the heart has to work twenty-four hours a day, virtually without missing a beat, for an extremely good reason. Whether you can make the same case for the beating heart and the thinking mind, I don't know. Why doesn't the mind simply do a minimum amount of work in the sleeping state? Why doesn't it just coast in neutral, or, better yet, just go to sleep along with the rest of the body? We know that it doesn't and that it is a myth to think that the mind must get tired just because the body gets tired. Yet in a way, maybe it does: if I grade a dozen student exams in a row, my mind is fatigued. But if I lie down to give my mind a rest, I notice that it will immediately start to daydream, and I assume that takes just as much electrochemical energy as grading papers. But it's much more pleasurable, so much so that I will probably drift off to sleep and before long I'll be dreaming, and in all likelihood I'll dream that I am grading papers or performing some bizarre task that imitates that rhythm.

So the brain had a chance to rest, and instead it maximizes the frustration that it was trying to avoid. I find it difficult to see how a dream like this does my mind or my memory storage process any good. Maybe it does, but there is still the possibility that consciousness, with the exception of the consciousness of deep sleep, simply has no choice but to think about things that concern it. It is, after all, the modus vivendi of the mind to cogitate. "I am, therefore I think—constantly," to reverse Descartes's postulate. Simply forgetting a person's name will drive a mind crazy, and it will put everything else on hold while it rummages around in its lost-and-found department, reappearing triumphantly (if it is lucky) with a name like "Jenkins! His name was Jenkins!" and the conversation can continue. That's the mind all over. It simply will not leave loose ends loose, and life, the living of life, is one long loose end.

So if a brain had nothing else to do it would think of something to think about. Perhaps the brain *is* like the heart and the other organs, after all: it has a specialty, and when it isn't doing that specialty it is for all purposes brain-dead. This is the issue at the heart of life itself: life isn't rest, life is liveliness; the central characteristic of life is always and everywhere to be *alive, to expend energy,* to convert one thing into another, to be constantly creating new cells, be they cells of tissue or "cells" of thought. Perhaps the question to ask, then, is not why we dream but why we always have to be thinking. If we knew that, perhaps we could take a step forward in our theory of dreaming. But now we might ask why a dream occurs (usually) as a narrative? Why doesn't it unfold like a photo album displaying "stills" of different people and places, or as a set of vignettes or blackouts? Or, as with congenitally blind people, as a set of textures, sounds, and presences? Or as a series of emotional intervals, a little like music? Why does it have to invent such elaborate plots? This makes the dream a very literary thing, as if it were imitating fiction. But it is clearly the other way around, on the evolutionary scale: first the dream, then the fictional narrative, the latter modeled on the former and by the same mind in both cases. And the main characteristic of narrative, or story, is that it is a form of thinking based on what Marvin Minsky calls the chaining principle (1988, 187–88). Chaining occurs whenever we imagine or try to explain something. Whenever we are concerned with the causes of things, with similarities (or differences) among things, or any form of dependency (A makes B possible), we are making chains. Making chains, beginning with the grocery list, is far more important as a principle of thought than being logical, Minsky argues, and the reason is that experience itself occurs as a chain. So anything having to do with experience involves us in a chain. Here is a simple chain: "Mother died in 1989, four years after Father." Here's a more complex chain: "You should see the cat. She found herself in the mirror and she's pawing it; then she looks behind the mirror to see where the cat is. She's so cute."

So we are enmeshed in chains; we are chain thinkers. To put it another way: we are in a narrative called life. A narrative is anything that endures and suffers change. We can speak as easily of the narrative of the algebra equation or the narrative of a football game, the city's narrative plan for five-year growth, and so on, until one is sick and tired of the word *narrative*. All that matters is that one thing leads to another and that something else follows from that. There's no escaping narrative. Narrative is remarkably like walking, which is a chain of steps in which one step is prepared by the one directly before it. So we are dealing with a fundamental way of organizing thought. Is it any wonder, then, that dreaming is a personal form of stringing things together in terms of causes, resemblances, dependencies, and interdependencies known only to the dreamer, the string itself being the path of least hindrance to the flow of association. In empirical reality, water, as we say, always seeks the lowest level; as the poet A. R. Ammons more colorfully puts it, "If anything will level with you water will" (1970, 10). In dream reality, the image, being a watery thing, "levels" with us. But the level it seeks has only to do with the gravity of association, the magnetic tug—weak or strong—that draws the image toward what we might call its *next of kin(d)*, or that "piece" of memory that bears the most pressing kinship with it. Beyond this, like DNA in Richard Dawkins's theory, the image doesn't care with whom it mates; it wants only to pass on, to be maximized, to be transmogrified according to the laws of dream probability which, as we will see, are the laws of metonymy and metaphor—at least that's our best way of saying it so far.

Indeed, to speak strictly within those same laws, one might say that metaphorical combination—as distinguished from symbolism—is to dream structure what hydrogen bonding is to the structure of DNA. We see this most vividly and frequently in the refusal of dream faces to remain the faces of single individuals (father, wife, friend, or daughter). This is probably the most common feature of dream behavior, and behind it we get a close glimpse of the source of the dream's vitality. The feature suggests that it is not the unique image (mother, father) that struggles to survive in the dream, but the class to which the face belongs in the memory of the dreamer, and the oscillations in identity that take place within the dream image are simply reflections of what we might call the class warfare taking place among "kindred" associations belonging to a common neural network.

This analogy between dreams and DNA leads me directly to the threshold of a larger idea that, in one way or another, will provide the basis for the rest of this book. The next step is to trace out the implications of Darwinian natural selection for the construction and behavior of dreams.

2 ·

The Myth of the Intelligent Dream

Some years ago, Richard Dawkins suggested that the DNA molecule is not the only "replicating entity which prevails on our . . . planet"; "a new kind of replicator has recently emerged" to which he gave the name of *meme.* A meme is

> a unit of cultural transmission, or a unit of *imitation.* Memes propagate themselves in the meme pool by leaping from brain to brain via a process which, in the broad sense, can be called imitation. . . . Selection favours memes that exploit their cultural environment to their own advantage. This cultural environment consists of other memes which are also being selected. The meme pool therefore comes to have the attributes of an evolutionarily stable set, which new memes find it hard to invade. . . . When we die there are two things we can leave behind us: genes and memes. (1989, 192, 199)

Dawkins thinks of memes in quite broad terms as any contribution to world culture—"tunes, ideas, catch-phrases, clothes fashions, ways of making pots or of building arches," poems, and presumably art of any sort. Thus memes are produced by science, art, and craft alike, any practice that "parasitize[s the] brain, turning it into a vehicle for the meme's propagation in just the way that a virus may parasitize the genetic mechanism of a host cell" (192).

I am not sure how literal Dawkins is when he refers to the transmission of the meme as being equivalent to the transmission of the gene. The natural question arises: Is gene transmission more biological than meme transmission? Probably so, in the "hardware" sense of the term: you can photograph a gene but you can't photograph the ideation that produces a new pot, a new poem, or the notion of God (one of history's most successful memes). But the question is interesting because it poses the possibility that Darwinian natural selection, as Daniel Dennett has argued in *Darwin's Dangerous Idea* (1995), may have more than genetic manifestations and that natural selection is something of a universal way in which all things, from cells to species to societies, go about evolving for better or worse.[1] Darwin, it may turn out, was looking only at single instance of natural selection. The dangerous thing about toying with this so-called dangerous idea is that analogies or likenesses between processes can lead one to overlook categorical differences that separate one process from another. Perhaps we can settle this problem temporarily by noting that mind is an emergent feature of brain, occurring at the "seam" where brain hardware turns into, or produces, thought software. Few people would argue that mind is less biological than brain because it isn't made *only* of fibers, tissue, and hard stuff. Or, as Dawkins puts it: "The old gene-selected evolution, by making brains, provided the 'soup' in which the first memes arose" (194).[2]

Before continuing, I should say that my interest in a Darwinian approach to dreams is substantially metaphorical rather than scientific. For one thing I find natural selection a useful way of getting us past the other metaphor that sees dreams as intelligent planning agencies with their own unconscious agendas.[3] A good deal of my preparation in these

1. In a review of Dennett's book, Colin McGinn suggests that "mountains, snowflakes, tectonic plates, hydrogen atoms, planets, galaxies—all exist because natural selection" (which could as well be called "natural *destruction*") "has operated in their favor" (1995, 3). McGinn also offers the intriguing suggestion that "genes *are* a type of meme [since] a gene is best defined as a unit of *information,* so that what is passed on to offspring is itself a semantic vehicle, containing instructions for body construction" (4).

2. In *The Extended Phenotype* (1992) Dawkins clarifies the issue to some extent, as follows: "A meme should be regarded as a unit of information residing in a brain. . . . It has a definite structure, realized in whatever physical medium the brain uses for storing information. If the brain stores information as a pattern of synaptic connections, a meme should in principle be visible under a microscope as a definite pattern of synaptic structure. If the brain stores information in 'distributed' form . . . the meme would not be localizable on a microscope slide, but still I would want to regard it as physically residing in the brain. This is to distinguish it from its phenotypic effects, which are its consequences in the outside world" (109); see also revised edition of *The Selfish Gene* (1989, 323).

3. Much of my work in the past ten years has been loosely evolutionist in spirit, at least with respect to the evolution of art forms (States, 1985, 1992, 1993, 1994).

matters came through a lifelong study of Kenneth Burke, who was at least a closet Darwinian in the sense that he viewed culture, art, and human experience in general in Darwinian terms as something that advanced "dramatistically" through, on the one hand, external or "scenic" influences (what Darwin would call "conditions of existence") and, on the other hand, through internal "motives," or the deliberate acts of "agents." Thus, in his discussion of Darwin in *The Grammar of Motives* in 1945, Burke writes, "For instance, 'adaptation,' 'competition,' 'struggle for life,' 'natural selection,' and 'survival of the fittest' can all be read and felt as *action* words [as well as blind *motion* words]. Or consider the almost 'dramatist' mode of expression in his reference to 'one general law leading to the advancement of all organic beings,—namely, multiply, vary, let the strongest live and the weakest die' " (1962, 153–54). Implicitly, then, Burke anticipates Dawkinsian evolutionary theory by positing the complementary forces of "blind" motion (the chance evolution of genes, history, culture) along with the internal and intentional motives of agents (memes). Indeed, as far as I can see, Burke's concept of motive is virtually identical to Dawkins's concept of the meme in that it embraces both individual and collective action. For example, compare Dawkins's idea of God, priests, and celibacy as "cooperating" memes (1989, 192–99) to Burke's idea that all gods are "names for motives or combinations of motives" (1962, 43) and that all saints are "motivational terms . . . that break down the universality of the [God] motive into narrower reference" (45).

Elsewhere, Burke coins the term *cooperative competition,* which is, in some respects, more Darwinian than the catchphrase given to evolution not by Darwin but by Herbert Spenser—"survival of the fittest"— which has a heavy overbite of the "tooth and claw" of a violent natural process. Cooperative competition is hardly as peaceful as the term sounds on first hearing. It is this force that makes a drama, or an evolution, and (I would add) a dream, possible. Cooperative competition is based on what Burke calls the agent-act ratio, whereby "the dramatist prepares for an agent's act by building up the corresponding properties in that agent, properties that fit him for the act." Shakespeare, Burke notes, is often praised for character drawing. But the illusion of life-likeness in his characters "really derives from his dramaturgic skill in finding traits that act well, and in giving his characters only traits that suit them for the action needed of them" (1964, 167-68).

Simply put, this is what one might call reverse Darwinism, but Darwinism even so. If you put Shakespeare's "dramaturgic skill" aside and read the passage from a Darwinian standpoint, traits, or genes, produce an action—an evolution—that occurs directly as a result of "corresponding properties . . . that fit [the agent] for the act." In other words, Shakespeare and evolution *do* the same thing: Shakespeare does it deliberately, with a design already in mind; evolution does it blindly, by simply capitalizing on new "advances" that accidentally occur in the gene basket.[4] But as proud human beings we have an inveterate habit of converting evolutionary blindness into "Shakespearean" foresight; for, retrospectively, these blind advances are interpreted as part of a vast plan, a long Shakespeare play written by God, as it were. Its theme is that nature gradually evolved, "act" by "act," and look what was produced as the grand denouement—us!

So there is nothing new in Dawkins's *concept* of the meme, except

4. I wonder, however, how deliberate Shakespeare's productions would seem if you were able to trace his aesthetic choices down to the microlevel of a "genetics" of the imagination. Did he really have much say in writing lines like "To be or not to be . . . ," or "If it were done, when 'tis done, then 'twere well/It were done quickly"? Or was he following intuitive hunches that originate in the body's "understanding" of sound and rhythm? When something felt "right" to him, in other words, was it a choice or a matter of obeying certain laws of form? These laws, one might argue, are in part the consequence of conventional practice but on what ground does conventional practice originate if not in racial usage, or in an era's "adaptation" of the universal principles of balance, development, crescendo, antithesis, and so on? I'm not trying to do away with the creative aspect of art, but to illustrate how difficult it is to separate biology from psychology, brain from mind, and inevitably, I suppose, genes from memes. You either have to see these things as sliding into each other, as being made of each other, or you have to posit a discrete border at which one "stops" and something turns up that we must call by another name.

the term itself; Dawkins's achievement, however, was to see the meme as a behavioral extension of the gene. In sum: blind advances in gene construction in turn prepare the organism for corresponding advances in meme or motive orientation—blind motion thus leading to directed action. My claim—scarcely original in this light—is a specific Burkian application of the Darwinian idea to dreaming: dreams are one of the private things we do in our struggle with memes (or motives, as you wish), and, like genes, dreams are selfish, blind, mental acts that capitalize on the strongest materials they cast up in their mini-evolutions. In short, dreams are "up to" nothing.

What drives the meme to replicate itself? Dawkins tells us that it evolves its "traits" in a way that is "*advantageous to itself*" (1989, 200), as opposed to being advantageous to the culture or to individuals. That is, we continue to have snuff movies and kiddie porn, presumably not advantageous to culture, side by side with so-called great art, which presumably is advantageous—all of which is to say that there are *appetites* for all of these things. Moreover, "bad" dreams and nightmares occur alongside relatively innocuous or pleasant dreams. The same "leveling" force must be driving both mimetic extremes, and it may have something to do with the inherent attraction of mimesis itself, as opposed to the particular things being imitated.

The word *attraction* should not be taken as suggesting a willful or voluntary fancy, a taste for something that could, if one wished, be left well enough alone; rather, it involves a human need that is as ubiquitous as shelter building or tool improvement. By mimesis, or representation, we are ultimately referring not simply to the making of art but to the process by which the brain records and represents what Paul Churchland describes as "the general and lasting features of the external world . . . by relatively lasting configurations of synaptic *connections.*" Out of this ongoing process, which Churchland calls "vector coding," we develop a dynamic library of "prototypical representations" that constitutes the standard by which we assess and react to the world (1995, 6). Memes are what one might call social vector codes. A meme's taking an evolutionary path that is "advantageous to itself" implies, among other things, a built-in tendency to structural perfection that appeals to the brain's quest for order, or its need to "match" or imitate the structure and complexity of experience in its mnemonic representations, whether in dream, art, science, or everyday behavior. In short, it involves no representation, and little or no thinking.

The proverb "What goes around comes around" captures certain "viral" truths relating to human experience. In one of its many meanings it describes the progress of a successful meme as it moves through culture: memes that "go around" (at least the successful ones) tend, like the flu, eventually to "come around" to everyone for whom the meme might hold potential interest. The saying makes its point, however, in the maximization and symmetry of its expression, which rounds things out to their full potential. Not sometimes or often, but always, the business of the proverb (and proverb is another term for meme, or motive) is to go as far as possible *in one direction*. Proverbs are not cautious constructions. Dawkins asks whether memes are competitive with each other, like genes—do they have rivals (alleles)? "I suppose," he says, "there is a trivial sense in which many ideas can be said to have 'opposites' " (1989, 196). But there is also a profound sense in which ideas have opposites—indeed, *require* opposites; for it seems to me that memes are needed, like proverbs, to cover all potentialities in experience. Thus "waste not, want not" is perfectly good for certain occasions, and its opposite, "easy come, easy go," is better for others. The truth is that we live in a world in which complementary ideas are needed to cover all bases. At times it is propitious for a person, or a people, to adopt a policy expressed by the proverb "Where there's a will there's a way"; at other times, it is necessary to bear in mind that "Man proposes, God disposes."[5] There is no reconciling the two maxims, and we need both options in a world in which, as another proverb runs, "nothing is permanent except change."

5. I owe these two proverbs to my good friend Paul Hernadi, who invokes them in *Beyond Genre* (1972, 156–67) and again in *Cultural Transactions* (1995, 102).

Proverbs, then, could be considered as the identifying "flags" under which memes and motives travel—the meme in shorthand form. For example, Dawkins notes that the meme for God ("an answer to deep and troubling questions about existence" [193]) is re-enforced by the memes for hell (from which God will save us), faith, sacrifice, and even celibacy (in the case of priests). And entries in any book of proverbs deal with all these topics ("Faith will move mountains," "The descent to hell is easy," "The blood of the martyrs is the seed of the church"). In fact, a book of proverbs can be thought of as a book of memes (or motives). So, yes, there are conflicting memes, and they are born of the diversity of human experience and the need to have a name and a "formula" for any conceivable experience. Indeed, the meme of God is balanced by its own "natural" opposite, for the concept of evolution is itself a meme.[6] This does not put its scientific validity into question, but it was only with the emergence of a species capable of positing the existence and behavior of what we now call genes that evolution, at least the kind developed by Dawkins, could have come into a conceptual existence. Genes are not memes, but the theory of evolution is a meme, irrespective of its foundation in objective science. And it is interesting to note that the meme of evolution puts us in the precarious position, with increasing technological resources, of being able to alter the direction and momentum of genetic evolution, for better or worse—more likely, for better *and* worse.

To sum up (proverbially): memes may be able to parasitize all of the people some of the time (geocentrism), and some of the people all of the time (religious doctrine), but a single meme is not likely to parasitize all of the people all of the time (especially those who have been parasitized by an opposite meme). In chapter 9 I will deal with further implications of this idea as the basis for a theory of personal and social conflict in (and out of) dreams. Here I am interested only in establishing that dreams and art are media in which experience is "replicated"

6. I was feeling rather smug about making this connection until I discovered that Daniel Dennett had gotten there before me in *Darwin's Dangerous Idea* (1995, 344).

according to certain patterns of design and maximization through the principle of mimesis (vector coding), which precedes all memes in point of origin if only because the urge to imitate, as Aristotle said, is natural to humans and like all urges necessarily precedes the pursuit of particular urgent things.

In fact, I can make the overall point clearer by looking briefly at the evolution of an entire art form. In about 330 B.C.E. Aristotle wrote, in a kind of *Origin of Species* for Greek tragedy, "It expand[ed] gradually [from the dithyramb], each feature being further developed as it appeared; and after it had gone through a number of phases it stopped upon attaining its full natural growth" (1967, 22). This is not good evolutionary theory (evolution never stops), but it has every earmark of a progress that was "advantageous to itself"—that is to say, to the complex meme called tragedy which, like God, is "an answer to deep and troubling questions about existence." Tragedy was, of course, advantageous to Athenian society as well, but how could tragic art have satisfied Athenian audiences if it were not exploiting its possibilities "naturally" and fully? Thus, the composers of tragedy were not only following current Greek tastes, giving Greek audiences what they wanted. They were also following natural rules, or forms, as Plato might have put it (if, alas, he had had any liking for tragedy), that appeal to the minds of tragedians and audiences alike because they are thorough representations of human nature. Good art is simply a good match between expression and our understanding of human experience; bad art is a poor match, but the same "creative" impulse *to match* underlies both renderings. As Dawkins puts it, "All that is necessary is that the brain should be *capable* of imitation: memes will then evolve that exploit the capability to the full" (1989, 200). Exploiting tragic mimesis "to the full" involved certain unconscious compositional procedures, most of which are still functional today.[7] Thus Greek tragedy—by which I really mean to say all art—was "selfish" in Dawkins's sense in that it looked out for itself and

7. My book *The Pleasure of the Play* (1994) is an extended discussion of this notion of the universality of Aristotelian principles.

evolved the mechanisms that brought it to its "full natural growth."[8] When something proved "good" for the form (e.g., the addition of a second, then a third actor) it was retained; when something proved less good, or outmoded (the chorus) it no longer made its contribution to the form. The *Poetics* of Aristotle is simply one document that illustrates how evolution used the imitation meme to its full capability.

Dreams, whatever their possible purposes, obey the same rules that poets obey, though they are applied under radically different conditions. It would be more correct to say that poets follow the same rules as dreams (with obvious differences). A dream is neither a gene or a meme. But it is a primary carrier of memes, or motives; a dream is one of the things we do about our memes, and the evolution of images it imitates in its narrative is "advantageous to itself" and not to the dreamer. This claim, of course, flies in the face of an entire school of dream theory.

What does it mean to say this? Simply that the dream is mine (in the sense that I am having it) but it has no obligation to evolve in a way that is beneficial to me: it evolves in a way that is "beneficial" to the dreamwork—which is to say in a way that exercises the dream process maximally. It can as easily hurl me headlong from a cliff as reward me with pleasure, depending on the theme it happens to be "selfishly" pursuing at the time. Now it could be that even nightmares are somehow advantageous to the dreamer in some respect we are not yet aware of (pain itself, after all, is a lifesaving property); but a nightmare may also bring on cardiac arrest. The point is that the dream doesn't care about any of this; it doesn't produce its images with my satisfaction or terror in mind but rather to realize the potential of the meme of imitation—which is simply to say that in a dream we catch the mind *objectively* engaged in the production of *subjective* images. The dream represents my mind working

---

8. I am not suggesting, even remotely, that there is not a deliberate and intentional side to the composition of tragedy as well. This amounts to an interplay between the intentions of the playwright(s) and the natural tendencies of the genre whereby the changes occurring in, say, Greek tragedy between Aeschylus and late Euripides are, like the march of any history, brought on by a combination of blindness and insight, in Paul de Man's phrase.

at a certain maximal pitch on the contents of my personal meme pool. By meme pool I am referring to the personal and social tensions the dream is carrying in its narrative, all of the contents and discontents, all of the motives, and all of the ambiguities and contradictions that come with living in a meme-infested civilization. There is no telling how many memes, or units of cultural usage, a dream may be carrying in its stream at one time, any more than one can say how many memes there are in Beethoven's Ninth Symphony, to use Dawkins's example (1989, 195). We may hypothesize that a dream begins with a certain tension or feeling that is somehow attached umbilically to a certain sector of memory (what Churchland would call a "prototypical hot spot" [1995, 83]) and hence to a certain quantum of relevant imagery (or what Burke would call an "associational cluster" [1956, 18]). Like an orchestra tuning up before the overture, it "exercises," and when the quantum reaches a certain pitch of affect and satisfies what Freud called "the conditions of representation," the dream pops into visual life and the evolution of tensions in the particular meme-motive pool begins. From then on the dream follows its own inclination, choosing the line of greatest attraction, which is also the line of least resistance. We have nothing to do with it, except to live it through. The dream is merciless: it excludes nothing that lies in its mnemonic path. To put it another way: the dream occurs at the pole opposite the repressive mechanism, which belongs to the day world.

Like evolution, then, the dream is a mindless process operating on and with mind matters. I take the word mindless as meaning strictly what it does to evolutionists: a completely unconscious, involuntary, innate, nonintentional natural process of "design accumulation" (Dennett, 1995, 62), something you simply cannot help doing. We can't really know what is behind the design because the design itself is not a consequence of prior thought and is subject to continual change as new images assert new priorities and disturb the priorities of old ones in the warfare of cooperative competition. But the most valuable lesson the theory of evolution has taught us is that design and order do not necessarily require advance planning of the sort that goes into preparing a picnic, organizing a conference on design, or writing a simple story for waking design-minded readers. As Daniel Dennett puts it, the evolutionary process "is not itself something intelligent but, wonder of wonders, something intelligible" (1995, 184). I will have a good deal to say about how dream images are linked together to produce a dream narrative. But none of the linkings involves a supervisory intelligence, or what Dennett would call a planner or a meaner, and here we come up against a common belief of students of the dream.

I am not referring to intelligence in the sense that the dreamer can be presumed to be intelligent and therefore that the dream is, in some way, a by-product of this intelligence. In this sense, emotions are also a by-product of such intelligence, but you could hardly claim that having emotions is a demonstration of intelligence. The intelligence I detect in the commentary from Freud forward bears on something else, some inherent demonstration that the dream is not only "up to" something, it also *knows* what it is up to.

What is the meaning of saying that something is intelligible but not itself intelligent? How can you tell an intelligent dream from one that is not intelligent? Would we expect Einstein's dreams to be more intelligent than the dreams of a person with an average or subaverage IQ? If we conclude that the answer is no, then it would appear that *that* kind of intelligence—measured by the IQ test—is not relevant to any conceivable intelligence one can detect in dreaming. And surely this is the right answer because dreams have nothing to do with solving problems in physics, and it is highly unlikely that Einstein's best work was done during REM sleep. But just for the sake of argument, how would we know that Einstein's dreams were, or were not, more intelligent than the dreams of Dudley Dimwit? What might be the characteristics of an intelligent dream?

Unfortunately, *intelligence* is one of those received words we use under certain circumstances without thinking about it ("Sue is an intelligent person," "Harold made an intelligent decision," "Is there intelligent life on other planets?"). Let us put intelligence into action by taking an unusual example that will help to isolate its qualities. We can't very well use human beings as our standard because we're all intelligent, and we can't reliably describe something we would have to use in order to describe it. As a simple illustration of intelligence, let us take the example of Lassie, who is a kind of ideal dog anyway. Everyone would agree that Lassie is an intelligent dog—not only as dogs go, but as humans go as well, as she's often smarter than some of the people she has to deal with. How do we know? What exactly does she do that can be called *intelligent?* First, she can tell when someone is imperiled or trapped, and she can either find a tool that will solve the problem or follow instructions ("Fetch the keys to the '62 pick-up, Lassie! Good girl!") or she will run back to the house and bring help. She can actually cajole the stupid humans there into moving into action, and she will lead them to the trouble spot by taking a short cut. In sum, Lassie sees both "before and after," as Hamlet puts it, and she has a set of virtually human priorities, and she can understand English. She can probably even do basic math with her paws. As Paul Churchland would say, she has an exceptional number of vector-coding and vector-processing networks, which is precisely the brain equipment needed in order to achieve intelligence (1995, 236). Lassie is one smart dog. She is just like us!

I can't bring myself to say that the dream I often have about being lost in the city is nearly as smart as Lassie. Oh, perhaps a little smart in the consistency with which the dream makes absolutely sure that all landmarks disappear when I look for them. But I think this could be explained by something much simpler than intelligence: dreams simply aren't good at maintaining stable environments. If you're lost in a dream, you're *really* lost because there's no "there" to find your way back to. In fact, one of the things I've noticed about dreams, though I haven't made a study of it, is that they tend not to return to scenes once they leave them. And I've wondered whether the reason for this may be that dreams have, in a manner of speaking, a short memory for their own inventions. They find it difficult to double back and knit the story into a unity. I've had dreams that do return to a scene, but they are more the exception than the rule. Dreams seem to be forward-driven; they're more like dumb oxen than smart collies.

In any event, we would be apt to say that a dream that displayed signs of intelligence—apart from having the neural equipment needed to do intelligent things—would have something like Lassie's powers. Call it situation savvy: the ability to plan ahead, look back, set up key events that would figure in the later narrative, build to a climax, maintain consistent symbolism, characterization, and so on. An intelligent dream wouldn't sniff along from one event to another unrelated event, like a junkyard dog; it wouldn't introduce characters it didn't intend to "use" in the narrative, and it wouldn't bury plot bones and forget where they were buried. In other words, it would resemble a story of the sort that intelligent parents tell their intelligent children before sleep (which usually feature intelligent animals); and we all know that children will not let you get by without using all the story parts you begin with:

"What happened to the squirrel?" Amanda will ask.

"What squirrel?" you ask.

"You said there was a squirrel with Mary Ann."

"Oh, that squirrel. Right. Well—"

Now some dreams do some of these things some of the time, but most of them contain dreadful lapses in probability and neatness, by general standards of intelligence. I'm not in the least arguing that dreams, to this extent, are stupid. I think the whole idea of intelligence in dreams is misplaced, just as it is when applied to the march of genes, but it has to be dealt with because a good deal of commentary on the dream assumes that dreams demonstrate a form of "in-house" intelligence. We *assume* they're intelligent. In fact, I would say that more than half of the people who study dreams professionally—and this is a conservative estimate—hold some version of this belief. Some of my best psychologist friends believe that dreams are intelligent.

Other than having Lassie savvy, the other way a dream might conceivably pass an intelligence test would be if one could show that it was abiding by *another kind of logic* in which these same shenanigans and errors become a symbolic code in which a hidden, or not so hidden, meaning is being projected. I will return to this topic in chapter 6 in another connection. But far and away the most famous instance in this line of thought is Freud's theory of censorship, the opposite extreme of an evolutionary explanation of dreaming. Freud himself argued that the dreamwork "is not simply more careless, more irrational, more forgetful and more incomplete than waking thought. . . . It does not think, calculate, or judge in any way at all; it restricts itself to giving things a new form." So far, so good. But this "new form" he refers to has something about it, to adapt his own figure, of the Lassie in sheep's clothing. Within the same paragraph, Freud tells us that the dream "has above all to evade the censorship, and with that end in view the dream-work makes use of a *displacement of psychical intensities* to the point of a transvaluation of all psychical values" (1900, 5:507).

Now how does this evasion, this "making use of," actually work? How could a dream accomplish *that* without some intelligence? It is fairly easy to understand how the dreamwork could move from image A to image B by some form of association (see chapter 4), but it is quite another matter to assume that a dream could (in effect) produce image A, anticipate that image B is coming, abort B, and substitute B-complex (a *displaced* version of B) so that the dreamer's sleep won't be disturbed. That seems to me to qualify as an act of intelligence, if only because it exerts *control* over the process that is occurring, and, moreover, this control is based on an interpretive reading of dream content from a *superior and external perspective*. Again, this is Sartre's complaint about the censor. The dreamer who is experiencing the dream knows nothing about this, and censorship, in its turn, presumes an intentionality behind the dream (it "allows nothing to pass without exacting its rights") that is distinct from any intention the dreamer may be having within the dream (avoiding a monster, reaching a goal, solving a problem, and so on). In short, try as we might to get around it, the censor is a little brain, a veritable Wizard of Id, with its own "ends" in mind, and so also is the dreamwork that tries to desperately to "evade" it. If the censor's business is to protect the sleeping dreamer from disturbing thoughts, then the only solution is to post an intelligent watchdog at the gate who can recognize and prevent the disturbance.[9]

Such a view seems to me outside the laws of falsifiability: obviously the censor's existence can't be proven or disproven, any more than one can prove or disprove the existence of flying elephants in another galaxy. For example, if I claimed there was a device or a discrete function in the brain that prevented me from using words I had never heard of, it would be as indisputable as Freud's censor, and for the same reason: no one could disprove it, and I could always muster my own "proof" by claiming that I had never used such words. So, too, the proof often used by censor advocates is that the dream didn't depict a penis but depicted a long object instead (more of this in chapter 6); therefore, the dream must have been censored because all long objects are symbols of the penis. It seems self-evident that the real intelligence in the matter occurs in the interpretation itself which is then reflected back to a supposed matching intelligence residing in the dreamwork. If the dream is intelligible, or interpretable, then it follows—according to this theory—that it is also, like the interpretation of the intelligibility, the product of an intelligence. At a minimum, an intelligent dreaming machine must (like Lassie) have a planner and a meaner, since the assumption is that you can't plan without knowing in advance what is to be planned, and you can't know that unless you have some idea about why it's worth planning. Otherwise, why would an intelligent intelligence waste its time?

9. Paul Churchland points out that the "immediate intuitive appeal" of Freud's theory of the unconscious is that "[i]t was just commonsense psychology relocated one level down [to the Ucs]." In other words, for all intents and purposes—e.g., avoiding the censor—the unconscious *thinks* precisely like the conscious mind "as represented in our commonsense prototypes for beliefs, desires, fears, and practical reasoning" (1995, 182). Churchland's book is devoted to showing that unconscious cognitive activity has no such "sentence-like [linguistic] and inference-like [rational] structure. . . . Rather, it is the transformation of one activation vector into another activation vector. Unconscious activity is there in abundance, but Freud's guess as to its causal structure was not remotely correct" (182–83).

My suspicions about intelligence in the dream process arise largely because I think dreaming, like evolution, can be explained without the assistance of a separate agency or capacity, and if that is possible there is no reason to add an additional "virtue" to dreaming. That's what the presumption of intelligence amounts to: it gives the dream process a "dignity" of being worthy of our own waking brains, as opposed to being a mindless cognitive process within the brain. The basic similarity between genetic evolution and dreaming — or the one that mainly interests me — is that both are unplanned processes that unfold algorithmically, to use Dennett's term, according to certain natural "rules" of elimination and selection. For the dream, these are substantially the "rules" of associational memory, and I place "rules" in quotation marks only because we tend to think of rules as having been consciously made by an intelligent agent. This is not true, as the "rules" governing the behavior of volcanoes, human hearts and lungs, bird migrations, animal courting rituals, and gravitation amply illustrate.

The essence of what I mean can be seen in a simple example: when you see a picture of a meerschaum pipe and you instantly think of your Uncle Harry you do so mindlessly, without "thinking" about it, as automatically, you might say, as cells dividing. Suddenly, there is an image, however unclear, of Uncle Harry there in your head, and you had nothing to do with putting it there — at least consciously. The association has about as much to do with intelligence as riding a bicycle; it is a process your mind cannot help performing any more than it can prevent you from dreaming. The rules governing associational sequences, then, are automatic and innate, but this does not imply that association is a simple one-to-one matter. If a meerschaum pipe reminds you of Uncle Harry, you can't know whether that is all it reminds you of, and it would be a strange image that carried with it only a single association. Uncle Harry was more than likely only the strongest association in your mind at that moment. Tomorrow, a meerschaum pipe might remind you of Magritte's painting *Ceci n'est pas une pipe,* or of a room that is memorable for the smell of pipe smoke; or it may remind you of something you simply can't pin down. Finally, once the meerschaum pipe has led you to Uncle Harry there is a whole network of associations buzzing around your image of Uncle Harry—places, events, qualities, emotions, and so on. And so it is with all of our mental images. An image is a representation (visual, aural, oral, olfactory) that is never only itself, never permanently carries the same set of associations, and is never the same thing for two individuals or for the same individual at different times. It is an immediate brain-state production. In short, even the images stored in our memory evolve in keeping with the history they accumulate and the sequences in which they occur. So it is easy to see why dreams behave as irresponsibly, as unlike Lassie as they do. They are following a different rulebook, and it is the book of neuronal activation and vector coding—or that's one way of saying it.

In any case, as the dream moves from image to image there is a kind of natural selection at work whereby the most "advantageous" images automatically survive and the weakest fall away or never arrive. What is advantageous to the dream is, again, not discernible in our recollection of the dream or in our waking priority systems. The advantage any image carries with it is that of associational priority, and this would depend on conditions absolutely unknowable from the image itself (recall the pattern experiment of chapter 1).[10] Dreams are very different from waking stories, but they are like them in the sense that each event constitutes at once an advance in the narrative and a limitation on the possible things that might happen next—barring disorders and exterior stimuli in the system. But unlike "intelligent" stories, dream narratives are powerfully driven by associational linkages stored in the memory of the dreamer. The thing we are tempted to call intelligence, and its

10. For a good overall sense of the neurobiology involved in these "authorless" transactions, see Timothy L. Hubbard (1994). For example: "Whichever elements of the network possess the strongest activation at a given moment would specify the content and type of dream imagery at that time. . . . There would be no need for a narrator, executive, homunculus, censor, or any other entity sitting out in the Cartesian Theatre witnessing, constructing, or making sense out of the dream. The course of the narrative would simply correspond to the sequence of activations (i.e., drafts) built up over time" (262–63). This is Churchland's thesis as well.

derivatives (meaning, design, the unconscious, and so on), is nothing more or less than the unfettered operation of associative memory: we dream what we already know and what is on our mind. Or, more conservatively, what the dreamer already knows is sufficient to produce any dream, including dreams that have produced intelligent inventions and discoveries, such as Elias Howe's sewing needle, Kekulé's benzene ring, Hermann Hilprecht's solution to the problem of the fragments found in a Babylonian temple, or Otto Loewi's discovery that the brain uses neurotransmitters to pass information through its channels.

But can we explain such intelligent discoveries and solutions to problems, if not through dream intelligence? Surely this is the acid test. First, there is nothing in the mindlessness of a dream that would prevent it from falling onto the solution to an intellectual or a psychic problem—now and then. The question would be: was this solution provided intentionally by the dream, which "thought" it out and presented it *as* a solution? Not necessarily. For it is one thing to say that a problem was solved in a dream, another to say that the dream solved the problem. For example, the solution could be something that had occurred to the dreamer before the dream in a subliminal level of recognition. This is no more mysterious than any piece of day residue subliminally entering a dream without our conscious manipulation; the difference is that the solution to a problem strikes one, after the fact, as being a *more intelligent act* than dreaming you're drinking soup from a car hubcap that you subliminally recorded from the day's experience.[11] Or did the solu-

11. There is also the incubation factor. Most solutions to problems do not erupt suddenly but are prepared during periods of conscious and unconscious thought. Quite often what prevents a breakthrough is the inevitable "tunnel vision" that occurs in thinking too precisely about the problem. As everybody knows, that's the time for a walk around the block or a short nap (during which you will probably dream about the problem). So the "Eureka!" of sudden discovery may follow a long period of gestation at a lower level of consciousness. In such cases, in a manner of speaking, the conscious mind is the "last person" in the cognitive chain to get news of the solution.

Roger Penrose advances the idea that there are two factors involved in making an original discovery or in solving a problem: "namely a 'putting-up' and

tion occur to the dreamer *during* the dream via an association that was irrelevant to the problem? Obviously dreamers don't put their intelligence on the bedside table along with their teeth and wristwatches when they go to bed, but for the most part they behave as intelligently in the dream state as they do out of it. But is there a difference between attributing the intelligence to the dreamwork or the state of dreaming itself and attributing it to the dreamer who is experiencing the dream?

Here, I admit, things become murky: what can you attribute to the dreamwork and what to the dreamer who is experiencing the dream? How do these two things differ? Suppose in a dream I see an object on a table and I immediately wake up and proclaim "Eureka! There's the solution to my problem!" (which I was thinking about prior to the dream). To whom (or what) do I credit this discovery? In a sense, there's only one thing going on (the dream) and I'm responsible for it. But responsible as what? As the experiencing dreamer or as (absent) author of the dream? Is there a difference? We probably ought to have a clearer case. Let's say that I take one of my pressing problems to sleep and in a dream a strange man I meet on a train tells me that my problem can be solved if I apply a grid-spreader to the turphenfoil of my new invention (which happens to be a Zeugma converter), thus guarding against the premature emission of fuchsia gas. I wake up abruptly and indeed there is the correct solution to the problem—clever even by waking standards. Here the dream has actually created a character who tells me the right solution, so there can be no doubt that the dream has solved the problem.

---

a 'shooting-down' process. I imagine that the putting-up could be largely unconscious and the shooting-down largely conscious" (1991, 422). That is, what is put-up, or proposed, by unconscious thought is not always reliable, but all good ideas originate at this source. So what is required is a "shooting-down" mechanism which passes judgment on what has been put up, crying either "Eureka!" or "Take that!" He adds that dreams are very good at putting up unusual ideas but they rarely survive the scrutiny of the shootist. (For the record, Penrose has never conceived a successful scientific idea in a dream—citing Kekulé, of course, as being "more fortunate.")

I can't deny that there is a certain intelligence at work here. The question is, where does the intelligence reside? Have we proven that the dream is intelligent, or that I am intelligent in the dream state? If I say that the solution came to me in a dream, need we then credit the dream with the intelligence? I think not. That is a little like arguing that if I couldn't solve the problem in my study but was able to solve it in the bathroom, the bathroom should be credited with the achievement. What we have proven is that intelligence survives *in* the dream state, in the same sense that my concern for the pressing problem survives. All we really mean is that *I can still think in the dream state,* which isn't saying very much because thinking in the dream state does not often produce reliable results. Ultimately, even though a strange man provided the solution, it isn't clear that I didn't think of the solution in the dream (or even before the dream) and put the words in the stranger's mouth, as I might have thought of it myself the next morning at breakfast. In fact, let's look at that version of the solution. Suppose at breakfast my wife, Nancy, says to me, "We should spread the Turf Supreme on the new lawn this morning." And immediately my unsolved problem of the idle gridspreader springs to mind and I see, through a pure coincidence of word sounds, that it should be attached to the turphenfoil of my new Zeugma converter. What's the difference? The immediate difference is that I didn't invent my wife, whereas I did invent the stranger in my dream who solved the problem. One is an innocent verbal accident, the other is a postulated agency, and both have "solved" the problem. Still, what *is* the difference? I made the connection, in both cases, with my own intelligence (if that's what it was). We haven't proven that dreams are smart, that they are capable of solving problems, only that they are capable of carrying thought about problems—and that they occasionally find solutions. At best the dream has played the role of a concierge or midwife.

In one of the most searching critiques of problem-solving in dreams, Mark Blagrove, a psychologist at the University of Wales at Swansea, argues that the "representation [for example] of indecision [in a dream] does not require the presence of indecision, nor any of its attributes" in the dreamwork itself (1992b, 211). That is, while Hamlet's dreams may be about his indecision, the dreams themselves would not be indecisive, any more than a novel about lust could be said to be lustful or Rodin's statue *The Thinker* made of pensive bronze. So, too, dreams may depict attempts to solve problems, and in some cases find a solution, without actually being in the problem-solving business. The truth is, it is *technically* possible to find the solution to a problem in almost any state of consciousness, short of chaotic hallucination or delirium, and there is widely held sentiment among scientists (and most people would agree based on their own experience) that solutions to problems come more often than not when you are doing or thinking about something that has no connection with the problem.[12]

One of the strange things about dreams, contrary to Rechtschaffen's idea that they are single-minded (1978), is that in the dream state we become, in another sense of the word, double- or multiple-minded. That is, we enter a state in which consciousness seems to be capable of contemplating its own productions as if they originated as independent veridical experience. In actuality, consciousness is always bifurcated to

12. The nineteenth-century physicist Hermann von Helmholtz described creative thought as occurring in three stages: saturation, incubation, and illumination. In *The Quark and the Jaguar*, physicist Murray Gell-Mann subscribes to Helmholtz's idea with respect to his own work in science. The solution to the problem, he says, usually occurred "suddenly, while we were cycling or shaving or cooking" (1994, 264). My claim is that one of these "sudden" moments of discovery might occur in a dream, but it is far more likely to occur, and with much greater reliability, while one is shaving or engaged in some such mindless activity that gives the brain maximal openness to "illumination." Dreams, in their own way, are rife with preoccupation and challenge, and one may be immune to illumination because one is too busy trying to solve the problem. Dreams, insofar as they are concerned with problem-solving at all, seem largely to be representations of the "saturation" stage of thought: they replay the problem over and over. However, it is quite possible that the relaxed, time-lazy medium of the dream might release creative solutions that had long been cooking without coming to a boil. Arthur Koestler offers a fascinating example of this in *The Act of Creation* (1969, 185–86).

some extent: that is, it is divided into conscious awareness and unconscious thought, which work together like the right and left hands at a piano. For instance, when a forgotten name or fact suddenly pops into your head "out of nowhere," it has come from somewhere "else" in your head, so to speak, though you seemed to have no part in giving birth to it. The dream state apparently transforms this condition into the visual separation of dreamer and dream world, whereby some part of our unconscious thought—and it is unclear what sort of "part" this is—is projected in the form of dream images and dream characters. The analogy that comes to mind is that of the ventriloquist who "throws" his voice, making it seem to come from the dummy. Of course, unlike the ventriloquist, the dreamer has no awareness of causing such an operation but experiences thought and action as belonging strictly to the dream character, be it person or inanimate object. In some ways, this is similar to the aesthetic phenomenon of empathy, or the tendency of the onlooker to attribute to the perceived object the feelings and actions that are going on in his or her own body (as when I say, "the mountain rises," instead of realizing that what rising is going on is doing so *in me,* not in the mountain). In the dream state this becomes something of a complete circle wherein the dreamer projects feelings (menace, desire) onto the dream image in the very act of imagining it and then reacts as if the feeling had originated in the image. Hence the false notion of the autonomy of the dream and our natural assumption that a dream is something in us with special powers of cognition. It is plain that the dreamer is ultimately responsible for everything that transpires in a dream.

I am not suggesting an actual division in thought of the sort that is often presumed between conscious thought and the dynamic unconscious (which seems to have a mind of its own). I refer rather to separate brain functions that are similar, for instance, to those involved in procedural (or "how-to") versus declarative (or "that") memory. As Steven Rose observes, "The way we learn *how,* and the way we subsequently remember *what* we have learned, are different in kind from the way in which we remember *that*" (1993, 120). Similarly, the way we produce mental images and the way we react to them may involve different processes. It is well known, from the Penfield experiments alone, that electrical stimulation of the cerebral cortex can produce vivid "memories" that are taken as real but may be nothing more than dream confabulations (130).

At any rate, this "doubleness" of the dreamer's consciousness seems to me a likely factor in the problem-solving business: who, or what, is solving the problem in a dream—when and if the problem gets solved? Does the dream solve the problem, or does the dreaming "I" solve the problem in the dream? (Who, or what, adds two and two and gets four?) Is it something in the dreamwork functioning, like a ventriloquist, through a dream character—an intelligence *behind* the dream? Or is the problem solved (if it is) by the dreamer who arrives at the solution on her own as a reaction to certain inadvertent happenings in the dream? In short, were Kekulé's dancing serpents the solution to the problem of the benzene ring, or were they simply a serendipitous accident that led Kekulé to the solution by an innocent chain of association? To maintain that the dream solves the problem seems to me to credit to the medium or form what belongs to the content—a classic case of the pot calling the kettle—a pot.

But perhaps the main question to be asked about problem-solving in dreams is how often do dreams solve problems in comparison to solutions that occur in the waking state? If it were an established fact that more problems are solved in dreams than in the waking state, or that dreams routinely solve problems that cannot be solved in the waking state, then one would be forced to attribute a special "talent" to the dream. But new examples of dream solutions to waking problems seem to appear, as Maurice Burton said of the Loch Ness monster, "with surprising infrequency" (quoted in Humphrey, 1993, 35). For every Kekulé who discovers the solution to a problem in a dream there must be a hundred Flemings or Pasteurs or Bells or Newtons who make great discoveries by being alert to chance occurrences in the waking state.[13]

13. The other thing we would have to know about these famous problem-solving dreams is whether the problem was solved during the dream or following the appearance of something in the dream that awakens the dreamer and acti-

Scores of my own dreams convince me that dreams are drawn to problems like moths to a porch light. A problem may be defined as a psychic disequilibrium of some sort and dreams seem to thrive on tensions brought on by social or personal life. This is not to say that all dreams do (see Hunt, 1989), but there are probably as many kinds of dreams as there are psychical states, and disequilibrium is one of the most reliable features of waking life, and hence one of the most common dream structures.

But there is a big difference between problem-putting and problem-solving, or, as Blagrove argues, between "attacking" a problem and simply representing the problem that is raising Cain with your sleep (1992a, 34). In my own case, theorizing about dreams leads to what I suspect is an exceptional amount of theorizing about dreams *in* my dreams. When I'm involved in a dream project I have interminable problem dreams. Finding successful solutions that survive the test of waking judgment occurs very rarely; for the most part my dream solutions turn out to be mindless in the *other* sense of the word. And more often than not, the dream doesn't advance a solution to the problem; it simply belabors the problem, repeating it in permutation after permutation—indeed, making more of the problem than it is often worth. The problem, after all, is the source of the irritation, like the grain of sand in the oyster; and the dream usually dramatizes the *irritation,* rather than the satisfaction of finding relief in a solution—or it will provide a temporary relief in the form of a quick fix that can work only in a dream (two plus two equaling five, for example).

For example, one night during the period when I was worrying about this very problem of dream intelligence, I dreamed that I had managed to sneak a camera into my dream and took a picture of the dream from the inside. Because it was a Polaroid camera the print immediately rolled out and I saw, with great satisfaction, that it was only a negative. Here was the ocular proof that dreams are not intelligent, for

---

vates his or her "intelligence." Because a dream event leads to a solution does not necessarily indicate that the event was conjured for that purpose.

if they were (so my dream logic ran), the print would have been a positive. So there was my solution, clean as a whistle. Then it occurred to me that I might have trouble getting a dream photograph back across the border into the waking world. What to do? Another eureka!—what better way to authenticate something than with a footnote? (Don't footnotes prove that your argument has solid support?) And there was the perfect substitute for the photo: a footnote added to my chapter explaining what I had found and proving my case. Hence the solution to my dream problem *and* my problem of getting the solution back to waking reality. And I immediately composed a footnote in my dream. That's what you're reading right now, though it has been promoted to my main text and substantially doctored by waking thought (the dream version went something like "Negfoto dream dumb")—the footprint of a dream photo that proves that dreams are not intelligent agencies. Now are you convinced?[14]

Finally, in the face of the scarcity of evidence we must conclude that the dream state, in most cases, is actually an impediment to solving problems. Freud is right: dreams are "more careless, more irrational, more forgetful and more incomplete than waking thought." To put it more kindly, problem-solving is something dreams are not meant to do, and when someone manages to solve one (or claims to have solved one) in a dream, we hear about it far and wide, like the sighting of a UFO. Moreover, the same handful of examples keep turning up as the proof: Kekulé usually heads the list (a highly problematical dream-discovery, to put it mildly; see Strunz, 1993), Howe is second, and Robert Louis Stevenson and Dr. Jekyll are never far behind).[15] All of this leads one

14. Freud might argue that this dream solution is a perfect example of wish-fulfillment, like the woman's mother-in-law dream, in that it filled my wish that my theory of nonintelligence be true. And it is, after all, a good solution to my problem: for didn't the dream throw up the right *kind* of solution (a silly one) in response to my problem? There's no quarreling with that, except that my dreams reliably throw up silly solutions, regardless of the problem.

15. For instance: "Many great inventions and creative ideas have come through dreams. For example, Elias Howe, inventor of the sewing machine, is

to believe that a problem has a much better chance of being properly solved when you are listening to Muzak in an elevator or riding a bus.

This said, however, there is an intermediary possibility that would be unwise to ignore. Like Franz Strunz (1993), I believe that dreams have a deep relationship to the creative process and especially to the "leaps" of mind this process seems to require. If we don't solve our problems in dreams, or solve them in foolish ways, who is to say, as Strunz argues, that the "Eureka!" of discoveries made in the waking state may not have begun in the liberties of thought commonly exercised in the dream state? There is no real way to find out when and if this is the case, but it is a possibility worth leaving open. "Dreaming and daydreaming," in which discoveries are often made, Strunz reminds us, "are not discrete states of consciousness. . . . [Rather,] they are phenomenologically continuous, deal roughly . . . with the same content and follow identical modes of processing" (291). Perhaps they have more to do with each other's business than we think. Ernest Hartmann (1995) has advanced a similar idea. "In my view," he writes, "a dream can rarely be said to solve a problem in its entirety. Rather the dream provides a new connection, which is then used by the prepared waking mind to solve the problem, create the new work, etc." (219).

At any rate, my point is not that dreams are dumb or unintelligent: they are simply nonintelligent, meaning that they don't have intentions and they don't have minds of their own that set tasks, and they aren't privy to intellectual skills or intuitions denied to the waking brain. They are thought processors without motives. Like Dawkins's "digital river" they may carry motives in their stream, but we should not confuse the motives with the stream. At best we might say that dreams release us to some extent from tight conventional thought processes; they allow us to make extravagant mental connections, but, like the sorcerer's apprentice, they sometimes don't know when to stop. But there is no evidence

---

said to have had a dream that showed him where to place the hole in the needle. Robert Louis Stevenson admitted that one of his best stories was the result of a dream that presented the plot to him" (Thurston, 1988, 13).

for carrying the notion of dream intelligence any further. The very question of dream intelligence, I suspect, bears on the common human need to anthropomorphize the world. When we find either great beauty or strong form in nature our tendency is to attribute it to a maker. In one stroke nature ceases to be natural (that is, mindless), and is endowed with human or divine attributes as a way of explaining how something as "awesome" as the Grand Canyon or as fragile as the human eye could have come about. The truth is that beauty and design in art—the thing the artist does to nature—is not, as Shakespeare's Perdita thinks, something outside of nature, but rather an extension of the rhythms and forms provided by nature in the first place. Cézanne stands before nature with his canvas and brush and steals one of its many secrets—for example, the truth that the apple, in Lewis Thomas's fine observation about Cézanne, "is really part fruit, part earth" (1975, 53). This occurs so often, and in so many different ways, that we end up thinking of nature's variety as a kind of art—which is to say, as endowed with intelligence. Yet, as Polixenes tells Perdita in *The Winter's Tale,* "over that art which [we say] adds to Nature is an art that Nature makes."

Later chapters will examine some of the ways dream designs may work without the benefit of a dynamic intelligence. Here my task has been to suggest that the assumption of intelligence (and its handmaiden, intentionality) in the dream is impertinent because the dream needs no such capacity to do precisely what it does. I subscribe to Montague Ullman's belief that "dreams are intrinsically honest exercises in self-reflection" (1995a, 60)—if by honest we mean something like involuntary and unrepressed expressions of what is on the dreamer's mind.

I'm not sure that's exactly what Ullman means, however. The word *honest* dialectically implies the possibility of "dishonest"—as in Freud's notion of the dream telling "falsehoods" by means of censorship—and to allow that dreams can be either honest or dishonest in *this* sense carries certain supervisory or intentional implications into the act of dreaming that belong more properly to waking life. A dream can't be said to be honest any more than an electrocardiogram or a sphygmomanometer can be honest (assuming they are not mechanically defective). How could the dream have such a choice? One can easily allow Ullman the word, and I have doubtless resorted to such anthropomorphism in this book (as in my sorcerer's apprentice metaphor above). But, if not constantly qualified or kept in a tight metaphorical context, these terms lead one to rhetorical characterizations that eventuate in an unspoken assumption of intelligence at the base of the dreamwork.

For example, Ullman argued (1995b), rightly I think, that dreams can "help us to understand the connection of the present to the past as we move into the future." That is, we can use the dream as a "healing potential," a claim I think few people would doubt, as dreams offer us a compelling view of our personal experience. But then we have sentences like these: "Our dreams resort to a variety of techniques to call attention to aspects of ourselves we are simply not attending to or not attending to enough, or not attending to clearly. . . . Our dreams seem to zero in on whatever has occurred that affects these connections [between past and present] and has not clearly risen up to waking consciousness" (30). Knowing (and admiring) Ullman's work, I take this as metaphorical shorthand, but it seems to me that it is just such language that unconsciously endows the dream with motives: dreams *resort* to techniques in order to *call attention* to ignored concerns of any kind; they *monitor* our oversights, select the pressing ones, and present them for our self-edification. Does such a capacity to survey our concerns not require an intentional thought process separate from the one that is doing the overlooking? Do dreams really "zero in on" particular kinds of oversight, while ignoring others? Why is it, then, that one's dreams might ignore a pressing problem like an upcoming diagnosis of a biopsy and worry about an appointment with an irate student? Innocent as the language may be in its intentions, I think it ends up privileging the dream state in a way that leads to the assumption of an autonomous mind function. We arrive at our concepts through our language, and this language is heavily laced with anthropomorphism. Moreover, I think we can make as good a case for the "healing potential" of waking thought, or even waking experience that one hasn't thought much about, as one can for dreams. This does not imply that we shouldn't use dreams to such an end—far from it—only that we are ultimately talking about an involuntary biological process that has no Cartesian powers that are distinct from or more perspicacious than those of the waking brain. At the very most, dreams have a far greater capacity for free association. But that is a difference in degree arising from the conditions of the sleep state, not a difference of kind.

I seriously doubt that Ullman would subscribe to any such notion of a separate dream intelligence. I am concerned here with the question of how certain shortcuts in our descriptive language—our metaphors, if you will—lead us (or others) to untenable positions regarding the nature of the dream. Years ago, Heidegger set out to find the origin of the work of art ("What and how is a work of art?" [1975, 18]). But he realized immediately that one could not encounter the work directly without understanding its "thingly nature," or that objective entity (sound, words, paint, stone, paper, and so on) that holds the artistic properties in suspension. Without this basis of thingness one cannot hope to get at the nature of the art which inheres somehow in the more-than-thing we call the work of art. So, too, the dream, which has much in common with the artistic process. We cannot understand what it is, or how it is what it is, unless we rid our inquiry of the infra-assumption, carried in the very current of our descriptive language, that dreams occur or exist or have being distinct from the rest of thought itself. Perhaps the most flagrant example of such mind division occurs with our conception of the unconscious. For all his warnings about not taking the unconscious as a spatial arrangement in the brain, Freud spoke about it spatially so often that it is still a widely held notion that the unconscious is a kind of "seething cauldron" of repressions and anxieties located *below* the preconscious and conscious systems in the same way that the cellar is below the rest of the house. Many people still think of the unconscious in a fairly literal way, that is to say as a *thing* that, if unlocatable in brain space, is still capable of sending cryptic messages from some sort of a neuronic transmitter cruising silently in the dark alleys of the brain.

3 ·

Chuang-Tzu's Doubt

Once upon a time, I Chuang-Tzu, dreamed that I was a butterfly flying happily here and there, enjoying life without knowing who I was. Suddenly I woke up and I was indeed Chuang-Tzu. Did Chuang-Tzu dream he was a butterfly or did the butterfly dream he was Chuang-Tzu? (1974, 48)

How can you determine whether at this moment we are sleeping, and all our thoughts are a dream; or whether we are awake, and talking to one another in the waking state?
—Plato, *Theaetetus*

I don't know what reality is.
—Rudolf Peierls (cited in Davies and Brown, 1993)

If you think about dreams long and hard enough your life gradually falls into two distinct parts or paraworlds, one peculiarly independent of the other, yet at the same time bound by certain dependencies. A good fictional analogue might be Alec Guinness's double lives in *The Captain's Paradise,* one of which supplies the "motive" for the other. And, if you aren't given to nightmares, you find yourself looking forward to sleep as if it were something more than a dormant annex to life brought on by fatigue and conveniently done in the dark when not much else is going on anyway.

Over the years I have wondered just how these two lives "belong" to each other. When we fall asleep and dream do we leave reality? Are dreams less real than reality? And if so, why is it that some dreams (nightmares, for example) seem more real than reality? In what sense might dreams be called real or unreal? The sociologist Erving Goffman once said that, contrary to Shakespeare's famous line, all the world *isn't* a stage but the ways in which it isn't are hard to specify (1959, 72). So, too, with the dream: it isn't easy to specify the ways in which dreams are (or aren't) a kind of reality, especially these days when we are tinkering with a new toy called virtual reality (which isn't a bad working definition of a dream). One can say with some empirical certainty that the dream is not real, but in what sense is it unreal? For, as Plato put it, "the resemblance of the two states is quite astonishing. . . . [We] are equally confident of [the reality] of both" (1937, 160). Here I am, leading two lives that are in significant ways different from each other, but are also identical in one overwhelming sense that I am the constant—and "confident"—center of both worlds. In one of these lives (the waking one), I know about the other (dream) life and I have both clear and vague recollections of some of the things I have done while I was living it, but in the other life (the dream life), the waking life simply doesn't exist and never did exist, even as a memory. In the dream I leave behind all memory of the world in which I am now thinking these thoughts and assume that I am awake and living the only life I have, in which I do much the same thing I do in my (forgotten) waking life, give or take a few impossibilities.

To be more cautious, let me add: *as a rule.* People who believe in a theory of lucid dreams will insist that in some dreams we *do* know about the other (waking) world. This topic should be addressed briefly before we move on, if only because lucid-dream theory is the one concerted means though which we have tried to "join" the two worlds. I confess that my usual reaction to lucid-dream claims is a skeptical one (1993, 32–33n), and probably for the reason that I've never been able to crash the party. I've had dreams in which I say to myself "I'm dreaming" or "This is all a dream," and a very few dreams in which I recollect my waking life while I'm dreaming. But I don't understand why such dreams can't be explained as part of the normal contents of memory, like anything else we dream, or why they deserve a special category. After all, people often say "I'm dreaming" while they're awake, and one would expect the same sensation of amazement to show up in dreams (if only as a well-worn idiom) when dreams become hyperdreamlike? That is, to say "I'm dreaming" in a dream is no more a veridical proof that one is lucid than to say "I'm flying" during a flight dream or "I'm falling" during a falling dream is proof that one is doing either. Obviously, you aren't doing either, yet you are convinced you are; in the case of "I'm dreaming," you *are* dreaming, but how do you know *in what way* you know this? Might it not be a memory of *having dreamed* in the past? In short, it might be—I'm not saying in all cases—a kind of escutcheon effect wherein a miniature version of something ("I am dreaming") is contained within a larger one (I *am* dreaming), like the illustration on the Quaker Oats box in which a Quaker is holding a box that contains the same picture of the Quaker, who is holding a box, ad infinitum.

Or, suppose you suddenly thought in a dream, "This is a dream!" and then you said, "I'm getting out of here, back to reality!" and you abruptly wake up—or *think* you wake up, but go on dreaming you are awake. Surely your "This is a dream" sensation would have to be classified as phantom lucidity. A number of experimental sleep laboratory reports I have read simply wake the subjects and ask whether they experienced any lucid reflectiveness during dreams, and if they say that they have this constitutes the proof of lucidity. But how could a subject know the difference between lucidity and the phenomenon of phantom lucidity? How far can you trust what is said or thought during a dream? The same sort of credulity exists in dreams when you think you've solved a problem in a convincing way—until you awake and discover that you haven't. In principle, then, anything an individual has experienced in the waking or dreaming life is subject to reappearance in a dream as day or life residue, including the sensation of dreaming itself.[1]

    1. For example, my photograph-footnote dream in chapter 2 may sound like a lucid dream. But I would claim that it is a near-perfect example of dreaming-that-one-is-dreaming. I had taken a "dream" problem to sleep as part of the day residue, dreamed that I was dreaming about the problem (which I was), but I had no other awareness of the empirical world, my bedroom, my wife at my side, nor did I regard the environs of the dream as anything more than a real place. In short, the difference between dreamland and the waking world was

A technique called Thorley's Lucid Dream Induction (LDI) has been proven effective in inducing dreams of this kind in people who have never had one. To simplify, it consists of various exercises that remind one of dreams during the day, so that one is primed with dream-thought prior to sleep. For example, criteria 1: "The subject should ask himself the critical question ('am I dreaming or not?') at least five to ten times during the day" (Zadra, Donderi, and Pihl, 1992, 86). And it apparently works. Subjects report having more lucid dreams (a dream in which one "realize[s] that he or she is dreaming while still in the dream state" [85]) than subjects who had not used the LDI technique. But I wonder if you wouldn't get similar results if you asked your subjects to say to themselves five to ten times a day—along with the other eight criteria for LDI—"Am I a Martian or not?" Wouldn't one anticipate a high incidence of Martian dreams from people who spent the day wondering whether they were Martians—at least when compared to people who hadn't thought about Martians at all?

Here is a personal example, a dream I have quite often: I become thirsty during a dream and decide to wake up and have a drink from the plastic bottle on my bedside table. I tell myself to wake up and drink. But frequently I cop out, I *dream* that I do just that, although it seems in the dream that I am actually drinking (this is called a false awakening). Soon thirst catches up with me and I realize, without waking, that I must have dreamed that I had had a drink. Finally, I resolve to wake and drink properly—and I do. If this is a lucid dream—I'm apparently aware that I'd been dreaming—then I've apparently joined the party. But it seems to me that I was only dreaming that I was aware of dreaming, or at best drifting in and out of sleep, and so fine are the gradations between the two states that I personally can't trust myself to say where

---

closer to being a difference between two real places than a real and an imagined world. How otherwise could I have fallen for the stupidity of substituting a footnote for a photograph—or for that matter taking a photograph in a dream in the first place?

one ends and the other begins. Hypnopompia (twilight sleep), I have discovered, is a land of many dimensions of awareness. In any case, I have performed this drinking routine so often that it has become a kind of Thorley's LDI. That is, I apparently associate the idea of being aware I am dreaming with the physical stimulus of thirst. I can't really see how this differs categorically from incorporating any external stimulus into a dream.

One can dream, then, that one is dreaming, or (the same thing) that one is awake in a dream. But true lucidity would seem to require something beyond the sensation of awareness that one is dreaming. Anyway, even if I'm right about this, it doesn't disprove the claims of lucid dreamers which sometimes (but not always) rely on far more complex criteria for verification (like signaling in dreams), and with some measurable success. I'm not really interested in discrediting lucidity in dreams, only in questioning the notion that thinking "I'm dreaming" during a dream necessarily means much more than that you're dreaming that you're dreaming.[2] Suffice it to say that for most of us, during

2. The most thoughtful approach to lucid dreaming I have read is offered by Harry T. Hunt in his chapter "Lucid Dreams and Nightmares" in *The Multiplicity of Dreams* (1989, 211-27). Hunt is less interested in the issue of "alertness and the simple knowledge that one is dreaming" (120) than in the phenomenon of "peak experience," which involves "a special sensory clarity, expansive emotional thrill, and sense of bodily presence" (119). Such lucidity is also possible in meditational exercises and in certain kinds of waking experience (i.e., out-of-body sensation). It "entails the same tenuous balance between our ordinary attitude of active participation (in which we lose ourselves in our activities equally in dream and wakefulness) and the attitude of detached receptivity that characterizes the goal of long-term meditation practice. We note in both states the same sense of clarity, exhilaration, and openness—an experiential 'sense of Being'" (120). I can understand this sort of lucidity perfectly and have experienced it several times in dreams (chiefly in flying dreams and dreams of sublime vistas), albeit without much alertness to the fact that I was dreaming. Indeed, what seems to fade away in such cases is precisely the distinction between states of mind. The clarity and exhilaration transcend all interest in terrestrial matters. For a recent review of the literature, see Gackenbach 1991. For a not-so-positive

most of our dreaming time, the real world is completely forgotten. If this weren't the case, lucid dreaming wouldn't be the fascinating topic that it is.

Our real problems begin with our notion of what reality is, and this leads unavoidably to the problem of consciousness. So already we are facing two complex and unsettled problems in philosophy. As with most questions of this sort (What is beauty? What is just? What is God?), you usually begin with a firm but unexamined belief that leads you eventually into the cul-de-sac of a self-fulfilling prophecy. You know what reality is in advance of asking the question. "Reality," you confidently say, "is what is *real,* what there *is,*" and to make the point you tap a nearby table with your finger. "*This* is real!" you say, and the table proves it by making a noise when your finger hits it. In effect, you have defined reality as what Descartes called the *res extensa,* or this massive, increasingly measurable presence around and within us, made of things infinitely small that go into the making of things infinitely large. And if this is the reality we refer to, then we have no case for such a thing as dream reality. For the dream has no mass, nor as far as we know does it send waves through the ether, nor can you manufacture a product in a dream factory that can be used in waking life. At best the dream produces a detectable electrical impulse. But the impulse isn't the dream as much as a sign that the brain is dreaming the dream, and the same (or similar) kind of impulse is produced whether the brain is asleep and dreaming or awake and watching the Super Bowl.[3]

---

research result see Barrett 1992. For the latest technique in eliciting lucid dreams by means of Dreamlight, see LaBerge and Levitan 1995.

3. According to the findings of neuroscientist Rodolfo Llinás (Llinás and Ribary, 1993), the human cortex vibrates at a steady rate of 40 cycles per second in both the waking and the REM sleep state. Both states are attended by bursts of representational activity that can be correlated with changes in the person's perceptual environment. These bursts are entirely absent in deep sleep, though the 40 Hz background oscillation continues. The only distinction between the dream and the waking state is that the bursts in the dream state are not correlated with the perception of external environment but presumably with ac-

So we seem to have cast all mental processes out of reality, or we have put them into a category Descartes calls the *res cogitans*—unextendable and indivisible thinking. Are thoughts, then, real? Surely not in the sense that the table is real. But look what happens to reality when we remove thought from the picture. Without us, the human bystanders—without human consciousness—the world becomes a totally different place. In fact, it isn't even a *place;* it becomes—nothing.[4] Or, if something, a multiplicity of "lower" species-specific worlds whose nature and substance vary with the perceptual equipment of each species. So there seem to be realities within, or beside, realities. The reality of the trilobite is "less" (that is, less sophisticated) than that of the frog, the frog's less than the lion's, the lion's less than the chimpanzee's, and so on, up the chain of being until we get to human reality, which is the final and most complete reality (because *we* have science). But the dream is only a memory of reality; it is like the people in Plato's cave who see only shadows of the real flickering on the dream wall. So we admit that the frog lives in a reality of a sort, without understanding its full extensability, but the dream doesn't go even that far into reality. The dream is just so much *res ficta* emitted by the *res cogitans.*

Chuang-Tzu's famous dream that he was a butterfly "flitting to and fro with a butterfly's goals and motivations" is usually cited as a kind of joke by people who appreciate it more for its punch line than for its possible seriousness. It is, we say, a quaint "saying." But behind Chuang-Tzu's little joke is the collective thought of a culture that perceives reality in very different terms from most Westerners who tend to

---

tivity in the dream environment. For a lucid discussion of this phenomenon see Churchland (1995, 219–26).

4. There is an irresistible joke about Descartes that may make the idea seem less lugubrious. One morning, fatigued by his philosophical ruminations on existence, Descartes repaired to his corner café for a break. He took his usual seat and presently the waiter approached and asked, "Would you like a cup of coffee, M. Descartes?" Descartes sighed, looked off into the distance, and pondered. Finally, he replied, "I think not," and abruptly disappeared.

find the Eastern view "inscrutable" and let it go at that. A "biological" version of Chuang-Tzu's doubt comes to us from Lewis Thomas's *Lives of a Cell.* Discussing the large proportion of mitochondria bacteria in the human body ("almost as much of them in sheer dry bulk as there is the rest of me"), Thomas writes that he, Lewis Thomas, could, from a certain point of view, "be taken for a very large, motile colony of respiring bacteria, operating a complex system of nuclei, microtubules, and neurons for the pleasure and sustenance of their families, and running, at the moment, a typewriter" (1975, 84–85). This *is* a joke (I think), but it does remind us that point of view is an unavoidable factor in any assessment of reality. Or, as Raymond Tallis (another philosopher) has expressed the point, "In a world observed solely from a physico-chemical standpoint, there are no viewpoints, no organisms, and no environments. The physical world, in itself, has no points of view. It has no privileged sites" (1991, 34).[5] So the mitochondria have nothing to brag about, either. All of us are ingredients in the same soup, called DNA, which has no point of view or awareness that it exists.

At the very least, Chuang-Tzu's quandary is a critique of consciousness as a point of view on reality. It might be rephrased as: if you can be fooled once, how do you know you aren't being fooled twice? Or, as the Western philosopher would put it, on what basis are states of conviction subject to external proof? In the *Theaetetus* Plato phrased the question like this: "How can you determine whether at this moment we are sleeping, and all our thoughts are a dream; or whether we are awake, and talking to one another in the waking state?" You *know* the answer (tap-tap), but the philosopher, who takes nothing for granted, would ask *how* you know that you know the answer. This leads directly to what philosophers call the problem of verifiability, or the idea that subjective processes require objective verification.

To put it simply: with the advent of single-celled life, the seed of a

5. For an eloquent account of the different levels of temporal reality see Fraser (1990).

point of view was planted in a heretofore unviewpointed "reality," and all subsequent points of view are variations on this rudimentary grain of subjectivity that somehow sprouted in matter. This means simply that the possibility of Descartes's dualistic division between the *res extensa* and the *res cogitans* was suddenly established in a fortuitous coalition of temperature and chemical and electrical energy (which have no points of view in themselves), and we have been having viewpoint problems ever since. And the real question may be what to make of the *res cogitans* being within, and a peculiar part of, the *res extensa*—a capability made of the *res extensa* which outgrew it and became its Other. So consciousness, in humans at least, now stands facing reality as if it were not *made of* reality but were simply contemplating it. And as if this were not bootstrapping in high enough style, quantum mechanics comes along and advances the idea that "Reality, inasmuch as it has any meaning at all," David Overstreet suggests, "is not a property of the external world on its own, but is intimately bound up with our perception of the world, our perception as conscious observers" (1980, 47–48). So reality gives birth to mind, and mind ends up giving birth to reality.[6]

All of this brings us, of course, to the infamous brain/mind problem. The brain, with all its biological wiring and plumbing, is pure *res extensa,* as Descartes himself realized; the mind, in contrast, is pure *res cogitans* and is quite separate from the brain, in dualistic theory anyway. Today, dualism is an increasingly unpopular position as the notion advances that mental events are determined at every level by biological,

6. Although one can find many sentiments of this kind among quantum physicists—the notion that reality amounts to the qualities we can observe and measure "in" it, or that reality will vary according to the questions one puts to it—there are probably just as many physicists, beginning with Einstein, who would dispute the notion that there is no objective *thing* "out there" behaving according to its own set of rules, completely independent of the measuring human mind. The important point is that the question ("What is reality?") has no simple tap-answer. Hence a careful and conservative physicist like Rudolf Peierls (in the epigraph to this chapter) can genuinely say, "I don't know what reality is" (Davies and Gribbin, 1992, 74).

hence chemical, substrates. It is no longer a matter of mind *over* matter: mind *is* matter. In the words of neurophysiological reductionist Paul Churchland, "mental phenomena [are] nothing but a particularly exquisite articulation of the basic properties of matter and energy" (1995, 211). In *Consciousness Explained,* Daniel Dennett draws a colorful distinction between brain-events and mind-events, or events in consciousness. Brain events are not "witnessed" or experienced because "*there's nobody home*" in the brain. It's all plumbing and wiring. "Events in consciousness, on the other hand, are 'by definition, witnessed: they are *experienced* by an *experiencer,* and their being thus experienced is what makes them what they are: *conscious* events" (1991, 29). What is required for something to qualify as an experience, then, is that it occur in consciousness as a mind-event. To borrow an example from Dennett's earlier essay "Are Dreams Experiences?": if an experience does not produce a behavioral reaction when it was said to have happened— if it is only recalled at a later time as having happened *earlier*—then it cannot be considered an experience (1976, 169).

Unfortunately, this view of consciousness turns out to be quite close to that of our view of consciousness in the waking state. And here is where dreams become problematical (for some people) because for the most part they are voiceless and virtually behaviorless from the objective standpoint. There is simply no way to verify that they are happening except through the presumed sincere report of the dreamer on waking or through some indicative measurements that can be made by sleep monitors (EEG, MEG, oculometer, and so on). Dennett offers this distinction: "Whereas nightmares accompanied by moans, cries, cowering, and sweaty palms *would* be experiences, bad dreams dreamed in repose (though remembered in agony) would not be, unless, contrary to surface appearances, their entry into memory is accomplished by engagements of the whole behavior-controlling system sufficiently normal to distinguish these cases sharply from our imaginary delayed hallucinations" (1976, 169).

I should add that the subjunctive language in which this statement is couched indicates that Dennett does not necessarily assert it as a personal belief, but only as something one could assert from a certain investigative standpoint. Or maybe he is floating it past us to see if anyone will agree. I will take the former to be the case, for as we will see (chapter 9), Dennett's own position on the matter seems unresolved. This said, then, one wants to ask what sort of observable behavior would this line of argument—assuming someone held it—expect to accompany a reposeful dream in which there was no cause for moaning, crying, cowering, sweating, or falling out of bed. Why should nightmares be classified as experiences because they are observably violent, and reposeful dreams not so classified because they are not? The criteria seem dangerously close to depending on the conditions of a sleep laboratory for confirmation, and this seems an implausible way of estimating whether other people are having experiences during dreams. "If it turns out that most of the functional areas that are critical to the governance of our wide awake activity are in operation [during dreams]," Dennett's hypothetical theorist goes on, "then there will be good reason for drawing the lines around experience so that dreams are included. If not, there will be good reason to deny [that] dreams are experiences" (1976, 169).

But how many "functional areas" are required to get dreams over the line into the category of experience? Too many and the dreamer is disqualified at the gate because he or she is no longer asleep; too few (say, the strictly electrochemical substrate) and the dream—if one is occurring at this point—cannot be called an experience because it is a pure brain-event in which "nobody's home" to do any experiencing. And, indeed, one can hardly say that one is *experiencing* such things as neuronal transmission or electrochemical activity, as opposed to the thoughts being carried along in these "motor" facilities. But surely when we reach the point that dreams are being formed, mental images are occurring, affects created, and thoughts thought, we must allow the high probability that dreams are being experienced. To eliminate reposeful dreams in which such physical activities as running, swimming, and climbing are occurring *without movement* seems to be drawing a line that is unnecessarily suspicious of the subjective—indeed, it eliminates almost everything but moaning and crying and sweating, or things that can be heard and seen by observers. Are these experiences to be disallowed because an objective observer could not validate them as happening while they occurred?

One wonders, on the same evidentiary basis, how one would classify a man reading a book in a hotel lobby? You can see he's awake and intentionally doing something, if only turning pages. The part you can't see is his mind converting the words on the page into mental images of characters and events. Would you doubt that he was reading even though you detect no moans, cries, cowering, or sweaty palms to verify that he was? Probably not; because he is awake, though perfectly motionless, you safely assume that he is reading *something,* not only a book but a book *about* something and that these somethings are passing into his brain as thoughts, though you have no idea what they are. Either that or he is faking the reading and is secretly looking at the woman who is sitting across the room reading a book, or pretending to. Either way, he is having an *experience.* And so is she.

The same seems true of the dream. You can also verify that a sleeping person is dreaming, up to a point, if you have the proper EEG or MEG (magnetoencephalograph) apparatus attached to his or her person. Why then deny that these indications, virtually equivalent to turning the pages of a book, strongly point to a dreaming consciousness? When the verificationists deny that dreams are experiences because they are unverifiable, it seems to me that what they are actually verifying is a *received* idea of experience (something objectively verifiable) rather than the subjective condition (dreaming) one was attempting to verify in the first place. One has only proven that a certain conception of experience does not apply to the case, and that seems equally true of the man reading in the hotel lobby. On such a basis one could as well deny that pain or grief or exhilaration are experiences unless the "subject" were crying out or thrashing around. And maybe philosophy would want to argue it this way for its own reasons, that is, not to disprove that dreams are experiences but to test the criteria by which we can rigorously say that they are or are not. But that does not get us to a possible ontology of dreaming. One is led to agree with Dennett's closing statement: "In the end, the concept of experience may not prove to differentiate any one thing of sufficient theoretical interest to warrant time spent in determining its boundaries" (1976, 171).

Still, I can see why philosophers would want to argue the experience problem from such an intrepidly rational point of view. My interest is more phenomenological, or, to be less fancy, more sympathetic to subjectivity. Put simply, I want to know what these things are that I have during the night. What I would challenge is the idea that dream consciousness does not qualify as consciousness, or more specifically, as *enough* consciousness. That dreams are illusions, in one sense of the word, there is little doubt; but I feel that they are also experiences in the sense of Dennett's criteria. And if they are experiences they are also participating in reality in the same ontological sense that waking thought is, though not in the sense that walking down the street is (unless the dreamer is sleepwalking). There is also little doubt that thinking during dreams or dreaming itself is of a different order from waking thought, but that difference doesn't seem sufficient cause to deny dreams the status of experiences.

The main difference seems to be that in the dream state you can't verify what you're experiencing. Presumably it might be possible to perform a tap-tap experiment on a dream table, to dream that you're verifying something according to objective standards, but verification isn't something that matters in dream experience because the question of doubt doesn't seem to enter dream consciousness: by virtue of its one-way street, dream consciousness has no other form of consciousness to verify. Moreover, it would be impossible to verify something in the dream state because (to set aside lucid dreaming) the dream does not admit of another form of reality to which it might be compared; hence the question would never arise. Even if we admit the experience of lucid dreaming, to the extent that the dreamer could make such comparisons, the further question arises as to whether he or she could then be classified as a dreamer-sleeper. How many capabilities that belong to waking awareness can occur in a dream before the dream ceases to be a dream and becomes, say, hypnopompic semiwakefulness or true wakefulness? To ask Norman Malcolm's famous question: can you say "I am dreaming" during a dream unless you dream that you're saying it?

An article in my local newspaper entitled "Thoughts on Dreams," by Lillian Chodorow, is relevant to my theme:

My artist sister Rose, who is in a nursing home, sometimes has such powerful dreams that she is convinced that the dreams are reality and nothing will convince her otherwise. This makes her life a lot more interesting than it is when she's awake within the narrow confines of her wheelchair and the home routine. In her dreams she skips around through time and space, from the past to the present and back, and is able to see and communicate with the beloved people of her early years. Who is to say which life is more real? (*Santa Barbara Independent,* May 4, 1995, p. 11)

Here is a variation on the problem of Chuang-Tzu's doubt which we may call Rose's Certainty. Here the quandary disappears and, if we can believe the author, is replaced by Rose's conviction that dreams and reality are one and the same thing, the dreams being simply more "interesting" than her adventureless reality. Even so, one could safely argue that Rose is hallucinating about what is real and that no one in the nursing home has ever observed Rose "skipping" through time and space. But does this deny that Rose is having an experience? This is the question raised some years ago by the phenomenologist Medard Boss. If we observe a sleeping person who is dreaming that he is skiing down a Swiss mountain, his dormant posture in the bed assures onlookers, beyond any doubt, that he is only hallucinating. But the dreaming person believes he is skiing "with consummate physical grace and pleasure, down an Alpine slope" (1977, 97), even as Rose believes that her dream activities were real even after waking. Still, both Rose and the sleeping skier, we say, are deceived: all reality contradicts their belief. Is one then wrong and the other right? Are the wakers right because waking thought is more accountable by being carried on in a certifiable environment and in cognizance of the orderly rules of nature, or because more than one person can confirm that Rose isn't skipping and the dreamer isn't skiing? If so, can we then take waking verifiability as the true criterion for what is real? This conclusion seems unexceptionable, except that it has not accounted for the possibility that real thinking—however deluded in the case of the dreamer—is carried on in both the dreaming and waking states by the same vitalized extension of the *res extensa,* the mind/brain. If there is a difference in the veridical content of the thought, there is no qualitative or quantitative difference in the thought process itself.

In 1974, Thomas Nagel wrote a now famous essay entitled "What Is It Like to Be a Bat?" which is concerned with just this frustration of dealing with subjective events in objective empirical terms. In the essay he notes that "we may have evidence for the truth of something we cannot really understand":

Suppose a caterpillar is locked in a sterile safe by someone unfamiliar with insect metamorphosis, and weeks later the safe is reopened, revealing a butterfly. If the person knows that the safe has been shut the whole time, he has reason to believe that the butterfly is or was once the caterpillar, without having any idea in what sense this might be so. (One possibility is that the caterpillar contained a tiny winged parasite that devoured it and grew into the butterfly.) (1974, 448)

We have here another situation similar to the seeming "metamorphosis" of Chuang-Tzu. But the situation also resembles that of the dreamer who is not manifesting any observable behavior, beyond sleep itself, and at the same time is having mental experiences that he will in all likelihood report on waking. This is not a problem for the dreamer, but rather for the verificationist philosopher who "opens the safe," so to speak, on confronting the waking dreamer. The question the philosopher will ask is how can this motionless "caterpillar," who appears to have been experiencing nothing (including sleep), also be this "butterfly" who now reports flitting vividly, at the same time, through experiences of life in a nonexistent world? Does one trust the subject's report and thus open one's investigation to what Dennett calls "a heads-I-win/tails-you-lose situation of unlikely infallibility" as regards what is *really* taking place? (1988, 221). Must science abandon its rigorously objective methodology when it reaches the domain of subjectivity? (Here we reach the point where psychoanalysis fails, at least in some opinions, to qualify as a science. How can one explain a mental event in purely physical terms?)[7] Is it utterly hopeless to attempt to say, "What is it like to be a bat?" Dennett thinks it isn't, within certain limits (1991, 442-48). Nagel expresses the dilemma as follows: "If the subjective character of experience is fully comprehensible from only one point of view [the subjective], then any shift to greater objectivity—that is, less attachment to a specific viewpoint—does not take us nearer to the real nature of the phenomenon: It takes us further away from it" (399).

Nagel sees a dim ray of hope in the possibility of an "objective

7. Marshall Edelson offers a spirited defense of psychoanalytic procedures. He argues that "the request for a biological explanation of psychological facts is incoherent," and that the methods and procedures of one domain cannot be applied categorically to another domain seeking answers to different kinds of questions (1984, 118). For example, the neural scientist is interested "in the biological mechanism for dreaming, in the nature of the design which is realized in the physical system." The psychoanalyst, on the other hand, "is interested . . . in what particular wishes or beliefs are manifested by a dream" (116-17), and these are "not questions that can be decided by collecting evidence"—at least of the "hard" sort demanded in neurological study.

phenomenology" that might "describe, at least in part, the subjective character of experiences in a form comprehensible to beings incapable of having those experiences" (402). It is not a matter of saying what those experiences might be *like* (as in the case of the bat) but of making "structural features of perception . . . more accessible to objective description" (for example, how might one explain *seeing* to a person who is congenitally blind?). This is one possibility of rapprochement—an attempt at a more objective description of subjective experience. Another possibility is set forth by Eugene Gendlin, who begins with the assumption that "any person should be able to corroborate any phenomenological assertion directly" (1982, 322). If this fails to occur the likelihood is that two different phenomena are mistakenly being described or two different formulations are describing the same phenomenon" (324). The important thing is that the two (or three, or four, or n) phenomenologists not be "committed to some logical model" that would be stubbornly re-applied in each case but rather be dedicated to making sure that they were addressing the *same* aspect of experience—let us say, the experience of flying in a dream (325). Experience, Gendlin maintains, "has *more order* than all our schemes put together" (331): there are always other aspects behind the phenomenon that have escaped us. "What we lift out [of an experience] is a product of the great order that is already there," much of it to be discovered (lifted) by future phenomenologists. In this, phenomenology is not unlike science, which is continually discovering new "aspects" of physical nature—like heliocentrism, curved space, gravity, and black holes— that weren't "true" yesterday because we didn't know they were there, largely owing to the poverty of our measuring instruments. "Universality," Gendlin says, "is not lost, but it alters. Instead of being a static structure shared by everyone always and already, it is *the capacity to become shared*" (333).

The same is true of our experience with art. How many poems remain to be written about daffodils, Wyoming sunsets, melancholy, and small-town life of the sort that E. A. Robinson made popular? The answer is as many as there are poets to write them. And this is precisely for the reason Gendlin gives: the phenomenon is always more expansive than our awareness. Or, to be more accurate, our awareness is invariably conditioned (like the instruments of the scientist) by our culture, and our culture is continually altering our perspective on the world. Therefore, future discoveries of the secrets hidden in a field of daffodils await a world whose meme pool and system of curiosities are always, on pure Darwinian grounds, different from our own. At which point daffodils and melancholy will yield new aspects. That is, the poet will "see" differently, and because to some degree we see the same range of things, we will be able to share in the poet's discovery. It will appear to be brand new, but it is only our perspective that is new. Indeed, it would be more correct to say that poems are not about daffodils, or melancholy, or skylarks; poems are about the people who see or know about these things—what we are able to see and feel in them.

The same notion can be applied to dreaming, along the following lines: there is no scientifically or philosophically rigorous way to verify that dreaming takes place (in the true subjective sense), because you can never catch the dreamer in the act of dreaming unless he or she is thrashing about in the bed (and even then, how do you know the thrashing is being caused by a dream?). And a dream is like music: if you stop it, it disappears. But it is possible to "lift out" of the experience of dreaming an assertion as to what dreaming is—not what it is *like* (some other thing) but what its characteristics are and what kinds of things go on in dreams. Say I report to you that I dreamed that I was flying over Niagara Falls. If you have had the experience before, though not over Niagara Falls, then we can "share" the experience of flying in a dream state. Instead of saying to me, "Ah, but we were fooled. Our dreams cannot be verified," you say, "I know what you mean: I have had such an experience myself," and we try to arrive at the most objective description we can, being careful not to confuse our aspect (flying) with still other aspects or to allow things to creep into our formulation that do not belong there. In short, we have not verified it, but we have shared it—not the thing itself, not a specific act of dreaming, but a certain experience of dreaming—the *type,* let us say, rather than the *token.* And presumably we might expect that a third and a fourth and an nth phenomenologist could, in principle, agree with us (if we have done our lifting carefully enough), that there are such experiences. If not, then we would have to check our formulations and aspects, precisely as scientists must be able to replicate the results of a given experiment. So something like a confirmation emerges: people dream, dreams are experienced, and dreams have certain sharable, or at least communicable characteristics.

But suddenly an unregenerated post-nth verificationist mole rises from our group and cries out, "You're all being fooled. If you can't prove it, it didn't happen!" We think about this and, being resolute in our sharing principle and anxious to reach full agreement, we recall that many people can be fooled as easily as one (therefore why not ourselves?) and that our verificationist might be a veritable Galileo in having the right answer in the face of the world's contrary belief. And though we have near-universal agreement that dreaming does occur, or that there are certain experiences that occur while we are asleep, we find ourselves back in the original quandary, which is to say that we have been lured back to the privileged world of reality. What shall we do? Tap-tap.

After a good deal of thought, it dawns on us that we may be troubling ourselves over language, not phenomena. Suppose, for the sake of argument, we grant that we are not having a dream experience but only *seem* to have one. What is lost? Actually, our formulations about what we formerly called dream experience have not been found false; we still agree about whatever it was that we seemed to be in agreement, except that we have lost our word for it. What, after all, is the difference between experiencing something and *seeming* to experience something, if all the senses are convinced in both cases? Wouldn't a rose by any other name smell the same—and so with grief, lust, fright, embarrassment, vertigo, acrophobia, claustrophobia, frustration, and all the emotional stuff that dreams are made of?

Is this, after all, a real problem or a *seeming* problem?

Why not let philosophy deal with the problem of what constitutes *experience* and confine our efforts to understanding *seeming* experience, or whatever it is we have always thought we were having while we were dreaming? But the verificationist raves on, claiming that we have simply adopted a homuncular strategy of deferring the truth, that we are naive geocentrists in thrall to subjectivity, and so on. We are getting nowhere, and we are getting tired—especially of the verificationist.

A solution suddenly emerges. It is admittedly drastic, if not draconian, something none of us has ever contemplated. It is a course of direst action. But we must make some headway if we are to have some understanding of dreaming, and this solution does take some cognizance of the verificationist position. So: we slip a drug into the verificationist's piña colada, we drive him in his deep sleep deep into the desert, we shoot him crisply between the eyes, and we throw his corpse into a dark abandoned mine shaft.

We vow never to reveal what has happened.

And indeed, what *has* happened? We are fully satisfied that the verificationist experienced no pain as he was blissfully asleep to the end and there were no signs of moaning, crying, cowering, or sweating. Moreover, he can hardly regret the sudden eclipse of his life because he now has nothing to experience regret *with,* his *cogito* having been thoroughly throttled. And because no one heard the shot and there is no corpus delicti to verify that a murder was committed, we assume that *it simply did not occur.* We now have perfect unanimity in our group and can proceed with our thinking about the seeming experience of dreaming—except that for convenience we decide to drop the word *seeming* and just call it experience (bearing in mind that in certain hyperscrupulous philosophical quarters it may not be held in such high regard). And because, as Lady Macbeth's Doctor puts it, "infected minds/To their deaf pillows will discharge their secrets—" the most we can expect in the way of punishment is a few unverifiable bad dreams.

4 ·

The Time-Space of Dreams

Having got over that hurdle—or at least around it—I turn now to one of the nagging questions about dream experience: how the dream gets from one image to another. How does the dream "think up" its next image when it appears to have all it can handle just maintaining the images already there? This is a complex question and it must be explored one step at a time. Here I would like to deal with the image itself, or what we might call the molecular level of dream formation. I will discuss chunkier problems relating to plots and imaginative composition in chapters 8 and 9.

I consider an image any visual or sensory event that occurs in a dream. For my purposes, an image might even be a thought or an emotion, for thoughts and emotions are usually accompanied by some degree of visualization, audition, or sensory awareness. Moreover, most of the time these dimensions work synchronously and occur in the dream as a multiplex phenomenon for which the term *image* is not entirely satisfactory.[1] In a dream, in other words, you can have what amounts to a sensory confusion without being sensorily confused. For example, I once *saw* an odor in a dream, and I naively remarked to myself (getting only half the point) that it didn't really look like an odor. What I am mainly interested in is how one dream event (of any sort) arises

1. Commentary on dream images has suffered from the inevitable comparison with cinematic and pictorial images, and the consequence is that we think of images as being exactly what we see or hear (Mother, Mother's voice, Dad's old Buick). But the image is born of a much more complex representational ensemble, most of its substance and meaning being invisible. For the image, which appears to be in one place, is "composed" in several brain systems at the same time. To get technical, we might think of images as arising from what Antonio Damasio calls dispositional representations, or "potential patterns of neuron activity in small ensembles of neurons [called] 'convergence zones'; that is, they consist of a set of neuron firing dispositions [or instructions] within the ensemble." So the face of a friend would appear to the dreamer as a face, but in neural terms it would be a firing pattern that triggers a "momentary reconstruction of an approximate representation [of the face] in early visual cortices" (1994, 102). And the same would hold true of colors, shapes, musical sounds, and spoken or unspoken words.

out of another. The reason this is a problem is that plots—a series of imagined events—don't come "out of" nowhere. Something is responsible for them, though it isn't easy to say what the something is, unless you assume that somewhere *behind* the dream there is an "author" supplying the dream with its images and events. And even if you assume that, you still haven't explained how such an author could string events along at the speed of thought without the least opportunity to revise or the knowledge of what comes next in the sequence. So what is the point of adding an additional author, as if doing so in itself constituted an explanation of dream authorship? You have simply passed the buck, whereas the buck should really stop at the site of the image itself, where consciousness is busily dealing with its own productions. In the image, Sartre says, "thought itself becomes a thing" (1968, 145). Precisely so, and that thing is the dream which is, so to speak, made "on the spot" out of thought. So we must begin by asking elementary questions about thought, which habit teaches us to take for granted, much as we do breathing.

Most of my dreams occur in anonymous places. I am at a party, or in a town, or with these people at the beach. It never occurs to me to ask where I am, and of course no one in the dream ever says, "Isn't it nice to be here at Henry's Beach again," the way characters do in plays. Dreams are even more careless than Shakespeare about telling you where you are: "A forest," or "A street," or nothing at all. The likely reason for this oversight is that it is unnecessary to identify place in dreams—as fictions almost always do—because you are already where you are and there is no more reason to inquire about that than there is for me to remind myself that I am sitting here in my study at the word processor. Who cares? So our first observation is that the dream treats its world, whether it is familiar (home, school, office) or not, as unquestioningly as we treat our presence in the waking world. No matter how bizarre, the dream world is always taken as valid and one's situation in it as having come about through thoroughly explicable means.

For example, let us say I dream that my wife and I have just bought this run-down house in an unspecified area at the edge of an unspecified town; but we apparently found it more attractive than other houses we were looking at (at least the dream gives me the impression we were looking at them). My neighbors are Mr. and Mrs. Familiar, which is to say I know them, recognize them as my neighbors (I met them just after moving in), but of course I have never seen them prior to the dream, and there is no scene in the dream in which I was moving in. So I couldn't have met them before, either in or out of the dream, unless there is a "part one" to the dream I have totally forgotten. But if Mr. Familiar were suddenly to walk into my dream house, I would immediately recognize him, no matter who he was or how he looked or behaved. I would say to myself, "There's Familiar again." And Familiar might respond by saying that he had just stopped by to drop off the saw he said he would lend me yesterday. And then I would recall that, indeed, we had talked about the dead tree branch threatening to fall on my greenhouse, and on the heels of that I recall that one of the reasons we had bought the house in the first place was that we had always wanted a greenhouse. However, this is pure invention on the dream's part because I've never more than casually wished I had a greenhouse in waking life—a pond with a fountain perhaps, but not a greenhouse. Thus the dream endows everything with a "known" past or cause, even though you never really know how you came to know what it is that you know.

In short, one thing happens (Familiar arrives with the saw) and this leads to an awareness that something else has already happened (Familiar was here yesterday; we discussed the dead tree limb, which leads to the motive for buying the house—it had a greenhouse). Time appears to be flowing backward; or at least past causes are springing up as explanations for present effects.[2] This sort of thing is a common occurrence

2. But note a further nuance. Though I recall that Familiar had been here yesterday, the dream does not "flash back" to yesterday. That is, the time and scene don't change simply because I recalled yesterday. I'm not saying this couldn't happen (as in a movie flashback), only that it doesn't happen often. The dream tends to maintain its milieu, its scenic integrity, at the same time that

in dreams. For example, you may meet an old friend, X, at a party, idly wonder how he came to be there, and then you recall—here we go backward again—that Y told you yesterday that X was already in town. Or you may be looking for a familiar face in a room full of strangers and a friend will suddenly show up; then you will remember that the friend had told you he would be there, though perhaps he would be a little late owing to a previous engagement. And you might even be told what that engagement was, though it has little to do with your original desire to see a familiar face.

This has always struck me as an extraordinary mental maneuver, even for dreams. It is one of those operations in which we detect the dream's indifference to temporal flow. To be truthful, the same operation occurs in waking life, as when the face of a stranger reminds us of a long forgotten friend and attendant events from childhood. The difference is that the memory recall in waking life is veridical, based on real past events (at least we remember them as such), whereas in the dream the past is invented, as it were, before our eyes. We are dealing here with another of those ways in which dreams bootstrap their materials from the inside while maintaining the impression that some dream events (such as my meeting Familiar) actually took place before or elsewhere, in the dream-yesterday. It is Familiar, in this case, who initiates the greenhouse theme, but of course Familiar is my own creation, so inevitably I'm responsible for the idea—including the familiarity of Familiar.

Still, it seems a long way around getting it into the dream by having Familiar show up with a saw, if that's what the dream is about. But it is highly unlikely that dreams think this way—in other words, that the

---

it permits parallel and auxiliary forms of mentation (thinking *about* yesterday in the dream-today). This may seem a trivial observation, but it establishes one of the more veridical qualities of dream experience: thinking occurs within thinking, or, to put it more finely, the composition process allows a reactive process in which the dreamer can have thoughts independent of the action in progress, just as we do in waking life. In short, the dreamer is *in* the dream but not *of* the dream. Thus the dream preserves the waking distinction between self and other, even though there is no "other" in the dream.

dream has an objective in mind and that in order to reach it, it sets up events in advance that will eventually produce it. This is the way writers write stories, in most instances, but stories have authors with the ability to plan ahead, revise, and make the events follow a believable sequence, even if they were written in reverse order.

A much more economic explanation is that Familiar somehow arrived with a saw in his hand as a result of an unknown piece of day residue involving a saw, and the dream simply "justifies" it with an explanation. God knows how the saw got into the dream, but we will look at that problem when we discuss the nature of day residue (chapter 7). In short, when the dream produces a character with a saw, for whatever reason, the consequent event will probably have something to do with cutting wood, and so on, one step bringing on the next by a process of likely association. This doesn't at all explain how a greenhouse got into the yard, but there is no way to trace these mini-evolutions in dreams in terms of specific causes because the causes of dream imagery are invariably far more complex than the images suggest. It would all depend on which "nodes" or mnemonic pattern had been activated and what sort of associative networks were activated in turn (again, see Hubbard, 1994). The point is that we might, from one perspective at least, think of dreams as a continual process of "justifying" their images, by responding in kind to what is already there.

Actually, this process has been given a very good name by Allan Hobson, who refers to it as the principle of self-organization (a term also used in chaos theory), or the tendency of any complex system to stabilize itself "without any higher control when the system is driven away from equilibrium" (Hobson and Kahn, 1993, 151). That is, the system "decides" to account for, or to justify, anomalous events by calling on memories that would explain the event and thus reduce friction, or bizarreness, in the system. The system doesn't know it is doing this, and even physical systems, like pots of boiling water and pendulums, have this ability to self-organize. It occurs as a natural response to incoherent or inappropriate things that find their way into the system and rattle around like loose debris. For example, the oyster, not known for having complex thought processes, self-organizes itself around an invading grain of sand by secreting a nacreous material that forms a pearl around the grain, thus reducing the friction of its presence. In the same manner, my dream "decides" to explain the saw in Familiar's hand by "secreting" a plausible explanation. And of course the very act of seeking an explanation turns into the explanation, whatever it is, and not all of them are plausible in the light of day. Not only that but, given the temporal elasticity of the dream state, its ability to combine its pasts, presents, and futures, I "recall" it as an event from a yesterday that never happened. That is, I recall, in addition, a memory of having remembered something that happened on a real yesterday. For one of the many structures etched in any memory is the *experience of remembering.* So it is quite possible to conceive of an event and then splice it into a past that never happened.

It is all a matter, then, of "filling in blanks" with various sorts of events, emotions, and cognitive processes that are "stored" in the brain. Thus, as Hobson and Kahn go on, there is "a large chance for novelty and innovation in dreaming as fluctuations play with a seeming infinite supply of existing images and story lines" (1993, 164). For example, had Familiar come with his wife and their children (if they had any) I would probably recognize them as well and say how nice it was to see them again. And what I would really be recognizing is a paradigm episode in which I once recognized other visitors on such occasions. Or, if Familiar had arrived at the house with a car jack I would have immediately recalled that we had talked yesterday about the oil leaking from my car and that he had volunteered his jack. Instead of having a "What's the jack for?" reaction, the dream would invoke a memory of a jack and a car and project it, self-organizationally, onto a false dream-yesterday. All in all, dreams are organized in much the way that liars defend their lies by "coming up with" appropriate secondary lies that support the original lie.

Thus the sensation of familiarity in dreams might be explained as the projection of a "generic" familiarity onto an unfamiliar object or person. As an illustration of the principle, take the rare brain condition called visual agnosia which literally de-familiarizes familiar things. For example, if you suffer from agnosia you might look in a mirror and be unable to recognize your own face. You would be perfectly capable of saying, "I don't recognize that person in the mirror"—that is to say, you recall language constructions well enough and you recognize the mirror as a mirror, but the person in the mirror is a total stranger. You are, as it were, selectively ignorant. Apparently the dream state, in nonpathological respects at least, is the reverse of agnosia in that it enables you to recognize things you have no business recognizing. This condition seems important enough to deserve a name, so (to continue the theme begun with my discussion of lucidity) let us call it phantom familiarity. The term is inspired by the phantom limb syndrome, in which awareness of an amputated limb persists after the operation. Awareness, in other words, is stored as a memory not in the limb itself, as it seems to be when we touch something with our fingers, but in the parietal lobes of the brain. So, too, the sensation of familiarity is stored in the memory and can be attached to any dream-object arousing the need for familiarity as a possible explanation for its presence. It goes without saying that the dream often neglects to cover its own bets and leaves us with inexplicable "stray" images and events. In such instances, as Hobson and Kahn put it, the self-organization mechanism of the brain is simply not working at an optimal level (1993, 154). But nobody's perfect. Dreams, in short, sometimes get headaches, just like people, and their efficiency falls off.

But we have not really settled the question of how the self-organization system gives birth to new images in order to satisfy this need for coherence. To put the question differently: what is it about the image that produces succeeding images? Quite apart from the business of self-organization, there is also the question of means, or what we might describe as dream "technology." And the closer we look at the dream image the more there is to it than literally meets the eye. I have been putting the word "stored" (as in "stored in the memory") in quotation marks, largely because it marks another of those metaphorical constructions that often leads to simplifications, if not outright conceptual errors. The problem in talking about dream images is that we tend to think of them in spatial terms, as we think of the images in paintings or drawings. The image is something we are looking *at*. It is there, occupying a certain space in your head, and if it were possible to sneak a specially designed camera into a dream you could almost photograph it, bring it back to daylight, and show people exactly what you'd seen. Indeed, in Hobson and Kahn's article there is a drawing of a customs house as recalled from a dream by the so-called Engine Man, whose dream journal Hobson has analyzed (1988; also 1993, 155). The drawing is intended to do just what a dream photograph might do—describe the incongruous qualities of the building as dreamed for someone who hasn't dreamed it—and as such it is a perfect instance of how we spatialize dream images in an effort to recapture what the eye thinks it has seen in the dream state. And of course such an exercise is doomed to failure because the image is not simply a visual construction, if it is that at all.

Still, there is every reason to think this way about dream images. In a dream we see a tree "over there" standing by itself in a field—that is, standing in space approximately a hundred yards from the dreaming eye. So it exists in dream-space which, if it is not the same thing as empirical space, at least shares some of its characteristics of "hereness" and "thereness." Moreover, dream images, like our impressions of the world, are continually changing as we pass them, seeing them from a new perspective, and so on. And the dream is very effective in imitating waking reality by changing the size of the dream tree appropriately as one approaches and is finally standing beneath the tree looking up into the canopy of its branches. Considering the fact that there is no tree there, or only a "mental" tree, it is quite a feat that the brain can duplicate the physical vicissitudes of the world as we experience them in three-dimensional space.

We tend to forget this in thinking about dreams, that the dream image, however much it may resemble things of the world, is as thin as thought, and that thought space is very different from real space. Indeed, our idea of memory itself is a spatial one. We think of memories as being "stored" in the brain in somewhat the way one might store provisions in a room or books in a library. Perhaps they aren't stored in particular sections, as the old memory houses would have it, and perhaps they are only excitations of certain neuronal networks, or perhaps we have a more "global" concept of memory storage than we used to have. But in the end our sense of memory is a spatial one, no matter what the form it takes. Your childhood memories are "stored" way back in the end of the memory house, middle-aged memories in the midsection, recent memories very close, not yet packaged for permanent storage.

Suppose, however, that we think of the dream image in temporal terms. If the dream image is "made of" memories and memories are necessarily of past events, perhaps the image has as much in common with time as it has with space. Once we see this we can appreciate better the fact that the dream image is not a thing but a dynamic process. Its very appearance in the dream depends on what has preceded it. It is, then, made of the dream-past, embodies the dream-past fully, and as such possesses the seed of the dream-future. How can this be so?

Let us look more closely at the nature of time by taking a page from the phenomenology of time according to Maurice Merleau-Ponty. "It is of the essence of time," Merleau-Ponty writes, "to be in process of self-production, and not to be; never, that is, to be completely constituted. . . . Let us be more precise and say that consciousness deploys or constitutes time" (1978: 415, 414). Time, in other words, never *is;* it is something that is constituted only by and in consciousness, and the passing of time is a process the brain imposes on events. Here is another passage in which this notion is worked out more thoroughly:

Instant C and instant D, however near they are together, are not indistinguishable, for if they were there would be no time; what happens is that they run into each other and C becomes D because C has never been anything but the anticipation of D as present, and of its own lapse into the past. This amounts to saying that each present reasserts the presence of the whole past which it supplants, and anticipates that of all that is to come, and that by definition the present is not shut up within itself, but transcends itself toward a future and a past. What there is, is not a present, then another present which takes its place in being . . . there is one single time which is self-confirmatory, which can bring nothing into existence unless it has already laid that thing's foundations as present and eventual past, and which establishes itself at a stroke. (420–21)

Suppose we edit, or adapt, this passage to present needs, changing the temporal words, like *instant* and *present* and *time,* into the word *image.* For example, the text would now read: "Image C and image D, however near they are together, are not indistinguishable, for if they were there would be no image; what happens is that they run into each other and C becomes D because C has never been anything but the anticipation of D as present, and of its own lapse into the past." And indeed, the dream image is, in this sense, an instant of time, broken off, as it were, from the various memory systems in which it exists as memory and placed in the dream. In saying this much, we are not arguing that imagery and time are identical, only that the image occurs in time, has its life in time: it takes time to happen, and hence obeys the "law" of time thanks to which it unfolds as something other than a still picture of something. So one might say that image C (the tree saw in my Familiar dream), like an instant of time, is not a "constituted" thing-in-itself, or if so it is constituted of its past, as the still photograph of a running horse is constituted, made possible, by preceding "instants" of running that are not *in* the photograph—except by inference—and by the ensuing instants in which the horse's feet will presently touch the earth and spring forth again, driven by the momentum of past leaps. So there is not one dream image, then another, then another; there is only a running image which is self-confirmatory and can bring nothing into existence unless it has already laid that thing's foundations as present and eventual past, and which establishes itself at a stroke. In the case of the photograph of the running horse, we are left with a single "still" image. Thus what has escaped the image is its constitution as an episode of time passing. (Whatever we mean by *running* is now a half-mile down the road.) Or, as Merleau-Ponty says in another essay, "Eye and Mind," "The photograph keeps open the instants which the onrush of time closes up forthwith; it destroys the overtaking, the overlapping, the 'metamorphosis' (Rodin) of time" (1964, 186). In the case of the Familiar-lending-the-saw image, what is really present "in" it, subvisually, is a set of associations drawn from my personal "saw" and "neighbor" networks from all "parts" of my memory. The image of Familiar carrying the saw—were I to draw a picture by way of showing you how it looked—is, so to speak, only the still photograph, arrested in time, stripped of its *passing* quality, and falsified as a fully constituted image.

A dream, then, is not a series of images, each independent of the others or attached to one another by causality of the sort one might observe on a billiard table; rather, a dream is a single running image, the demonstration of an evolving process of association. And this is the sense behind Sartre's remark that "a dream . . . is a world," which is to say that "every dream image appears with its own world" (1968, 216), having, as it were, been hauled from a pre-oneiric tissue of associations borne gene-like within it.

So the image as present is constituted of a certain past and a certain future which are beneath visualization. One can never know what the image is carrying; one can "see" only the path of its endurance and transformation, much as one can see the wind only in the movement of trees and grass. My image of the chemistry laboratory in the basement of my boyhood home is not a photographic "still" but a dynamic representation of all the time I spent in it as a boy and all that I have thought about it since. I see it "clearly," in one sense, but what I see in my mind's eye is not what is there in a single mental frame—a photograph of the lab itself with all its bottles, jars, tables, and apparatus. What is there, if something can be said to be *there,* is a motivated history that has condescended to "appear" as a certain graphic quantum of itself. I can inhabit it, get around in it; I know where my microscope, my bunsen burner, and my shelves of labeled bottles and wooden canisters are (were), but these are memories, recalled habits of the body, with little more than the status of the phantom limb. I am not seeing the lab; I am *experiencing* it and the picture in my mind struggles into existence as a dim analogue of the time I have invested in it. And so it is with the images I create of my mother, my friends, and my English teacher Miss Boles, whom I always see at her desk from the perspective of my seat in the last row on the right side of the classroom. They are all faint traces invaded by history and emotion which give them a false palpability. If they were not constituted thus, there would be no image, for the image is nothing more than a symptom of the past contained within it, as my riding a bicycle today is a symptom of all the trials and errors by which it gradually came to be second nature to me. To be riding a bicycle in a dream, therefore, is to be riding a known past into an oncoming future recalled from a distant yesterday.

How, we must ask, does image C run into image D? How does C become "the anticipation" of image D as about to be present? That is, to come back to my dream, how do we get from saw to greenhouse? One thing is clear: the oncoming "future" image (D) does not arrive in the way that a salesman arrives at the front door. This would imply a strictly spatial, not to mention empirical, sense of the image as something discrete and autonomous with a mind and constitution of its own. Like the future itself—any future—the image does not come out of nowhere. It emerges from the past, and this is the sense in which C is its parent and carrier, though D is not detectable in advance by the dreamer as being "in" C, any more than my act of thinking is detectable in the thought-content I am thinking about.

For example, as I sit here thinking about the next sentence I will write, what passes in my mind is not a groping or a searching for words, as if the appropriate words were "out there" or in my head waiting to be discovered. It is not strictly a matter of "Where to next?" but a matter (as distracted speakers always say) of "Where was I?" It is a matter of harnessing a certain momentum implicit in the preceding sentences, as with the running horse. I see that I have gotten so far in my thought and that what has to be thought next is not open to *any possible thought* but must somehow be prepared by what I have already written. Perhaps what I have written is inadequate, a dead end. This is possible, indeed quite frequent, and in such cases I must erase and begin again. But beginning again means precisely fashioning a sentence with a future somehow contained within it. Writing, finally, is an artifact of thought; thought itself knows no such boundaries as words but is dispersed in time. Thought is either tri-temporal or defective. There is no such thing as a present in which thought is bound up in itself. Here is an example from an article by Jose M. Arcaya on time and memory that argues against the notions that memory is "stored" or (necessarily) past experience:

When I see my friend Dan's face, with whom I have had no contact for the past ten years, I perceive in his present features the outlines of my more youthful companion of a decade earlier. In this regard the past "shadows" the present because it is through his here-and-now experience that I derive glimmers of the man he used to be. However, as I continue my looking, memory starts to predominate and, beyond the white hair and wrinkled skin, the youthful indications of my former classmate emerge. Here presence "shadows" the past as memory predominates. Indeed, past and present shift before my gaze as I behold my friend—not knowing when I am seeing a memory (how he used to be) or remembering a seeing (how he is still despite superficial changes in his present appearance). (1992, 309–10)

Moreover, Arcaya might have added, even the shadow of the future creeps into his seeing-remembering of his friend in the expectation that the friend is *still* aging, *will continue* to age, and over and above the immediate perception hovers the "known" fact, born of the past and directed to the future, of a destiny in-the-making: this process that has aged the friend in the past ten years is even now at work before one's eyes in the dotted line of his not-yet-complete life. When we say, "My, how he has aged," there is in the back of the mind an understanding that aging is an *ongoing* process leading to a terminus. In short, the present does not really exist apart from the past and the future. All worldly objects, including memories (especially memories), are temporal intersections. So the very idea of there being a present that is "empty" and free of the past or the future is, as philosophers since Augustine have realized, a false one. The something that is present in the present can be apprehended only in terms of a consciousness that is, for the moment, tri-temporal, bringing to the perception a unique past and a unique set of expectations. Even the past, as Arcaya says, "does not necessarily precede the present or is subservient to it" (309), for it is the past that edits what is seen in the present and forms our expectation as to the possibilities of the future—again, as in the case of the pattern experiment in chapter 1. We are taught by our past to expect what it is that we are expecting.

Granted, the experience of seeing an old friend is not the same thing as making a dream-image. But the tri-temporality of the experience must be the same in either case. If we understand the dream image correctly we see that it is not finally a matter of the image being a virtual object, sufficient unto itself, a thing called to perception by a reminder (the saw and the tree limb) but a site of remembering in which time is "taking place" not as a present but as a passage. At this level, even the concept of the image as symbol is inadequate because it points, as symbols usually do, to certain meanings already "stored" and sealed off from time and the ongoing revision of the past by new experience—for example, the absurd idea that long objects represent penises in dreams, despite the fact that they are immersed in the entire history of the individual. To come back to my dream, the greenhouse was not something posterior to the saw carried by Familiar, something my mind *then* thought up; the saw was the anticipation of the greenhouse, lodged invisibly in it by virtue of an "interlocking of retentions" (Merleau-Ponty, 1978, 422) which is simply beneath identification. There is no way to determine the specific "motive" for the evolution in my dream from Familiar to saw to dead branch to greenhouse, which we may consider as a typical progression found in most dreams. What is certain is that behind the progression is an interlocking of retentions and associations so subtle and multilayered that the image sequence itself is but a crude artifact of all that was going on in the dreaming mind.[3] Once we have this in mind we can see the way in which the seemingly bizarre images common to dreams are bizarre in visual space alone; beneath their visual "surface," however, they are the battleground on which conflicting memory associations may be competing for survival or prominence.

To return to my original question: how does the dream "think up" its next image when it appears to have all it can handle just reacting to the images already there? It turns out that the business of reacting to images already there—the dream itself, in short—consists largely of watching a "future" image hatch from a "present" image. As dream participants we experience this "hatching" as a series of events that are happening in the dream: I am lost, I encounter a policeman who tells me where to go, and so on. On another level, the level of the dreamwork itself, what is happening is a pattern of association in which certain potentials in the memory are activated as a visual field. It is not images that are recalled but memory sequences, and I will have more to say about such sequences in the following chapter. To put this another way, the plot advances through self-fulfillment. In a way, we create such plots in waking life a good deal. For example, we sit and observe people and, if the mood is right, we begin anticipating what will happen next—what gestures, movements, or sounds the person will make. What we are doing, really, is using our past observations about the person to predict

3. Consider our emotional engagement at the end of *Hamlet* when Horatio says, "Now cracks a noble heart." The moment-image achieves its power only because the entire history of Hamlet that we "retain" comes rushing into the moment. Such a history, I suggest, accompanies all images, indeed all experience, and attempts to confine the meaning of an image to specific symbolizations are inevitably simplifications.

future behavior. We don't truly predict of course; we are more likely to say to ourselves, "I thought she would do something *like* that," recognizing that the past behavior is of a piece with the new behavior only now unfolding. Even so, you may feel a little burst of self-satisfaction at having been so astute in your anticipations. You *feel* like a prophet because the effect is that of prophecy in the sense that whatever happens next is consistent with the quality of your expectation. The fact is, it could not have been otherwise and hence it is self-fulfilling.

The last thing I want to create here is the impression that an image contains its successors in the mechanistic way that the Russian doll contains smaller versions of itself. Nor is it a "biological" matter of the single seed containing, in potentia, the mature tree which predictably follows. The dream environment, as Hobson says, is chemically dynamic and unstable. It is complicated still further by a variable input of energy, virtually no input of sensory stimuli, a degree of randomness and chaos in mentation processes, and the vagaries of the cycle of sleep itself. In other words, many things can befall a dream en route to its future, and were it possible to know the potential of the dream's "seed" image, if there were such a thing, we could not predict what adjustments would have to be made along the line by way of maintaining coherence in the system. Suffice it to say that the dream, at any instant, is a spectacle of consciousness in flux. Merleau-Ponty warns us against taking consciousness "as a multiplicity of psychic facts among which [we can] establish causal relations." He cites the case of Proust's Swann, whose love for Odette *causes* his jealousy, which in turn *modifies* his love. Rather, "what we have," Merleau-Ponty says, "is not jealousy aroused by love and exerting its own counter-influence, but a certain way of loving in which the whole destiny of that love can be discerned at a glance. . . . Swann's [love] bore its degeneration within itself" (1978, 425). In short, Swann's was a jealous love from the outset.

And so it must be with the saw image which bore the greenhouse within it. It is not a causal series but a certain psychic potential in which that series was evidently the most probable course of evolution, given all the conditions pervading my consciousness at that point in the dream. For example, the saw image might have come from a saw-like sound overheard in sleep or from an abrasive contact of skin and the buckle of a wrist watch. Systems, as we now know, are continually reacting to disorder that inevitably finds its way into the heart of its order.

It may be useful to view this process of mindless composition from a somewhat more pragmatic perspective. The evolution of a dream plot has much in common with the wave function in quantum mechanics, or at least we might learn something from the comparison. Wave function does not refer to material things like sound or water waves. In quantum physics, waves "are a measure of *probability.* One talks of electron waves in the same sense as crime waves" (Davies and Gribbin, 1992, 208). Indeed, David Overstreet has drawn an analogy between wave propagation and thought propagation in the literary process:

A wave function propagates as a thought occurs. The actualization of the thought follows a wave function in that each word thought is independent (any image capable is possible), yet the probability of one image following another is related to its associative connection and syntactical appropriateness. . . .

In literary terms, when a writer puts pen to paper, there is a potential for writing any work, new or old. But when the image is made language by writing the first word, the wave function collapses [narrows]. While each following word has infinite possibilities, the wave function of possibilities has collapsed into the most favored statistical group, the probable. . . . Quantum mechanics could predict the odds on different words or types of words being used, but it could not predict exactly which word. (1980, 47–48)[4]

In essence, this is what I've been saying here. I cite the passage in order to illustrate that dreams, like electrons, are best regarded as being

4. I wish to thank my friend and colleague Dan Davy at the State University of Kansas for pointing out Overstreet's article to me.

governed by probability rather than certainty, and that the same can be said for literary writing as well—though fiction writers have the added advantage of being able to roll the dice again (called revision) until the *ideal* probability (the best metaphor, the best description, and so on) arises. This is another way of saying that dreams are self-organized and that the self-organization requires no mysterious skill to produce a probable thought process. In fact, in terms of pure energy expenditure, it is much more difficult for a system to create an improbable sequence than a probable one, if only because an improbable one necessitates a violation of the self-organizing principle.

There is a further corollary to this connection between dreams and electrons. Dream probability, as we have seen, is closely aligned with time, or the tri-temporal composition of an image. But how is it that the image can be both itself, a discrete entity, and a coalescence of past and future associations in a fleeting present? Is this not a confusion? It isn't if we regard the problem as being one of perspective rather than one of "solid matter." It has been a commonplace of quantum physics since Heisenberg that it is impossible to measure both the wave aspect and the particle aspect of an electron. You can measure one or the other, or one *then* the other, but that's that; like our running horse, if you seize the particle aspect, the wave aspect instantly disappears, and vice versa, and nothing can bring them together in a single perception. This frustrating situation leads to the innate uncertainty that Heisenberg saw as haunting the subatomic world.

So, too, with the dream image. There are similarly two ways of looking at and identifying it. And it is an interesting (and understandable) fact that dream study has been dominated by the particle approach, which regards the image as a discrete entity in space (sign, symbol, displacement of something else)rather than as a process-in-time. I am not suggesting that dreams and electrons "do" the same things, only that both have particle and wave aspects and that a full account of the dream image—were one possible—should be concerned with both. For it is in their cooperative competition that the integrity of the dream, as well as its fundamental uncertainty, finally lies.

To come back to the example of Uncle Harry and the meerschaum pipe (chapter 2), in the empirical world these are two different things: pipe and Uncle Harry. In the world of dynamic memory they are "chained" to each other; they participate in each other, and they occupy the same neural network. Again, this is a gross simplification; for many other "things" occupy the same neural network and all of these "things," including Uncle Harry and the meerschaum pipe (not to mention Uncle Harry's wife, Edna, and Edna's sister Blanche, and Blanche's daughter Sue), occupy countless other networks as well. In other words, in the mind's eye Uncle Harry—clearly as you may see him in the dreaming eye—is a *distribution* of mental energy, a *potentiality* that can come to "life" in *n* number of contexts. What would emerge as "probability" from any dream involving Uncle Harry or the pipe would depend on what sorts of related, or co-chained memories had been activated, what sorts of "first" and "following" words, in Overstreet's example, set the dream wave in motion along an ever-"collapsing" contextual path. This is the fundamental uncertainty at the subatomic base of all dream images, but it is also the source of dream intelligibility.

In conclusion, suppose I ask you, "Quick: what do you think of when I say 'Kansas City'?" You might answer "beef," "the Chiefs," "humidity," or "Uncle Harry." But whatever it is will have come from a pool of associations you have no power to control and no conscious part in devising (if you play the game fairly); moreover, your response will certainly carry with it further engrams, or traces, of "attached" associations that will constitute, ever increasingly, the probability of the dream wave. Are these traces *there* or *not there?* The answer is: both. They are *influentially* there, somewhat as the electorate and lobbyists are "present" in the goings on of government.

Part of a short verse by the seventeenth-century Welsh poet Thomas Traherne might, with a liberal jot of imagination, be considered as a mimetic model of atomic life in the dream state. The poem itself has nothing to do with dreams (though a verse from Traherne's poem "Dreams" serves as the book's epigraph); it is entitled "My Spirit" and is about Traherne's own soul, which he likens to "an Endless Sphere, Like God Himself." This is close enough to the mystery of time and imagery to erase the distant hesitation I feel about putting it to my own secular uses:

> It acts not from a centre to
> > Its object as remote,
> But present is, when it doth view,
> Being with the Being it doth note;
> > Whatever it doth do,
> It doth not by another engine work,
> But by itself; which in the act doth lurk. (1958, 50)

The poem summarizes my theme beautifully. But, more to the point, it also *acts out* my theme in precisely the way that I am saying the dream image contains the three phases of temporal consciousness within its own "engine." One of the poem's more obvious delights is that when you reach the last line you have a marvelous respect for the coherence in systems. In fact, one might say that the poem is about self-organization. It doesn't want to "go" anywhere but to keep folding back into itself, as physicists say, in a causal loop, as if it were about nothing but itself, or about anything that should be looked at as itself, as it *is* in its Being, and not about some remote object which the poem will eventually get around to naming. Even so, the closing couplet rounds it out perfectly, as couplets are supposed to do. Suddenly you see that *work* was hiding *lurk*, as *remote* was hiding *note*, and *view, do*—a very simple instance of the pleasure of rhyme, when it isn't forced, or when the point being made is sizable enough to justify the ostentation.

But the poem is also an instance of the pleasure of time as well; for time and rhyme have similar constructions in that both are reversible, or at least reciprocating engines. It is purely accidental that *time* and *rhyme* rhyme with each other (like dream and meme); but then rhyme is always something of a planned accident looking for somewhere else to happen. More important, time and rhyme *work* and *lurk* alike. Past time lurks in the future and "rhymes" with it when it comes about, having been one of its causes and, like Jose Arcaya's friend Dan, retaining its original features; and *rhyme* needs time, or a point in the future, in order to happen. Time and rhyme are both ways of planting, in the dual sense of putting down clues and of preparing a harvest. In any case, as psychic experiences they are not progresses but oscillations and self-augmentations. You simply can't separate *work* from *lurk* because they fulfill each other. You can't go back and read *work* the same way once you've gotten to *lurk,* any more than you can recall the past as if it were still a present uncontaminated by all the futures that have arrived to change it. Finally, you don't ever know whether *work* is the cause of *lurk* or *lurk* of *work,* because the chronological order, you now see, was simply a deceptive framework for a series of returns to a "centre" called "It" about which we know very little except that it never leaves itself.

The same thing, I take it, can be said of the dream, the main characteristic of which is that its images are made of memories altered by the passing of time and re-presented during the time in which seeing takes place. But sight itself is only the tip of the neuronal iceberg. The dream is the act by which the mind gives up its images only to take them back to itself, thus converting memory to expectation and back to memory again. This is the sense in which the dream is wholly present in what it "doth view" and not controlled by an absent puppetmaster "stored" somewhere else in the brain who is pulling its strings. The dream is simply the full operation of the dreaming brain in which "lurks" all the resources of memory that compose it. The dream is not something *made* by the memory; it is memory itself changing before your eyes.

5 ·

The Harrison Ford Syndrome

One night in a dream I found myself at the same house as Harrison Ford. Physically he didn't look remotely like Ford, but he was still indisputably Harrison Ford. And there was a group of people in one corner of the room watching a display and light show that seemed to be a promotion for Ford's Indiana Jones movies. Ford was more or less lingering on the fringe, preoccupied with something else. Beyond this I couldn't see anything clearly except now and then puffs of smoke and sparks emerging from some sort of video arcade game obscured by the crowd standing around it. But I knew what was going on because I could hear trumpets blaring the Indiana Jones theme: Ta ta *ta* ta—ta ta *ta!* It was the music that caught my attention, not Ford, and a moment or so later I awakened, humming the tune to myself. And it was, I now remembered, the right music. The shocking thing is that I didn't know that I knew the music before I heard it in the dream. In fact, I can't sing even a few bars of the score from any movie I knew well, except perhaps *Casablanca, Jaws,* or *Singin' in the Rain,* because I have almost no memory for background music in movies. And I certainly couldn't have ta-ta'ed my way through a few bars of Indiana Jones in the light of day. But my dream had the music right, though it had Ford's face and body all wrong.

Here, it seems to me, is a real dream conundrum. The dream apparently calls on a form of memory that is at least partially unavailable to the waking brain; and even though I know perfectly well what Harrison Ford looks like and could probably draw a decent likeness, the dream gave me a person I had never in my life seen—or at least could not recall seeing. You could say that the dream "settled" on this person to "play" Ford because it also had someone else in mind, and this is what came out: a Harrison Ford compromise. But of what was it a compromise? Between Ford and who (or what) else? All of these negotiations are hopelessly beneath detection; the dream simply offered what it offered and I haven't a clue as to why Ford was there in the first place. In any case, it is a common dream experience to be able to identify a person—friend, mother, wife, son—as himself or herself even though there is little if any resemblance. Not only that, you may be perfectly conscious of the confusion in the dream and you might say to yourself, "That's Mother, but it doesn't look like Mother. But it *is* Mother all the same." And you're not even surprised by the stark stupidity of such a contradiction.

Maybe it is, finally, just a matter of Allan Hobson's acetylcholine discharge; maybe the dendrites were firing in a confused way, the way static lets you hear only parts of a radio transcription. So the Indiana Jones music comes through as clear as a bell, traveling, as it were, on a different frequency, but Ford gets lost along the trunk line, even though his identity, being less dense, manages to squeeze through without his body. So I get *Ta ta ta ta — ta ta ta* and a complete stranger who is and yet isn't Harrison Ford.

While I can't dismiss this as an explanation, it does occur to me that maybe the dream state abides by entirely different rules of recognition. And it may be useful, before charging these confusions up to riotous electrical and chemical behavior, to ask what sorts of perceptions one *couldn't* have in a dream owing to this fundamental condition. Or: what could be the conceivable use of such confusions? In waking life we recognize familiar people through a complex procedure, primarily through visual means, and only at a certain proximity. At three hundred feet you can't tell even your mother from Harrison Ford. But vocal recognition is important as well. Mother will, or should, always sound like herself. Then there is another form of recognition we might call behavioral or attitudinal recognition: if Mother isn't behaving like herself I will likely suspect something is up. She's Mother, but what is wrong with her?

In the dream state we seem to have a different perceptual apparatus. Somehow this complex, multilayered act of recognition gets splintered or short-circuited. Unfortunately, the word *short-circuited* suggests that an error of some sort has taken place. But I am using the term in Umberto Eco's sense of a cognitive "leap" or "short circuit of preestablished paths" which allows the mind to traverse mnemonic networks very rapidly (1984, 81): a matter of economy rather than error. It's a little like the perception of the frog that can't recognize a bug right in front of it until the bug moves. That is, perception is geared to need. Frogs apparently don't waste their weaponry on an object in their line of vision until movement establishes that it is edible. Maybe it is more complicated than this for the frog, but the idea might apply to dreams in the sense that something (an object or a person) becomes "itself" only when the dreamwork gives it some psychic passport. It isn't necessary for it to look like itself as much as that the mind connects it with a certain idea of itself. How often, for instance, do we say of a photograph, "It doesn't look like you"? Yet the camera didn't lie. Obviously, what it failed to capture is *the flow* of identity in time, the continuity through which identity expresses itself. Dream images, as we have seen, are not photographic stills; they are, as it were, sensory composites, and it apparently doesn't matter which "sense" of the person is captured.

I recall another frog story from my high school biology class: if two frogs are engaged in coitus (so the lesson runs), you can sever the back leg of the male and there will be no pain and no interruption of the act, beyond the incidental awkwardness of performing one-legged coitus. Apparently the frog's nervous system, being comparatively elementary, has a priority list at the top of which (at the moment) is sex, and any other sensory imposition has to wait for acknowledgment. Pain afterward, maybe, but not during pleasure, if that's what the frog is having. I'm afraid to check the truth of this story with a biologist, and I don't really want to because it's such a good analogy to the Harrison Ford problem, or part of it, and it doesn't matter anyway. That is, the dream has thought of Harrison Ford—God knows why (that's another matter entirely)—and filled its circuitry with the Harrison Ford *essence,* and then created a sloppy facsimile to give the essence a corporeal home— somewhat the way movie stars write their autographs. Or maybe, like my first frog, it just applied the Harrison Ford energy to the first moving object, like lightning striking the tallest tree, and voilà! Instant Harrison Ford. But then we have the problem of where this moving object came from in the dream's design. Did this dream person show up before the idea of Harrison Ford, and if so, who was he before the Ford-essence waylaid him? If there were no dream person to call Harrison Ford—or, more correctly, to allow me to recognize *as* Ford—where did the idea of inviting Ford come from? Ah! From the music! But then, I don't *know* the music—or I thought I didn't. And if I apparently did remember it in one of my memory compartments, why was it being played on this particular dream night in a dream that had nothing otherwise to do with Ford?

I suppose these are tedious questions. But if you think about the problem at any length, these questions bear on the characteristics that distinguish dreams from other sorts of experience. I am convinced that the dreamwork isn't separate from the dream we experience. If it were, we would be back with the ghost in the machine paradox, and this would be much more difficult to explain than this silly Harrison Ford problem. So there is nothing in the dreamwork that "thinks" these matters out in advance of the dream show, or that makes decisions (however instantaneous) and produces an image. But this doesn't mean that there aren't orders of thought over which we have no conscious control. The probable thought model to go by may be that of our invention of sentences, which come to the lips or the page seemingly out of nowhere. Yet something in the brain knows the difference between a hawk and a handsaw. Surely the image must occur simultaneously with the dreamwork. You dream what is going on in your head, and you don't have two heads. So Harrison Ford pops up and fails to bring along his likeness. It stands to reason that a real, recognizable Harrison Ford is irrelevant to this particular dream experience. Or perhaps it *is* an error of sorts, not so much an error that enfeebles the dream or its sense but one that is an inevitable part of thought itself.

It is rather like the error you make when you forget where you've put your glasses or car keys. Or, on a slightly higher level, the kind of unplanned error an artist might make with a paint brush, of which there must be thousands in a single Van Gogh painting. They aren't certifiable errors, like mistakes in your checkbook, but aspects of personality or self-expression. And the brain that makes such "errors" is the same brain that you dream with. So we can't assume that there is an explanation for why all these things happen in dreams without allowing for glitches and errors. When you look around you, you observe errors and inefficiencies, large and small, that are part of any human activity, and there is no reason that the dreaming brain should be thought to be super-efficient or that *everything* it casts up must mean something.

But then how can we explain the even more frequent cases in which Harrison Ford (or any recognizable person) shows up as himself and, like Mother, looks, sounds, and acts like himself? It isn't very helpful simply to say that such cases are more "error-free" than the others. Or that the dream, in giving us the real article, is simply operating in a more efficient mode. This is a possibility, but it seems like a typical "waking" argument and a far too convenient way to settle the question. Maybe errors aren't really errors but something else. Before we cry "error" we ought to consider the possibility that error and efficiency may be inappropriate categories to apply to dreams. For instance, suppose Shakespeare, instead of writing Hamlet's famous line

> O, what a rogue and peasant slave am I!

had written

> O, what a dunghill idiot am I!

The latter happens to be the version that appears in the soliloquy in the infamous First Quarto. Scholars have strong suspicions that Shakespeare didn't write it and that it was falsely remembered by an actor who was adapting the play for a tour. But presuming that Shakespeare may have written it, would "O, what a dunghill idiot am I!" be considered an error on his part in not finding a metaphor in keeping with his genius, of sending an idiot to do a rogue's job? In fact, can we assume that the First Quarto version is inherently inferior, or is the inferiority the consequence of our familiarity with the famous version? Suppose we had never heard of the famous version: wouldn't we simply accept the "dunghill idiot" as being the correct and only version and if, thereafter, some smart revisionist would suggest that a better version would be "Oh, what a rogue and peasant slave am I!" (from the bad quarto) we would roll our eyes and scoff at the very idea that this tin-eared poetaster could conceivably find "rogue and peasant slave" superior to "dunghill idiot" with all its stunning vulgarity and its brazen relevance to the theme of cankers, worms, and offal eating at the heart of this "rotten" community? What have rogues and slaves to do with Hamlet's problem? What a dunghill idiotic thing to suggest.

In short, to think in terms of errors is to assign the dream—or art—to the logic of checkbooks, calculations, and things that should have gone a certain way, in terms of efficiency or normative expectations, but owing to some unforeseen interruption of the process went another way. One might speak of an error in meter, as when a poet gets his iambs and dactyls mixed up, but that's a special matter of the logic of poetic conventions, not to be confused with the images the poet puts into metrical form.

Beyond error, of course, there is the question of randomness. Can something random be going on in dreams? My own hunch is that any randomness in dreams must be related to the question of priority. We all have priorities; indeed, we are a priority-driven species. Apart from fundamental priorities like oxygen, food, rest, and safety, priorities vary with the person. To keep it simple, let us say I go to a restaurant and cannot decide whether I want the chicken piccata or the veal milano. They are equally attractive on this particular night and I am absolutely stalemated. Meanwhile, the waiter is taking orders from the others at the table and getting closer to me. It is finally my turn. I stutter, then I ask my wife which would be better (as if she were going to eat it), but of course she's no help. I ask the waiter what he recommends and he tells me that both are excellent. The waiter waits; everyone laughs. So finally I blurt out: "I'll have the New York steak, medium rare."

The logic here, I suggest, is that two items have the same priority and simply cancel each other out, leaving room for a third to sneak in.

The truth is probably that I wanted to order New York steak all along but was ashamed to do so because I always order steak and it makes my wife smile ironically and I lose originality points. Actually, I've adapted an old military strategy: get two countries or armies to go to war with each other and then move in and take over while they go at it. So I set up this false border clash between second-choice adversaries, and when they've exhausted themselves I moved in with my beefy artillery, accompanied perhaps by Indiana Jones music, and get what I secretly wanted all along. If this is unconscious thinking, it's at least honest thinking and it doesn't refer the choice to some mysterious second thinker off in a secret war room.

Now something of this kind must go on a great deal in dreams at a much faster speed. Moreover, the process is entirely unconscious—not in Freud's sense of the word, but unconscious in the sense that the dreamer doesn't know it is going on, or more correctly *how* it is going on, for the "motive" must be at least partially in mind as an attitude. This is the sort of unconscious, for instance, that helps you to drive a car or to play tennis, or write a paragraph on the unconscious. I notice above that I quoted Hamlet's line on the hawk and the handsaw, and then about eighteen lines later I quote him again in a completely different connection. I didn't plan that; Hamlet was just walking nearby in one of my mental hallways and when I wanted a line to illustrate the principle of error he was right there. And I suspect that dreams make choices of that sort as well: there are groups of "nearby" things (including the whole day residue waiting in line for "processing") that swarm together by virtue of the theme of the dream in progress, like yellow jackets around a picnic ham.

This is rather technical business, and it might be useful to develop the principle in more detail. The semiotician Umberto Eco has argued that metaphor is made possible—indeed, can only occur—by virtue of subjacent metonymic chains. That is, resemblance can occur between two things only when there is a pool of contiguous things or images from which to draw (1984, 74). To put it simply, one can metaphorically explain why two people are "joined" in matrimony by saying that they are compatible, have similar tastes, views, and so on (in short, they "resemble" or are "like" each other). Or, you can explain it metonymically by noting that they accidentally happened to be at Penn State in the same year. Both of these reasons are correct, but the metonymical reason (based on contiguity, or on their being in a common place) necessarily has priority over the metaphorical one. That is, both people would have to have been together at Penn State, or someplace else, before they could discover each other and make a nice metaphor. So all successful metaphors, so to speak, have to go to Penn State. If you were to say, metaphorically, "My love, my flame," any recognition of the possible meanings of that metaphor would arise by reference to the semantic conditions through which passion has come to occupy the same metonymic chain as heat, burning, glowing, fervor, brightness, warmth, dancing danger, and whatever other connotations of "flame" may come to mind. Indeed, without an underlying metonymic chain a metaphor becomes as incomprehensible as Borges's Chinese encyclopedia. How would one half a metaphor know where to look for its other half if it weren't already wandering in a field of potentially resemblant and "nearby" things? Otherwise, it would be like looking for vegetables in the meat section of the grocery store.

Douglas Hofstadter would probably call such a chain a "semantic network" or a group of "partially isomorphic symbols," any one of which would be capable of triggering any other by virtue of their synonymic exchange value (1980, 370). Metaphor, then, would be a movement between two semantic networks that possessed the potential for certain overlapping meanings. A phrase like "My love, my desire" wouldn't be a very good metaphor, but more a tautology or a synaphor because both elements are drawn from the same network, making them virtually synonymous; whereas "My love, my flame" is (or used to be) a good metaphor because it uncovers a quality shared by two networks that (at one point in time) were not normally coupled. Of course, a network would be much larger than my terms indicate, and they would not be "stored" as words or images but as something *energetic* in the brain for which we have no precise word. Moreover, each member of a semantic network can be charged in various ways, and the type of charge will determine which other members it will attract (371). For example, if you're awfully fond of snakes and you make a metaphor like "My love is a coiled snake," it will mean one thing to you and something quite different for most other people.

But one might want to ask how the person who first coined the metaphor "my love, my flame" got from one semantic network (love) to another (flame) without having *something* in mind. It's easy to see why it works after you know the metaphor; but how do the creators of good metaphors find the right network, not to mention the right metonym in the network? Did the poet think, "Well, love is warm, and it's dangerous, and it's bright," and then pose the riddle "What's warm, dangerous, and bright?" and arrive at *flame?* This is a real mystery. And it is complicated by the fact that many people, perhaps most, are not good makers of metaphors, as Aristotle was the first to notice. It apparently requires a strong sensitivity and a mental ability to break out of fixed categories. And it may well be that the dream state actually enhances our metaphorical susceptibility because it frees the mind from the constraints of waking thought.[1]

Finally, it would be simplistic to assume that having an image in mind is a matter of a specific symbol being turned "on" as opposed to "off," present or absent from thought during any metaphorical transaction, for a particular member of a semantic network (say, *glowing* or

1. It occurs to me that Dawkins's meme pools operate in this same way. For example, the God-Hell-faith-sacrifice-celibacy meme pool I discussed in chapter 2 is really a metonymic grid of interreliant memes that give birth to each other as a way of assuring the safety of the Mother meme, which in this case is surely God. How do you ensure the sanctity and worship of God but through a concept of Hell? How do you teach the worshiper to persevere in the face of dangerous anti-memes (like evolution!) but through blind faith, and so on. Thus a meme pool gets metonymically built up of interchangeable "parts," each of which becomes in turn a metaphor for the others.

gaseous in our flame metaphor) might be half "on" and half "off," or suggestively present, or present only in the sense that the context does not *contradict* its being an aspect of meaning. The thought of a gaseous loved one isn't very alluring, but a glowing loved one does suggest a certain radiance. In any case, an image's connotations might be rather like trees in a landscape painting which become less articulated as the view retreats to the horizon, until finally you know they are trees only by the context. They no more look like trees individually than they look like Harrison Ford, and it may well be that my Harrison Ford was simply one of those unarticulated dream images because he was (and remained) on the periphery of the plot. The dream cast him in a role, so to speak, but his "part" was somehow exigently cut.

So when you say "My love, my flame" you may be referring primarily to the warmth or brightness of your love, but you can't be sure that you aren't subliminally trailing a quality related to consumption, or destructiveness, that involves still another semantic network down the line that may include death (as in *liebestod*). This is an extremely important feature of semantic networks in that it accounts for the depth and inexhaustibility of the metaphorical image, as well as the complexity of one image's relation to another. Indeed, here is another way to look at the problem of temporality that we examined in the previous chapter. Image C giving way to image D, and so on, could be described as an evolution taking place within a metonymic chain, whereby the dream moves within a chain, any one of whose members implicitly contains all the others. For example, a dream taking place on a farm will be drawn to the properties and possibilities one finds on farms, and specifically farms and farm experiences already "stored" in the dreamer's memory. Hence the "et cetera" effect of all metaphors: what the mind's eye sees is only the exemplar, or sign, of an unarticulated field of related things (I shall return to this idea in chapter 7). One of the beautiful things about any metaphor is that there is always more to it than you can ever know. Indeed, tracking down all the implications of a metaphor would be as difficult and unending a task as tracking your ancestors back to Eden.

Anyway, I assume that's how Hamlet got back into my argument. And if you examined this entire chapter, you would probably find a dozen places where a metaphor or allusion or sound secretly brought along a relative for possible later employment; or, to put it a better way, by virtue of being in a text, a metaphor or image or sound contains, contiguously, potentially, metonymically, *all of its kindred,* and it wants only a provocative context in order to give birth. Metaphors work like key in music; unless they are hopelessly "mixed" or crash dissonantly into one another, they set the tone and range of an entire stretch of thought.

In *A History of the Mind* (1992) Nicholas Humphrey eloquently describes how dream images might be formed in the mind. His name for the principle is "binocular rivalry." A simple illustration (his own) might be putting your finger in front of your right eye while you are reading a book. Immediately, you seem to see the page before you "through a transparent 'ghostly' finger." Since your vision is focused on the page (unless you re-focus it on the finger), what the left eye sees is dominant, but even so the right eye is still registering the same image *through* the finger. And so too with imagery, in and out of dreams. The thing about the dream image, however, is that there is no competitive stimulus arriving from the outside world to dilute it and so the dream image has the field to itself. This would account, not only for the peculiar vividness of the dream image, but the tendency of dream imagery to persist in the vision (like the real world), whereas in waking perception it is extremely difficult to close your eyes and hold an image in mind for more than a few seconds (111–12).

Finally, binocular rivalry would account for the strong susceptibility of the dream image to invasion or contamination by other internal associations that arise in the mind—all images, as I have said, being saturated with associations. And as the dreaming mind is obliged, neuronally, to honor the competitions and complexities that accompany all dream images, it offers the dreamer not a world of stability and accountability but the struggle of images for dominance and the parade of images passing into their "familiars" and opposites on the current of what Humphrey calls the "dream idea." Hence the bizarreness of dreams is a function of thinking an "idea" through for the first (and only) time. If it were possible to visualize on a screen of some sort all the thinking that has gone on in my head during the composition of this single paragraph (the word changes, the dead ends of thought, the inadequacies—all the things my reader has been mercifully spared), what you would see would be as bizarre as a dream. Unfortunately, we tend to think of dreams as final drafts rather than the works in progress they necessarily are.

A variation of the idea may well account for Harrison Ford showing up in someone else's body. There is no way to tell who or what is occupying an image in a particular dream, but there is bound to be some process of activation (search and selection) taking place as the dream unfolds. One might say that its very unfolding, what we experience as a dream, is the visualized surface of this sorting process. In other words, the march of events in a dream plot is really a march of metaphors (another way to say what I was describing in chapter 4). If a dream were ordering dinner in a restaurant, tossed about (as I was) as to its priorities, it might solve the problem by ordering all three—steak, chicken piccata, and veal milano. In waking life this would be called gluttony. But in a dream you can eat all of them (and much more) at once. If you are of three minds, or three stomachs, about something, the dream doesn't make a choice, unless one is clearly dominant; it blends the possible choices into an unrecognizable hash. Hence the seeming bizarreness of most dreams: bizarreness, one might say, is the soup kitchen of dreams. What necessitates this is the unbelievable speed of neuronal transmission. At a real restaurant I can delay, fuss, and finally make a choice. The waiter will remain patient, or politely ask if he should come back when I've made up my mind. Not so the dream waiter, which is to say the dreamwork. The neural networks of the brain are exquisitely sensitive, nothing nearly as gross as the networks of my computer, which normally processes exactly what I instruct it to process, and far too slowly.

The difficulty is that one can't know all the contents of a metonymic chain because metonymic fields, like memory itself, are continually changing and making room for new connections. For example, Eco notes the unlikelihood of anyone before Copernicus conceiving the metaphor "the peripheral sphere" in describing the Earth because Earth possessed no seme of periphericity at that time (1984, 85). Moreover, metaphors—at least original metaphors—are not created out of a single metonymic chain but by an arcing principle that joins two unconnected chains either by an absent "middle term" or by elements within a single chain that have only a remote resemblance. A metonymic chain, then, is a complex and dynamic thing that has a periphery and thin boundaries, as Ernest Hartmann would say (1984), and is held together by what Douglas Hofstadter calls "conceptual nearness." The trouble is that "there are many different kinds of nearness" (for example, antithesis, paradox, opposites "reminding" one of each other—that is, "My cold flame") "and different ones are relevant in different contexts" (Hofstadter, 1980, 371). What may be near in one person's experience may be far-off in another's. For example, a metaphor like "My love, my tire iron" would pose an extremely difficult cognitive leap, except in a rare personal case, say, in which I had met my love while changing her flat tire. This would be an example of contiguity being formed by an absent middle term—not absent for the maker of the metaphor, of course, but for any outsider hearing it for the first time. Metonymic chains behave much like Hofstadter's "semantic networks" in that each member "can be activated in many different ways, and the type of activation will be influential in determining which other [members] it tries to activate" (371).

Indeed, one might say that a day in one's life is a gradually evolving metonymic chain consisting of events, thoughts, sights, and so on, that share, if nothing else, membership in a common time zone; thus recalling something that happened yesterday might trigger a memory of something else that happened yesterday ("That reminds me, I have to pick up my mail"), though there is no other relationship of similarity. And as more days ensue, yesterday's metonymic field blends into a larger field encompassed by a week, weeks into months and years, and so on, ever fading in specificity like trees in a landscape painting, until "triggered" forth by the sudden recall of a "middle term" (a phrase from a song, the smell of a cup of tea, or the look on a face). The complete holdings in an individual memory thus form a vast kingdom of metonymies from which one might draw metaphors that any other individual (having different holdings) could not appreciate. Who else but the dying Charles Foster Kane—and of course the audience watching *Citizen Kane*—could appreciate the metonymic depth of the Rosebud image as the glass snow scene slips from Kane's dying hand at the end of the movie. The image sums up the full force of Kane's acquisitive history, his life being one long metonymic chain of getting and spending, bound on both ends by the metaphor of the innocent child's sled. But note that the sled achieved its meaning for Kane only as his life moved further and further from the orbit of its childhood simplicity.

In short, metonymic fields are formed at least partly by accidental associations. And it is thanks to such associations that we are able to recall different nonresemblant events that happened the same day or year. Moreover, if we can accept this idea as a partial cause of images, we may see dreaming as being similar to artistic projects (mentioned above) in which unplanned slips of the brush (the work of Francis Bacon comes to mind) find their way onto the canvas and the painter incorporates them into the painting as if they had been intentional. Thus art is enhanced by "errors" in technique which produce fresh opportunities for further development. Indeed, in many cases this unplanned or accidental quality makes the work interesting and frees it from submission to the imposed order that one finds in amateur art or art made by computer. One might theorize that dreams normally don't represent real places or events because dynamic metonymic and metaphoric motifs are always interacting; that is, any "piece" of reality that finds its way into a dream, accidentally or otherwise, is subject to ongoing metonymic alignments with what is already there. David Sylvester once asked Francis Bacon if his cleaning woman couldn't as well have thrown paint at his canvas (as Bacon often did by way of beginning a painting) to achieve the accidental quality one feels in a Bacon painting. Bacon's answer was basically that she might be able to throw the paint but she wouldn't know what to do with it afterward (1975, 97). For Bacon, painting is "a continuous question of the fight between accident and criticism" (121). And one can assume that the dreaming brain may work this way as well. There is always the accident of the stray association that creeps into the dream on the coattails of another image; there is always the dream's "critical" tendency to integrate it, via self-organization, into what is already there; and as a consequence of this integration, whatever the dream may have been tending toward before it occurred will necessarily be altered.

I'm not trying to limit the possibilities of dream displacement to this logic but rather simply suggesting that things may become related to each other in dreams by more than one cause, and the materials of the immediate day residue must have a powerful advantage similar to that of people who are at the head of a theater queue. Given the speed with which dream images unfold, the principle of "first come, first served," must exert at least some influence on both the content and order of the dream plot—not to mention the possibilities of "meaning." And once such couplings have occurred, arbitrary in one sense yet contextually provoked in another, new developments would presumably take place that might shift the original intention. Add to this that a single dream cannot be limited to a single residue, or even a single metonymic chain composed of several residues—that there may be even larger metonymic chains beyond these drawn together by the experience of the whole day—and we see the impossibility of ever tracing a dream to a single source or even a single *set* of sources. Moreover, we can account for so-called errors in sense (bizarreness) common in dreams through a principle we might call *metonymic deflection,* or the influence of a secondary semantic chain that alters a dream image in some way yet maintains the theme of the dream from an emotional standpoint. The dream simply splits the difference without the least concern for accuracy because dreaming is fundamentally a process of connecting networks that are exerting some affective influence on the dreamwork.

Rudolf Arnheim discusses one of the more interesting experiments along this line of metonymic deflection in *Visual Thinking* (1969). In this experiment, one of Arnheim's students asked selected observers to describe their impressions of two paintings by artists with entirely different styles (Dubuffet and Rembrandt) placed side by side. Then one of the paintings (Dubuffet) was replaced by another in yet another entirely different style (Chagall), and so on. In each instance observers revised their descriptions of the retained painting to emphasize a feature common to the immediate pairing but not evident to the eye in the previous pairing: for example, "a strongly stylized painting by Karel Appel made a Modigliani figure look realistic, whereas the same Modigliani looked suddenly flat when confronted with a Cézanne portrait" (61). While the experiments "were designed to illustrate the psychological mechanism on which metaphors are based in literature" (62), we might see them as confirming the role played by metonymy, or context, in metaphoric formation. A similar operation is surely involved in the transformation of dream images as one image succeeds another, with the result that the new image changes the dreamer's perception of the old one. By such means thoughts occurring to the dreamer about a dream companion might radically change the companion's appearance without changing his or her identity. How can one account for the dream image of Mother suddenly changing into a stranger, while remaining Mother, unless by a clash of metonymic fields? And the proper interpretation of such a displacement would not be that Mother has become estranged from me but that Mother's image has been compromised by a competing dream thought with a similar affect. Of course, if I continue to have dreams in which Mother turns into a stranger we can bet that something more pathological may be taking place.

Meaning, or form, then—and I see these as virtually reciprocal— are created out of things that are brought into conjunction with each other by a combination of the metaphoric and metonymic principles.

We tend to see dreams as manifestations of some form of psychic intentionality: that is, they express something that is "on" the dreamer's mind. However, the metonymic process, as I've been treating it here, opens the possibility that dreams may create meaning as much as they are created *from* meanings (or psychic pressures) that exist implicitly in the unconscious as a wish, fear, or desire. Moreover, such meanings would always be relevant to the dreamer's life because the dreamer usually dreams in personal terms—that is, from the metonymic holdings of a unique memory. There are simply no such things as irrelevancies in dreams for the simple reason that the coherence of dreams cannot be judged by waking standards of formal or thematic unity. Dreams are not confined to the making of waking sense, but to realizing, or enacting, the most suggestive potential for the images they cast up.

Perhaps I can explore this idea more fully by turning to the close poetic companion of the dream. One of the favorite devices of the surrealists for liberating the imagination from conventional patterns and arriving at new, unfamiliar image combinations was the coupling of randomly selected images arranged in a structure. The idea was that the imagination cannot resist processing arbitrarily joined images as if they were normal phenomena. To this end the surrealists invented a game called "the exquisite cadaver" (after the first image produced by the game) in which randomly selected nouns, adjectives, and verbs were arranged in standard sentence form—noun/adjective (subject) + predicate (verb) + noun/adjective (object)—and then allowed to invade the mind. The product of this game was always a bizarre image that was similar, they said, to those of dreams. Here is a typical example generated in my own classroom: "The gossamer swan devours the metal night." It makes no sense at a glance, but as you encounter the words you can't resist trying to form a picture in the mind's eye—which is to say that one creates a kind of sense out of nonsensically arranged semantic units. Sometimes, of course, you produce an image that resists all pictorial conversion, like, "The western pencil coasts the exotic whistle." But even these tease the mind into making pictures. As John

Searle says of our reaction to metaphorical statements: "Where the utterance is defective [bizarre] if taken literally, look for an utterance meaning that differs from sentence meaning" (1979, 144). Nights aren't made of metal and swans aren't gossamer, but if you allow the images to have their way with your mind, you can see a sense in which nights (like metal) may be dark and impenetrable but that something like a light filmy swan just might throw its curtain around all that dark density and "devour" it. Come to think of it, Western pencils (writers?) do hug the shore where exotic (Eastern?) sirens whistle fatal songs.

I am hardly suggesting that dreams occur on some such random provocation. But a dream would have even less trouble making emotional or perceptual sense out of such a string of images simply because dreams are like birds that don't observe property lines established by civic law; rather, they fly wherever the provocation leads. Then too, as Hobson and Kahn put it, the "dreaming brain, cut off from the external world, is ultra sensitive to stray images and thoughts. It thus has the ability to jump from one class of images/thoughts to another; that is, to bifurcate to entirely new and probably unrelated images/thoughts" (1993, 158). I would add that dreams are able to "understand" bizarre images because they understand them in a different way than the waking brain. Dreams seem to have what the surrealists called an "absolute availability" to receive images and to incorporate anything (including such confusions in sensory stimuli as an eye that smells) with anything else. My only quarrel with Hobson and Kahn is that their definition of bizarreness — "highly unlikely elements in the dream narrative" (157) — is conceived from a mental standpoint (waking) that lacks precisely this dimension of thought. So it seems odd to accuse the dream of "failure" when it is only doing something with input that the waking brain, at best, must work to achieve.

Actually, the surrealists reversed the whole problem of poetic inspiration: contrary to what is generally thought, they claimed that "in the poet illumination [meaning] follows creation, rather than preceding it" (Alquié, 1965, 100). Could the same thing be true of dream imagery?

One facet of dreamwork may be the natural inclination of the mind to make sense of whatever occurs to it, or to find the "conceptual" link between what are, in some cases at least, accidental associations. I hope it is clear by now that by *accidental* I don't mean random, or unmotivated, only that certain images may enter dreams because they were metonymically attached to another image. They come as companions of an invited guest, so to speak, but they never crash the dream party without provocation. For it seems reasonable to assume that thoughts and images often occur in the brain as a result of "hanger-on" attraction—actually the disorder that is inherent in any dynamic system (compare chaos theory). And this may explain how some images enter dreams on other than thematic grounds and once there are converted to thematic uses.

In short, rather than assuming that a dream selects and joins things from the memory in order to serve the needs of a theme or wish that is *already in place,* suppose that the dream's business is to find a justification or "utterance meaning"—in short, a narrative structure—for images that, for one reason or another, get metonymically "stuck" in the memory and cannot be ignored. Indeed, among such images may be a high quotient of subliminal stimuli from the day's experience that was not even noticed by the dreamer at the time. The brain achieves this feat personalistically and narratively because there is no other way to organize dynamically evolving image systems. The most extravagant example, again, might be the accident of the falling headboard that becomes the guillotine in Maury's execution dream; or, less radically, the capacity of dreams to convert sounds and stimuli emanating from the waking world (a ringing telephone, a distant siren, a kneading cat) into "relevant" dream images. If it is true that unplanned exterior input influences dream construction, then it seems probable that unplanned *interior* collisions can influence them as well.

In other words, dreams are always having to deal with the "emergencies" cast up by the dynamic nature of the process. As Hobson puts it in *The Dreaming Brain,* the dream is really just doing the best it can "under the adverse working conditions of the brain in REM sleep" (1988, 214);

that is, it is trying to "establish orientational stability" (273) by dealing with constant changes in image development. Again, my only reservation about this description is that the word *adverse* suggests something deficient about the dream state (adverse to what?), as opposed to seeing it as a mental state that is designed to achieve an altogether different kind of stability than that sought by the waking brain. Ernest Hartmann puts this general idea another way by saying that in waking goal-oriented or avoidance-of-danger situations, thought ignores peripheral portions of the connective net (what I'm calling a metonymic field or chain); whereas in dream thought, the peripheral portions of the net are likely to be explored and ordinarily distant connections made (1996, 149). We have somehow tended to place meaning (or intention) first in the dream process, as though meaning exists prior to the image and then expresses itself through a relevant image, but perhaps meaning is created by the brain's need to "make sense of" or to self-organize images and thoughts that are to some degree serendipitously joined. In short, it's the "exquisite cadaver" game all over again.

I imagine neural networks to be as sensitive as the spider's web, which is literally a secreted extension of the spider's own body and therefore a network the spider "feels" to its farthest reach. If an insect touches one thread on the periphery of the web, the spider is instantly on the spot (being, as it were, already there in principle) with the coup de grâce and the necessary packaging for shipment to the central storehouse. So, too, the dreaming brain feels an image it casts up to the length of its network. In the theory of Rodolfo Llinás, a neuroscientist at New York University, the brain fans the image across the entire cerebral cortex in a single unified moment.

I recently had a stunning insight into this business. One morning just before dawn, as is her wont, Abbie the cat came into our bedroom from her own sleeping place elsewhere in the house. She jumped noiselessly onto the night stand beside me, and I awakened, perhaps not fully but enough to hear her bathing, which is also her way of getting my attention. The sounds were empirically audible and catlike.

Then I opened my eyes and saw her colors and markings moving synchronously within a cat shape, even though it was pitch black in the room and impossible to see anything—unless I had been a cat. Here, I thought, might be the solution to the Harrison Ford problem, which had been on my mind at the time. It was the licking, the music of the bath, that brought on the image of the cat, though I could see nothing. And I thought immediately of those conjurers who can raise the spirits of the dead if they possess only a token, a piece of clothing or jewelry, a shard of the dear departed, some real *locus* through which the spirit might be conducted to a palpable appearance. It must have been the sound that metonymically brought on the image of the cat. Thus my ear had told my eye a lie. What made this possible, I can only assume, is the sensory versatility of the hypnopompic state of mind, that brief twilight between sleep and waking in which one can conjure images of dream quality even though one is well on the way to being awake.

Elated by my discovery, I immediately ventured a further experiment. "I'll conjure Simon," I thought (Simon is a colleague and friend who lives nearby). So I closed my eyes and conjured, and, sure enough, there was Simon loping across my backyard from his house on the next street—even coming, though I had not planned this, from the right direction! Alas, as he approached I saw that it wasn't quite Simon; he hadn't Simon's face at all, though he had Simon's gait. So I rearranged a few details—the hairline, the head shape—and I got a better likeness, a semi-Simon. But that was the best I could do. I don't know whether my hypnopompic powers had run out or I had neglected to provide an adequate token or a musical accompaniment. In any case, it was a vast improvement over my Harrison Ford.

6.

"Sometimes a Cigar . . ."

Almost everything about dreaming resists our attempts to understand it. Hardcore verificationists aside, we know when a person is dreaming, and for how long, and we are even able to measure, with an oculometer, such things as eye direction in dreams—meaning that we can tell when the dreamer makes a right turn or goes up a flight of stairs or, in one well-known case, is watching a tennis match. And we know a good deal about the neurochemistry of dreaming. But we have no clear idea, for example, what determines the choice of dream content. It is a commonplace that dreams will pass over the most serious tensions of your day and take you on a pleasant picnic or put you to work weeding a garden growing on your living-room floor.

This apparent triviality and indifference of most dreams to crisis are probably the central factors in the persisting belief that dreams are symbolic constructions. Just as a poet can talk about life or love or death through humble objects like clouds, flowers, and worms, so the dream speaks in symbolic tongues. Thus the triviality of dreams is typically translated into a nontrivial language of signs: the picnic isn't really a picnic, or not *just* a picnic, and the garden in your living room is a warning that you are planting your hopes and goals too close to home, shutting out the sustenance of the outside world. But the problems that arise from such a belief are considerable, and foremost among them is the problem of symbolism itself. For instance, how is it possible that a symbolically naive dreamer, someone who hasn't heard that water is a symbol of interuterine life, or flying a symbol of sexual excitement, can conjure a symbol that would be unrecognizable as such if he or she were confronted by it in waking life? If a waking poet uses an image symbolically, the chances are very good that it is done intentionally, at some level of awareness or "rightness." And waking readers of such images will know, on the grounds of convention and literary competence, that the storm in *King Lear* (for example) was brought on not by a convergence of low and high pressure systems over the English Channel but by the "storm" raging in Lear's mind. Actually, this is the same process of inference that allows waking people to interpret an *x* in an algebraic equation as a hidden number with a certain value to be determined by further analysis. But an unsophisticated dreamer—that is to say, most dreamers—may miss the point of a dream symbol entirely, in which case the question arises as to what the purpose of the symbol may have been. For whose benefit would the dream make such a symbol?

I have spent a good amount of time dealing with symbols in art and literature, but I seem to have no luck recognizing symbols in my dreams, either during them or after I have awakened. The most obvious answer, assuming they're there in the first place, is that I'm not supposed to recognize them: that's the very reason they're symbols instead of just plain things. Or maybe the fact that they are my symbols disqualifies me from identifying them, in the same way in which my tics and faults may be obvious to others but not to me. Still, one would think that symbolic images in our dreams would carry some sort of aura of hyper-implication, like the glow of a star, an affect that would say, "There's more to me than meets the eye," something to identify them, as they sail past, as being different from the run-of-the-mill thing-in-itself. Other-wise there is no way to tell a symbol from a nonsymbol—in which case it isn't clear whether we're dealing with a symbol at all or, as Harry Hunt puts it, with something that has been *turned into* a symbol" (1989, 9), either by an interpreter or by the censor in the dreamwork (in which case it would be called a disguise or a displacement). And once some-thing has been nominated as a symbol, regardless of what it is, it is apt to take on this special aura to which I referred. Somehow, you begin to look at it in a different way.

It must be said that psychoanalytic theory could account for the patient's lack of awareness that something is a symbol of something else in a dream (or in waking experience) by saying that censorship, or repression, doesn't create the symbol, it simply erases the symbolic re-lationship between the symbol and the symbolized referent (snake as a symbol of penis), which had been known in some way before the dream. "It is the symbolic *linkage* which is repressed," writes Hans W. Loewald. "Repression [when there is repression], far from bringing symbolism about, disguises symbolism by interfering with the symbolic linkage and hiding the symbolic function of the symbol. Defense is responsible not for creating symbolism, but for disrupting it, disguising it, and distorting it" (1988, 54). The consequence is that the symbol doesn't really become a symbol for the patient, as it had been for the analyst, until the repression is lifted and the relationship between two objects, images, fantasies, and so on, is restored.[1]

In any case, we still have the symbol, and it behooves us to look more closely at what we have on our hands. From one standpoint there is very little in the world that isn't symbolic in one way or another. For example, there is what one might refer to as personal-unconscious symbolism. You can have an attitude toward something—spiders, ladders, high places, even parking meters—without knowing or having thought about what that attitude is. To come back to the illustration above, if I ask whether you like snakes, you may say, "Not really." "Why?" I ask. "Well, they're slimy. They have no knees. I don't know, I just don't like them." There is probably something deeper than sliminess in your

1. In what follows I am concerned primarily with the classical psychoanalytic conception of symbol as a disguise mechanism. I am by no means suggesting that newer psychoanalytic approaches hold the same view. Indeed, in the "school" of dream psychology that seems most rapidly on the rise, the dream is seen more and more as an integrative instrument that functions primarily as a means of organizing experiences and memories into patterns that lead to ego stability. As such, symbolism is conceived as a way of expressing feelings and connotations of experience through an appropriate but not exhaustive image. Moreover, the whole business of a manifest/latent dream structure undergoes a shift that in general pays much closer attention to the manifest "surface" of the dream and less to the latent. An excellent treatment of this mini-evolution can be found in Fosshage (1992). For Fosshage (as for Stolorow and Atwood [1992] and others) the dream plays the "profound role in psychic life" of developing, regulating, and restoring psychic organization (264). Fosshage's paper appeared originally in 1981 and contained many references to the "neglect" by classical psychoanalysis of new ways of conceiving the dream. One notices now (apart from integrationist theorists) very little abatement in the standard view that dream images are basically sexual in symbolic content and that the same manifest/latent structure in dreams still obtains.

dislike: snakes are the quintessential reptiles and reptiles are among the most primal of the nether-creatures. No wonder it has come to be associated, in literature, mythology, and painting with evil, poison, stealth, and death—not to mention sexuality, and especially male sexuality. Hardly anyone, short of a misanthropic herpatologist, would say that snakes were the symbol of joy or friendliness. Virtually all primates raised in captivity, including humans, associate snakes with fear, violence, and pain (Dennett, 1991, 385). So if you dream of snakes it is likely to be a bad dream.

But maybe not. As Freud was among the first to notice, dreams are quite apt to serve up contradictions; you might have a friendly conversation with a snake in a dream, which I have done, and snakes are right up there on my top ten fears list. But you would probably wonder, on waking, how such a thing could have happened, given your feelings about snakes. In any event, having an attitude toward something is a form of symbolizing, at least when the attitude is condensed into an image. We are surrounded by things we see mainly in symbolic terms: all lambs and doves are gentle, dogs are friendly and outgoing, cats are private and unknowable (cats are actually furry snakes with knees, masters of stealth). But there are exceptions to these rules as well: pit bulls and all kittens and tabby cats, for instance, violate the standard symbolism of their species. But even in becoming exceptions to the rule, they have their own symbolic weight ("nasty as a pit bull," "cute as a kitten," and so on).

So this is one form of symbolism there can be no argument about because it comes with the culture. Even so, a normal person may not understand why he or she is frightened of tulips and feels spiritually liberated in the presence of mailboxes. This is a form of unconscious symbolism, but it is symbolism even so. What is symbolized by the object or the image, what it stands for, is one's entire personal experience with it, and this is the sort of symbolism that begins shortly after birth and requires no literary training. It is probably not possible to take ten steps without encountering something that has symbolic value for you.

"My, what a enchanting yard," you say on your morning walkabout. But how did the yard come to be enchanting? Why not the yard next to it? The secret is locked in the landscaping section of your memory. And if you searched it you would probably find that the enchanting quality came from certain visual effects that could be related to things remembered from books and movies, like bowers, stone walls, intimate walkways, weeping tree branches, plashing fountains, and so on, all part of the symbolic machinery of romance.

One of the most perplexing experiences I have occurs when I walk up or down a well-lighted staircase flanked by white walls tiled up to the handrail. If the tiles are irregular or colored or mosaic or black or blue, the experience doesn't occur, or occurs with less intensity; the tiles have to be white (or offwhite) squares, though the size isn't important. And there has to be relatively bright light. When these conditions are met, the experience occurs without fail in museums, public buildings, and in campus libraries, and the feeling is always the same: a vague sense of apprehension. It is always disturbing but somehow diffused, something I have come to accept.

I have some idea about where it may have originated. In my hometown, my dentist's office was located on the second floor of the newspaper building. You reached it by just such a staircase, and it was here that my mother would take me in the days when the metal novocaine plungers were the size of today's bicycle pumps and the dentist's drill was activated by a long wire pulley running over your head in elbow stages from a motor concealed under the chair, or perhaps operated by the dentist's foot, for all I remember. The odd thing is that today a visit to the dentist is, of itself, little more than an inconvenience. The dentist's office itself holds no symbolism for whatever might have happened to me at the top of those stairs—or at least dentists' offices don't *seem* symbolic of a particular experience or feeling. But on the tiled staircase in the library I have this unsettling feeling of something being— *wrong.* It is not associated with pain but with an ominous impersonality, a sort of institutional torpor, and this is why I wonder if I don't have the memory all wrong, or at least partly wrong. Is it the dentist's office that awaits me at the top of the stairs (or the bottom, for it works going down as well as up), or is it something else? Is it something I did, or that was done or said to me, on these stairs? Could it have been at the hospital rather than the dentist's office? My tonsillectomy in the sixth grade, for example, or my wrist operation in high school? Did my gurney pass along such a hallway en route to the operating room? I also have a memory of there being an elevator just to the left of the stairs, a small cage-like affair with a steel accordioned gate that slid noisily back and forth into the wall. I have some apprehension about that (enough to remember it was there), and it now occurs to me that it was probably the first elevator I had ever seen, as the newspaper building where my dentist was located was the only building in town with more than four stories. The memory is obviously confused beyond any hope of sorting it out. Anyway, one would think that the feeling would wear off, like novocaine itself; but it is always more or less the same, even when I consciously anticipate it, and when I use the stairs I have taken to smiling on discovering that the stairwell is still sending its message. "Ahh, you're still here," I say to it, but of course it simply goes on being its clean, antiseptic, institutional self, a preface to a room I never enter. Still, there is this vague expectation, this weak dread that at the top or bottom of the staircase I might walk directly into surgery, instead of Periodicals.

This sort of symbolism I understand, and dreams are filled with it. Indeed, every dream is inescapably fueled on such private symbolism. It is the principle of the tri-temporality of the dream image (chapter 4) in another of its many forms. Properly speaking, of course, my staircase isn't a symbol; it is rather an instance of the figural image we call metonymy, in which a part stands in the place of a whole or an object for an attitude or a feeling, depending on which definition of metonymy you use (metonymy is sometimes called synecdoche). If you want to call it a symbol it would do no harm, but such things should be distinguished from symbols in the standard psychoanalytic sense in which symbolic meanings are generally the same regardless of who is doing the dreaming. For example, in Freud's and most other symbol dictionaries, the staircase is a symbol of the genitals or sexual arousal. Even Calvin Hall, who doesn't agree with Freud about much of anything, agrees that staircases are sexual symbols. Why? "For the same reasons," he says, "that airplanes [are]. They involve ascension and descension, which is one of the principal features of the sex impulse" (1966, 55). By this same logic anything that goes up and down, from mercury thermometers to teeter-totters to the sun and moon would be sexual symbols. The main idea is that things become symbolic by virtue of resembling something else, and most of the time, in psychoanalytic usage, the something else has to do with sex. (If it's wider than it is long, as some wag has put it, it's a penis.) So if I had a staircase dream (and I haven't), I would be told that it had something to do with sex.

But here is just the point: given my personal experience with the tiled stairway (assuming it had to do with the trauma of tooth or tonsil removal, or something equally painful), surely the personal symbolism would take precedence over the general symbolism. Now I've played right into Freud's hands here because tooth removal (and teeth in general) in his lexicon are also strong symbols of sexuality; dreams of tooth removal, particularly, are symbolic of masturbation (1900, 5:387). So my staircase dream (were I to have one) would, on Freudian grounds at least, be solidly sexual from "mounting" the stairs in the first place to what happens behind the (apparently green) door at the top.

If you take a sampling of things Freud lists under "Symbol" in the index of *The Interpretation of Dreams* you get items of this sort (which I choose more or less at random): animals, asparagus, boxes, burglars, clarinets, eyes, flowers, fruit, hats, house keys and locks, luggage, money, neckties, relatives, rooms, snakes, tables, tools, water, weapons, whips. Almost invariably these occur in dreams as sexual symbols. The first thing to be said about this list is that it consists largely of common things encountered on a daily basis by nearly everyone. None of these things, as we normally experience them, would be construed as arousing sexual implications. No one would claim that asparagus is a popular vegetable because it resembles the male member. I see the resemblance, and as Freud himself put it, "No knowledgeable person of either sex will ask for an interpretation of asparagus" (1900, 4:184). But if this were the case, almost all our food (passing, alas, through the gateway of our teeth, entering the womb of the stomach and the long snake of the intestine, and so on) would refer to sex. Life would be one continuous subliminal orgy of sexual substitutes and before long the whole world would resemble a brothel. My point is simply that, as Jung once said to Freud, or Freud to Jung (you hear both versions), surely sometimes a cigar is just a cigar, meaning, I gather, that a cigar is sometimes a good smoke, just as asparagus is sometimes a delicious vegetable, especially when "suppressed" in butter and garlic. I am sure that even psychoanalysts eat and enjoy asparagus without the least arousal. But the psychoanalytic assumption is that when asparagus and all these other things occur *as images* in dreams—that is, when they are unconsciously *chosen* as images, however involuntarily, by the dreamer—they are no longer their edible, smokable, usable selves. They take on symbolic meanings.

George Steiner has written a critique of such assumptions about dream symbols. Referring to a book (published in 1966) about dreams of German people during the Third Reich, Steiner wrote, "It does not take long to discover that patients dreaming of the loss of limbs or of the atrophy of arms or legs are not displaying symptoms of a Freudian castration-complex but, more simply and terribly, revealing the terrors inflicted on them by the new rules demanding the Hitler-salute in public, professional and even familiar usage" (1983, 20). This is such a highly charged example that it probably biases the case; but the lesson it carries for all dreams is that there is probably an immediate historical or personal cause for dream images that has nothing to do with sex, even though these so-called sexual symbols run through the dream like rabbits. And how could it be otherwise? On this logic I've tried to think of something that might *not* be a sexual symbol on the grounds of resemblance alone and I come up empty-handed. In fact, even an empty hand seems, on reflection, to have ominous sexual possibilities (at least in the context of the paragraph above).

This whole question was settled—in my opinion—some years ago by Charles Rycroft, who scuttled the classic psychoanalytic concept of dream symbolism in a short pungent paragraph.

The construction of lists of sexual symbols is in any case a pointless and misleading activity; pointless because such a list would in principle be infinitely long, there being no reason to suppose that there are any objects which could not be used by someone somewhere to construct a sexual metaphor; and misleading because objects whose images are used as sexual symbols do not in any real sense become sexual— any more than objects used to construct metaphors become endowed with attributes of whatever they are used to describe. Roses remain roses, despite being perennially invoked as metaphors for girls and lips. (1979, 79) [2]

2. An object is symbolic only when it is regarded as a symbol; what is less obvious is that resemblance to a sex organ or to the sex act doesn't make the object symbolic even when the connection is self-evident. Symbolism is only one strategy, among many, to cover such connections. For example, if a movie switches from two lovers in bed to a playground where the teeter-totter is "in play" (to return to my earlier examples), or to a mercury thermometer rapidly on the rise, the audience will certainly make the connection between the two. But this isn't symbolism; it's closer to irony or even satire, and Alfred Hitchcock gets a great laugh out of it at the end of *North by Northwest* when he cuts from Cary Grant and Eva Marie Saint climbing (finally) into bed in their train compartment to a shot of the train plunging into a dark tunnel. The train and tunnel aren't any more symbolic of the sex act than the sex act is of tunnels and trains. They are bisociative, as Arthur Koestler would say, in that two independent phenomenal chains are brought to a sudden convergence. Koestler would probably refer to such cut-and-paste operations as *optical puns,* or "one visual form bisociated with two functional contexts" (1969, 179). Puns, whether optical or verbal, can be either comic or deadly serious, or both at once, as when Shakespeare's Mercutio, having been mortally wounded by Tybalt, says, "Ask for me tomorrow, and you shall find me a grave man."

Unfortunately, built into the "list" principle is a tendency to use the list as one uses a dictionary: all images have established definitions in the same way that all words have dictionary definitions. It is Rycroft's view, and my own as well, that we have confused the concepts of symbol and metaphor and that "dreamers use images of objects with which to make metaphorical statements about themselves" (86). This may seem like a quibble over terminology, but as we shall see it renders the whole concept of dream symbolism supererogatory.

To begin with, there are many cognitive and constructional problems with the concept of dream symbolism. How would a dream go about selecting, say, an asparagus spear as a sexual symbol? Exactly what mental acts would be necessary? First, it would seem that the dreamer would have to know that asparagus resembles a penis. Fair enough. But now we must ask why the dream would choose asparagus instead of a real penis, and beyond that why it would choose asparagus instead of a carrot or a banana or something else. For there are so many sexual symbols in the world of things that a secondary choice would have to be made among them. In other words, it doesn't do to assume that the censor "orders" any old phallic substitute; its nature would have to be provided metonymically by the dream in progress, and then the question arises as to whether it was a displacement or a legitimate part of the dream. How can you tell a symbol from an image? In poetry, this wouldn't be a problem. Poets deal in symbols and metaphors. One of poetry's primary aims is to defamiliarize the world so that we may see it from a fresh viewpoint. It is this innovative way of embodying meanings that gives poetry its primary value. So poets are always looking for new and unusual ways to say what are basically very old things. Poetry thrives on subtlety, on the oblique reference, on allowing the reader to discover the meanings, and asparagus or some other suitably gifted vegetable or object would be a perfect vehicle for a sexual metaphor — were it not that the connection was by now withered to the impotency of a dead metaphor.

But a dreamer is not a poet. The dream has no audience, and therefore no need to be clever. So we must ask why or under what conditions dreams would resort to this sort of symbolism. Let us return to the symbol dictionary for a moment. Classical psychoanalysis commonly assumes an entirely different kind of symbolism that we may call typical or "fixed," as it is referred to by Jung (1974, 31–34). Typical and fixed symbols are not exactly the same thing, but both share the ideas that dream images — Rycroft's argument notwithstanding — are symbolic *in advance* of dreaming and the meanings are usually sexual in nature. How does one know this? Does one know it biologically, perhaps through a racial memory, without knowing one knows it? This idea has its adherents, but most of the time one hears about racial memory as one hears about the unconscious: that is, without much reference to any cognitive or memory-forming process that might explain how such knowledge enters the mind without the person's awareness, or how it is passed along from generation to generation through genetic evolution or whatever other process might be available. We have all spent time in the watery amniotic sac; therefore, water's fundamental meaning consists in this symbolism, which is apparently not erased or eroded by the thousand subsequent ways in which water figures in our daily lives.

In order to talk about typical symbolism, it would be good to have an typical case, so let me stick with snakes by turning to a dream that figured in the controversy between Frederick Crews and the Freudians in 1994. Dr. Herbert Peyser of New York City reported in the *New York Review of Books* the dream of a female patient who was upset about her forthcoming marriage to a man her mother did not like. In the dream the patient is taking a shower. As she emerges from the shower, she is followed "by a snake coming through the bathroom wall, and [she awakens] with great anxiety." Peyser's interpretation is that the dream represents her "ambivalence toward the phallus in particular and toward men in general: that aspect/representation of the matter which is clean and good (the shower) is seen positively but is bland, and that aspect/representation which is 'wicked,' even 'evil' perhaps (the snake) is seen negatively but is highly emotional" (1994, 35). Of course Peyser knows a good deal more about the woman's psychic history than we learn from this brief report. I am here interested strictly in the implicit assumption that the snake and shower represent a phallus, and in *how* we might know that as a valid analytical datum.

There is no suggestion that snakes or showers had ever been a topic of discussion in the analytical sessions prior to the dream; moreover, the tone of Peyser's commentary suggests that he takes the symbolism as an assumption, so I gather that he derives the phallic content of the dream from the standard symbolic meanings established for showers (or at least the mechanical apparatus involved in taking showers) and snakes. In any case, Peyser heard the account of the dream and formed his opinion, but did not "intrude" it (he says) into the analytical session. (Later, the woman confirmed that his diagnosis of her "ambivalence" problem was correct.) So the shower and snake represent a phallus. Even more relevantly, we might invoke Wilhelm Stekel's sense of the snake as "symbolic of the woman who is false to her husband, but never of the husband who is false to his wife" (1967, 398n). This would fit the case very well because it turns out that Peyser's patient has been having a "wicked" affair with another man even while she is planning her wedding. But the main question is whether the woman's dream substituted the snake and shower for a penis, or (more broadly) for her own sexual "wickedness"? Obviously, we can never know the answer. But I suspect that Peyser, confronted on the one hand by the woman's sexual duplicity and on the other by the dream, arrived at the phallic meaning of the dream as naturally as a doctor would diagnose a temperature of 103° as a sure sign of fever. This does not, of course, solve the diagnostic problem (what is the woman's attitude toward the phallus?), but it establishes the symptomatic ground on which a diagnosis can be made. Or maybe it was the other way around: the notion of ambivalence occurred to Peyser first and the shower/snake images supported the claim, assuming they are read as variations on the phallus—shower equals good (but bland) phallus; snake equals wicked (but exhilarating) phallus. So the shower and snake would, in that case, stand in a relation to the psychic problem (phallic ambivalence) as smoke stands to fire. I wonder whether, in some cases (perhaps not Peyser's), this relation might become confused to the point where one attributes to the smoke what belongs only to the fire. In short, a case (to reverse the adage) of saying "Where there's fire there must be smoke," and finding it among images that bear some resemblance to the operational "end" of the sexual problem.

I can imagine someone saying, "What difference does it make? The diagnosis proved correct." This may be true, but that does not validate the idea of typical dream symbolism because one has proven the phallic nature of the images only by means of the conclusion one draws from other analytical data. I'm simply suggesting that this is a natural risk in matters of evidence and symbolic attribution, not only in psychoanalysis but also in literary study, where interpretive ingenuity knows few restrictions. Indeed, it is almost impossible to resist treating images as being "fixed" or "typical" symbols because once they have been invoked in that connection they retain their reputation for sexual reference as surely as a criminal retains a record of past convictions. Proof is no longer necessary. I am not dismissing the possibility that the appearance of a snake in the dream may have been caused by thoughts about sexual organs or relationships. I'm sure that is quite common, and I doubt if there is a symbol as universally accepted as a sexual symbol in psychoanalytic and literary theory as the snake. Even Loewald, in his discussion of the snake/penis symbolism, agrees that snake and penis "show an emotionally significant resemblance to each other, so that one may represent the other" (1988, 49). My skepticism arises from a nagging feeling that there must be as many reasons for dreaming of a snake as there are dreamers and that many of these don't have the remotest connection to sex. And if that's the case, what can we make of the notion of typical symbolism?

The whole idea of "typical" symbolism bristles with problems. It is comparatively easy to identify typical images: all you need to do is to count the number of snake or shower images that appear in a sufficient population of dreams and put them on a scale with other images found in the same population. And I suspect that snakes would be right up there with dirty bathrooms and strangers in frequency of incidence, certainly far ahead of things like carburetors or panda bears. Typical symbols, however, introduce the added factor of an image with a single meaning, or at least a single *range* of meanings. Otherwise, how would you know it was a symbol and not a plain image with an infinite number of meanings? It isn't at all clear how you would know one from the other, as both images and symbols look and behave alike. Obviously, the attribution of symbolicity would have to come either from an analytical hunch (the woman is having problems with phallus-bearing men, ergo the long thin image is a phallic symbol) or from an advance belief that certain images always carry certain meanings. You might have more luck trying to find typical symbols that go with typical relationships. But now you've doubled the problem because how would you go about determining what a typical relationship was? At any rate, somewhere in the mixture there has to be a certified "known" from which to depart.

Melvin Lansky observes, "One cannot know [that] a symbol [is] a typical symbol unless the meaning of that manifest material has been demonstrated to be the same in a large enough number of cases to warrant the adoption of an empirical generalization, namely, that . . . the dream element is an instance of a typical symbol with a specific meaning" (1992, 480). The difficulty here (and I think Lansky is aware of it) is that how can you determine that the meaning is "the same" in any number of cases except by the same inferential process that interprets the image *as* symbol in the first place? When, and under what conditions, could you safely say that the symbolism of the snake (to put aside the shower) was typical or atypical? If you had at hand, say, two thousand cases of snake imagery in dreams, how would you go about proving that a given image was a sexual symbol and another was symbolic of something else, or nothing at all? You simply can't examine symbols and put them into phyla, as you can disease symptoms or plants or insects, because the characteristics are not determined by the symbols themselves but by the psychic state of affairs of the maker. "There need be no resemblance," Marshall Edelson writes, "between symbol and state of affairs; in this sense, the relation between them is arbitrary" (1984, 92). And even if you could establish the typicality of a symbol, wouldn't you run a risk thereafter of thinking "typically" wherever you encountered a new variation, as opposed to looking at each case individually? I realize that psychoanalysis has to make some generalizations, by the very nature of its business, and that in the analytical give-and-take there are ways to confirm assumptions within a reasonable doubt—some of the time. The problem is that the successful assignment of meanings to dream symbols for diagnostic purposes (1) doesn't prove that the image was a symbol with that meaning, or even a symbol at all, and (2) doesn't authorize its generalization to dreams at large as a typical structural phenomenon.[3]

The assumption behind typical symbolism is usually that the dream is repressing a forbidden or unpleasant impulse in a compromise formation: the snake is *like* a penis (or, if you will, the whole male) and it isn't. But how is this possible in cognitive terms? How can one part of the brain (the part making the dream) know something is a substitute

3. It is important to keep in mind that psychoanalysis is dealing with exceptional instances of dream formation and that something radical may happen to the associative system when severe mental illness occurs. Perhaps trauma has an effect on the dreamwork similar to fever, hallucination, or delusion in waking mentation, and that the "metaphor machine" can get "corrupted" and perform unusual operations approaching what we might call a strong or obsessive symbolism. A compelling example might be the case of the schizophrenic woman who dreamed repeatedly of being "burned down into isolated fragments," as discussed by Stolorow and Atwood (1992). It would seem reasonable to assume that here was a striking case of "fixed" symbolism (though I still prefer the term *metaphor*), and if you read the details of this unfortunate woman's case you can understand why. Suffice it to say that my skepticism about psychoanalytic conceptions of dream symbolism relates only to the assumption that because a device is appropriate to clinical practice as a means of healing trauma, depression, etc., it can be presumed to reflect the true nature of dreams in general. So in what follows I am not criticizing psychoanalysis as much as the idea that one can make a "transference" from psychoanalytic assumptions (like symbolism) to dreams of "normal" people, if I can be permitted that archaic category in a purely relativistic way.

for a repressed thought, something slipped in *instead of* the real thing, and another part (the part experiencing the dream) not know it? This of course is Wittgenstein's complaint: "Consider the difficulty that if a symbol is not understood [by the dreamer], it does not seem to be a symbol at all. So why call it one?" (1966, 44). You could argue that the brain doesn't *know* it is dealing in symbolism, in the conscious sense of the word, but what sort of operation would then lead it (technically the preconscious censor) to go in search of an acceptable substitute? How would the preconscious censor perform this operation? Surely part of the mind is doing a lot of sophisticated thinking at the same time that it is trying to keep something hidden from another part of the brain. Moreover, one part of the brain knows that a snake, for example, is a symbol of a penis and the other part will be fooled into thinking it isn't. Or perhaps there is an assumption that the dreamer wouldn't have to know—that is, have in mind—that a snake is a symbol of the phallus any more than he or she would have to know that a pistol fired bullets. It's self-evident.

Anyway, there is a cognitive distinction between conceiving an image through association or resemblance and conceiving an image in order to avoid something it resembles: the former is a ubiquitous, virtually automatic brain function, the latter requires the additional step of something like foreknowledge followed by a cover-up after the resemblance has been established. Even in Loewald's idea that it isn't the object (penis) that is being repressed but the linkage between the symbol (snake) and its referent (penis) there is a presumption of a disguising agency. Moreover, if the woman in Peyser's account was awakened from the dream in "great anxiety" it is hard to see what the repression accomplished in her behalf. What good is there in suppressing the object if the affect remains unaffected? Would a real penis breaking through the shower wall frighten her more than the snake? And this is hardly an isolated case: in fact, I find it *typical* that a dream of this degree of endangerment awakens the dreamer in "great anxiety." Finally, if this additional cognitive step (censorship) is possible, requiring (on the brainspeed scale) at least an infinitesimal flash of foresight, then one wonders why the censor doesn't routinely protect the dreamer in other kinds of dreams with nonsexual and violent subject matter—why, for example, it doesn't anticipate a plunge of the dreamer's car over a cliff, and throw up a detour sign to avert the disaster. If repression is a function of maintaining sleep, then it must operate in all cases of serious threat and not only in those which happen to involve long slim things called penises and repressed things like vaginas of which the empirical world offers endless likenesses.

But let us say that the snake in the woman's dream does have full-scale sexual connotations. This is not proof that a displacement through censorship has taken place. (Peyser doesn't go into this matter one way or the other, but I'm assuming that he sees the phallus as becoming a snake—and a shower—through some such displacement.) One might explain the transformation by saying that the snake was directly express-ing the woman's fear and that a snake, for any number of reasons (day residue, personal experience, and so on) was ready to hand on this par-ticular night. In other words, it wasn't a disguised penis, it was a situa-tion equivalent of the sort that dreams continually manage to find in any context. Well, you might argue, doesn't it amount to the same thing? No, it doesn't: the snake, I'm suggesting, not only has a certain super-ficial resemblance to a phallus. It is also a congeries of even stronger qualities: the snake is sudden, sinuous, solitary, sinister, voiceless, elu-sive, limbless, venomous, hypnotic, and above all strange. Of all crea-tures, the snake is least like us; indeed, it is not the venom of the snake that arouses one's fright but the bizarreness of the instrument by which it is administered. The snake might rightfully be considered the incar-nation of (dangerous) otherness. (For anyone who is not convinced, I recommend Maurice Richardson's *Fascination of Reptiles* [1972].) So the "symbolism" of the snake is various and complex, and there is no reason to assume, even remotely, that when it appears in a dream it has anything to do with a phallus, even when the dream is sexual in theme.

Now if this were the case the snake wouldn't be a symbol at all, but (as Rycroft would say) a straightforward garden-variety metaphor, however frightening. And metaphors are not symbols, typically at least: they are means of describing something qualitatively in terms of something else. In fact, there is something antithetical about symbols and metaphors: by their very nature symbols are built on a set of pre-established meanings or referents (the cross was not a symbol before the Crucifixion), whereas metaphors are, or at least originate as, one-of-a-kind freshly minted connections and are devoted precisely to transcending established (or symbolic) ways of looking at things, at least in art. As Eco puts it, "metaphor appears as a new semantic coupling not preceded by any stipulation of the code" (1984, 69). Symbols are conservative, metaphors are revolutionary; symbols preserve, metaphors colonize. In short, metaphors are antisymbols, though perhaps we could say that they turn into symbols when they're *dead*—meaning when they have lost their semantic motility (like the phrase "dead metaphor" itself). When Macbeth says to his wife, "O full of scorpions is my mind, dear wife," the word *scorpions* isn't being used primarily as a symbol, even though one knows that the scorpion has a nasty reputation. It doesn't stand *for* something else; it elucidates in a striking image how the mind can be "stung" and poisoned by fear and guilt. The scorpion is the equivalent of Macbeth's entire mental state, not a device for repressing it.[4] I wonder if this might be the case in the woman's snake dream as

4. To make Macbeth's mental state as vivid as possible to the spectator-reader, Shakespeare takes a horrid image from nature and plants it in Macbeth's head, where scorpions normally don't belong. The image succeeds because nothing is as powerful as a sudden and apt juxtaposition that is at once specific and general enough to allow the imagination room to play with the possibilities, rather as a dark alley tempts one to conjure the worst dangers. This business of allowing room for imaginative play is apparently a "good" thing, systemically, because it allows the mind to adapt the image to the unique associative networks already there. Indeed, could we not consider the pleasure of receiving a new idea or metaphor as consisting in the stimulation of dormant or "sleeping" networks—what Ernest Hartmann would call "making connections" (1995)? Such metaphors communicate precisely what logical thought connections miss in pinning something down to the nth degree.

well, if you agree with the idea that the dream was about her "ambivalence" problem, which I have no trouble accepting, knowing as little as I do about the case. That is, she may have been saying to herself, "O full of snakes is my mind," snakes being the most "horrid image" that occurred to her as a way of summing up her "poisoned" and sinuous situation—not a phallus but a locus of the endangerment inherent in her "phallic" bind. It would be interesting to know, in this regard, what the woman's life-relationship to snakes was; I think you would have to know *at least* that in order so say what the snake *may* have been doing in her dream. Maybe Peyser would agree with my line of thinking, or some of it, and maybe not. I'm not quarreling with his diagnosis of the woman's problem; I'm simply using his dream example to illustrate the difference between symbolic and metaphorical thinking.

The more integrative dream theory I read the more I am convinced that David Foulkes was right when he said that symbolism of the sort that psychoanalysis regularly invokes isn't involved in the production of dreams (1985, 95). The concept of the symbol is as outmoded as the censor that gave rise to it in the first place. Obviously symbols appear in dreams as frequently as they do in waking life. But for the most part they are what we might call standard symbols (the flag, the heart, the cross, the Star of David, and so on) that have become a normal part of the language of signs. Like dead metaphors, as John Searle says, they have "lived on" and are accepted to the point where their original symbolism is idiomatically taken for granted (1986, 98). Moreover, as Rudolf Arnheim reminds us, any image might act "as a *symbol* to the extent to which it portrays things which are at a higher level of abstractness than is the symbol itself" (1969, 138); and in this sense, I suppose, everything in a dream, including the dream itself, could be considered as a symbol. But such broad conceptions of symbolism, easily allowable, have little to do with the specific claims of classical psychoanalytic theory in which the symbol functions primarily as the handmaiden of the censor. To put it simply: what looks like an act of censorship from one standpoint might more economically be considered, from another, an act of recall or correlation. It is the same process, to an opposite end.

Not all conceptions of dream symbolization are of the substitutive or disguise variety. For example, Herbert Silberer advances the idea that there is a kind of symbolism that helps the brain to gain knowledge. "In the course of the development of intelligence, the mechanism of symbol-formation effects an understanding of that which is as yet not understandable." Moreover, in states of fatigue, tiredness, or "other disturbances, symbol-formation serves as a substitute mechanism, which enables ideas and complexes to manifest themselves in spite of the disturbed condition of apperception" (1951, 233). This seems a reasonable claim, but it is a far cry from the kind of symbolism I am concerned with here which entails substitution for disguise purposes, *this* standing for *that* because *that* is somehow unacceptable to the dreaming mind.

The symbolism Silberer is talking about, however, strikes me as being more a metaphor-formation than a symbol-formation capacity. For instance, consider its similarity to what scientists sometimes refer to as "theory-constitutive metaphors" whose utility "seems to lie largely in the fact that they provide a way to introduce terminology for features of the world whose existence seems probable, but many of whose fundamental properties have yet to be discovered [i.e., black holes, light waves, baby universes]. Theory-constitutive metaphors, in other words, represent one strategy for the accommodation of language to as yet undiscovered causal features of the world" (Boyd, 1986, 364). Or, along the same line, there is Eco's idea that all metaphors "produce, prior to knowledge, something which, psychologically speaking, we could call 'excitation' and which, from a semiotic point of view, is none other than 'information' in the most proper sense of the term: an excess of disorder in respect of existing codes. . . . Metaphors imply additional knowledge without knowing how to demonstrate the legitimacy of the argument" (1984, 86–87). Maybe this is not what Silberer has in mind, but without the capacity to form this sort of imagery (call it symbol or metaphor) we would probably never have reached the stage of the creature in *2001* when he discovers the potential of the thigh bone with which he accidentally fractures an animal skeleton and then realizes, in a flash of intuition, that this "tool" can be used to make war as well. And I am far from claiming that such images do not occur in dreams, but even when they do and manage to offer solutions to problems, we cannot claim that it was the dream that solved the problem (chapter 2).

Rycroft is right: what the mind really makes in dreams is not symbols but analogies, metaphors, and models, all of which are straightforward integrative mechanisms involving the automatic retrieval or activation of memory structures rather than their suppression. "Symbolism," Rycroft concludes, "belongs in fact to the realm of the humanities, since it hinges on the fact that people can perceive similarities between things that are scientifically and rationally speaking dissimilar" (1979, 159–60). I would amend this idea slightly by saying that symbolism (of this sort) belongs not only to the humanities but also to waking life at large and that it is precisely the symbolic capacity that is lost or seriously diminished in dreams, and what replaces it is the capacity to make metaphors, which are, as Burke says, ways of bringing out "the thisness of a that, or the thatness of a this" (1962, 503). The basic property of metaphor is that any word or image can be used to uncover a resemblance at any level and in any context; whereas the property of the symbol, like that of synecdoche, is to make possible the portability of large things (abstractions, wholes) into smaller or at least more specific "parts." One might allow that both processes occur in dreams to the extent that symbolism is not conceived as the hard language of sexual desire or the servant of repression.[5]

5. It is not symbolism per se that bothers me. In fact, we can allow all sorts of amalgamations between the metaphoric and the symbolic in dreams, as these are finally only names we have given to cognitive processes that are unlabeled in nature. What is most problematic about the fixed or typical symbol concept is that it doesn't work when you get far beyond sex, and it works there only because sex organs come into play, if only indirectly, in the sexual thematics of the dream, and because sex organs have shapes. So automatically sexual dreams

This isn't a theory of dreams (it doesn't tell us what dreams are *for*); it's only a claim that dreams are formulated by associative thought processes that have nothing to do with repression. If anything, dreams seem to be antirepressive mechanisms, seekers of equivalence rather than seekers of avoidance through disguise. It seems to me that dreams do not attempt to minimize repressed material; if anything, they maximize it. From this standpoint, the snake in the woman's dream might better be described as an instance of hyperbole. That is, to the extent that phalluses may have figured in her dream state of mind (or even if they didn't), the dream may have gone the phallus one better, so to speak, by producing an image that was even more alarming in its immediacy and its ominous intentionality than her ambivalent thoughts about her sexual "wickedness" — in short, an exaggeration of what she was trying to repress during the day, as opposed to a failure of censorship during the dream.

Actually, this phenomenon has an established name, given to it by the psychologist Ignacio Matte Blanco: "maximization of magnitude," (MM), is the tendency in emotional thinking to "idealize" or maximize any experience. Most things that are good or bad, pleasant or fearful, will be so to the maximum degree. Thus, love and hate are always

---

contain a set of symbol-seeking instructions ("Find something long and slim."). But what about dreams of shame, grief, fear, or lostness, which are probably as frequent as sex dreams and equally in need of repression (if you hold that as a cause of dream symbolism)? Such dreams have no anatomical referents, hence have no symbolic equivalents in reality, except perhaps in obsessive dreams with recurrent elements, such as the schizophrenic woman's fire dream in note 3 above. But even such cases take us back into the realm of what I have called personal symbolism, as the woman's obsessive dream of being burned into fragments can scarcely be called a "typical" symbol of this kind of schizophrenia. Finally, it is notable that when Freud dealt with shame dreams, as Melvin Lansky has shown, he typically "short-circuited" the theme of shame and traced the dream back to "childhood sexual desires and sexual competitive feelings and their attendant conflict as though the *wish* in question were for sexual consummation" (1996). Among other things, this enabled Freud to find "typical" sexual symbolism in every shame dream.

maximized; "fear of the dark," Matte Blanco says, "however much rea-son may tell us that it is fantastic, populates darkness with the most terrifying monsters with unlimited potentialities for evil and capable of rendering the subject completely helpless" (1975, 242). This doesn't mean, of course, that all our emotional experiences are extreme, or that there is no middle ground between, say, love and hate (such as ambiva-lence). It means only that it is a human tendency to dwell on extremes in cases where risk, danger, or desire are involved. If the theme of your dream is falling, it will probably not be a fall from a two-step ladder: the dream, using all its MM resources, will arrange a soaring building or a cliff at the sea's edge—something really horrific. Or, if you dream you are showering and find thoughts of sinuous sexual problems emerging, some lurking danger in the thicket of your affectional life, the dream might just oblige by concretizing your thought in the dreadful image of a snake breaking through the shower wall and pursuing you across the bathroom floor. Now that's frightening!

At one point in thinking about this problem I naturally wondered how many people studying dreams today actually believe in the idea of the fixed symbol. My guess is that extremely few, if any, psychologists and probably very few psychoanalysts do. In contrast, a belief in *typical* symbolism—which I take to be a looser version of fixed symbolism—is probably a different matter, for I detect evidences of typical symbology regularly in dream interpretation. (The very identification of something as a symbol implies that its symbolism is "well-known.") Then there are many professionals who practice and write books on dream therapy, or on how to understand your dreams through interpretive decoding. At my local bookstore in Santa Barbara I was surprised to find a flourishing dream section occupying a six-by-four-foot shelf. There I found some thirty or forty books on dream interpretation alone, including at least a half-dozen dream dictionaries, one having sold more than a million copies (all were in paperback in new or recent printings). Most of these books' authors are very cautious about advancing fixed meanings to symbols, and they urge the reader to interpret any dream image in personalistic and contextual terms. In many cases, this turns out to be a bit like the Surgeon General's warning on a package of cigarettes; for the book goes on to suggest the common meanings of the most vigorously dreamed symbols. (One book listed a half-dozen meanings for snakes depending on whether the snake was coiled, striking, dead, or moving away from the dreamer.) Moreover, in about 90 percent of the books on the shelf, there was what one might call a "symbolic perspective," or an assumption, usually implicit, that symbols, along with dream events, are the main element in dream interpretation, that they are the hinge between the manifest and latent levels of the dream, that they usually carry a more or less standard "cluster" of meanings (often listed in the text), that they always *stand for* something else, and that dreams *use* symbols either to disguise meanings or to summarize meanings otherwise unrepresentable. So prevalent are these assumptions, in one or another combination, that the concept of the *symbol* has apparently come to stand symbolically for the dream and for dreaming. I think this is the case because without some such construction as the symbol, the need to interpret could not be satisfied. The common question, "What does my dream mean?" implies that dreams are symbolic constructions.

But if you drop the concept of symbolism entirely—that is, of an image standing for something else, for anything *absent*—what do we have left? My hunch is that nothing has been lost, or changed; the dream continues to produce images that bear on our desires, fears, and concerns, and we see that what we took as symbols are only images like those that appear in daydreams and waking cognitive processes of all sorts, had we the dream's capacity to frame them for visual attention. Images function like words in sentences: no word is detachable from the advancing sense, the meaning of each word is limited by the surrounding words, and as soon as you remove a word from its context in a sentence it degenerates to its inert dictionary meanings and its connotative power is lost. Words make *sense*—as opposed to having meanings—only in their combinatory force. Images are the music of thought played by the dreaming brain on the organ of memory, and a single image means no more (or less) than a D flat "means" out of the flow of a unique musical composition. In short, an image means what it *has meant* to the dreamer *as modified by the unique and unrepeatable occasion* of the dream in progress and this meaning is *never* reducible to other language constructions. The lion can lie down with the lamb or rip it to pieces, as the dream occasion indicates, and even these extremes do not begin to exhaust the metaphorical power of lions or lambs.

One of the virtues of this view is that the principle of equivalence (as opposed to displacement and substitution) can explain why the dreamer is left so completely out of the loop in the "symbolic" trans-action. Nothing is being hidden from the dreamer, and there is no division in the dream process between naive dreamer and smart censor. The brain is simply doing what it must in order to think: it is moving, again "mindlessly," from one image to another that is on some unfixable level related to it. But this isn't really a form of symbolization, except in the most general sense. It is primarily a mechanism of association, conden-sation, and recall; dreams seem incapable of selecting an object, a place, or a person—thus representative of something in the dreamer's waking experience—and leaving it unmolested by other things it is like. Very quickly, all images in dreams become contaminated by their "similars," which is to say by other members of the same category (metonymy) or by their resemblance to things in categories outside them (metaphor).

In the same volume in which Silberer's essay on symbol-formation appeared there are several papers on hypnotically induced dreams that gave me some concern about my skepticism toward dream symbols. In the experiments of Karl Schroetter (1951) and Gaston Roffenstein (1951) subjects were told under hypnosis to dream of explicit sexual acts but to do so in disguised form—in short, to dream "symbolically" of the acts, rather than explicitly. Roffenstein's work with a twenty-eight-year-old single nursemaid "of subaverage intelligence" (1951, 252) produced a result, he claims, so successful that it "proves symbol-formation in dreams" (256). In one dream the woman was asked, under hypnosis, to dream of performing fellatio with her previous employer in such a way that the dream could be told to "any stranger without embarrassment" (252). Here is her dream: "I sit in the kitchen. suddenly the bell rings; the master calls me. I got to his room. He asks me to sit down on a chair. On the table I see many bananas. The master tells me to eat. I take one and peel it. It tastes fine" (253).

It should be said that Roffenstein had only limited success in this series of experiments in confirming his findings. Still, what are we to make of such a clear instance of "Freudian sexual symbolism," for here, surely, we have the "goods" in hard factual form? My suggestion is that such experiments don't prove much beyond the notion that dreams use appropriate visual images. I can scarcely deny the strong similarity between eating bananas and performing fellatio, but is it therefore a symbol in the sense of something that is *substituted* for the penis? How, for example, can we know what bearing the hypnotic instruction that the subject should distort the sexual content may have had on the dream? In Schroetter's experiments the subject was sometimes *not* instructed to "symbolize," and the dreamer dreamed in "symbols" even so. This suggests to me that the dream may have no alternative but to "symbolize" its events. In short, it probably makes no difference whether the subject is told to disguise her dream or to dream it any old way. The dream will produce a "symbolic" version of the command—which is to say, it will deal in resemblance, in the same way that a subject, being told to dream of a horse, might dream of a horse-cow or something associated with a horse or simply something one could ride. In any event, all the experiments prove is that one can induce dreams that follow certain instructions fairly well. But this does not seem any more remarkable than a dream of an event from the dream day that had subliminally "hypnotized" you, or got your attention in a particular way. The business of the dream, to come back to Ernest Hartmann's theory, is not to dream *about* something, even in disguised form, but to make connections among memory networks, and single images like the banana/penis image of the nursemaid's dream are only the molecular variation of what dreams do with places, people, real events, and temporal life in general.

In any case, it is no easier to say what dream images mean to the individual dreamer—why this image appears and becomes fused with that image—than it is to say why individual societies categorize things according to different systems of classification. For example, the Osage associate eagles with coal, Lévi-Strauss tells us, because coal produces fire, fire is associated with lightning, and lightning is one of the eagle's attributes (1966, 59). Thus if an Osage were to dream of an eagle (or of coal), there is a good chance that it might appear as a black, firey winged object hurtling to the earth. Or maybe not, for the Osage are no more likely to dream only what their culture tells them about an object than anyone else, and in any case one eagle would always be different from another in the multiplicity of its connotations. But if you make such allowances for the Osage, and for all cultures, then it seems you must make them for individual dreamers as well. And before long, the idea of a symbol dictionary, or a set of "typical" meanings associated with a given image, however resemblant of a sex organ, becomes, as Rycroft says, pointless and misleading, and, I would add, destructive to any understanding about what dreams are or how they work.

There are a hundred texts on symbol theory that could illustrate my overall suspicion of typical symbolism and of symbolism in general as it is "typically" applied to the dream. But the best one that comes to mind was written by Emerson: "The quality of the imagination is to flow, and not to freeze," he said. "Here is the difference betwixt the poet and the mystic, that the last nails the symbol to one sense, which was a true sense for a moment, but soon becomes old and false. For all symbols are fluxional; all language is vehicular and transitive, and is good, as ferries and horses are, for conveyance, not as barns and houses are, for homestead" (1989, 367). A dyed-in-the-wool symbol-hunter might interpret this passage as saying that horses and ferries are symbols "standing for" things in motion and that barns and houses stand for things at rest. The truth is that they don't stand for anything; they are the incarnation of motion and rest, horses and houses and such "like" things being what is necessary in order to have motion and rest, among countless other things and states they might embody in still other contexts. The main deficiency of symbolism is that it teaches us to look through something rather than at it; hence the experience of the dream is swallowed in the welter of its possible significations, and the dream becomes an adjunct to one's experience rather than an intimate part of it.

Finally, there is another obvious consideration: symbolism, in order to exist at all, requires some degree of awareness of the referentiality of the image. The dream is, among other things, a mechanism that cancels such awareness by putting the imaginary in the place vacated by the real. The proper question to ask of symbolism is the one asked by Nelson Goodman of art in general and symbolism in particular (1978, 66–70): not *what* is a symbol (anything can be) but *when* is a symbol? If the symbolism of an image is lost on the dreamer and known only by the mysterious censor and, subsequently, by the dream interpreter, then it is legitimate to wonder whether the interpreter may have invented both the symbol and the censor.

Before leaving this subject, I want to examine an even more formidable claim of symbolist thinking: the categorical notion that defecation and urinary dreams are primarily instances of sexual symbolism. Here we are no longer wandering among the innocent paraphernalia of the everyday world (hats, doorways, showers, and fire hydrants). Of course psychoanalysis doesn't take the most direct route to this conclusion; that is, the proximity of the sexual organs to the excretory parts of the anatomy, or the fact that the same "private" organs are involved in both sex and elimination, or the possibility of a certain pleasure (the relief of release) common to both. Psychoanalysis backtracks to the primal scene of childhood and the anal stage of the oedipal formation, to the narrow world of infantile sexuality bound on one side by the nipple and on the other by the nappie (with the father ominously poised somewhere between). Hence the classical psychoanalytical theory that urinary dreams are caused by a sexual stimulus that has regressed to infantile urethral eroticism (1900, 5:402).

If this is the case, however, we have a remarkable coincidence on our hands. Here is a common dream experience I have a half-dozen times a month: in my dream I become aware of an urgent need to micturate (as Freud would say), a scenario that was signaled up from the bladder. I probably had this urge before the dream began, but it invariably finds its way into a dream, so I suppose my urinary apparatus, having failed to get my attention in deep sleep, simply waits for the onset of an REM episode. But it is the one dependable thing I can say about dreams: when I have to "go," the dream's plot will directly reflect the somatic urgency and the dream will go through some variation of the Tedious Search for a Bathroom—invariably unsuccessful. And at some point, without fail, I will get out of bed and put an end to the scenario—and its incentive.

Surely we have here an unequivocal, unmistakable cause-and-effect situation that has nothing to do (at this point at least) with infantile urethral eroticism. Or are there exceptions? Does the micturation dream always originate in urethral eroticism? Sometimes? And, again, how does one know the symptoms of a urethrally erotic urinary dream from those of a full-on, run-of-the-mill *I've got to go right now!* urinary dream? And when Freud tells us he rarely feels the need to urinate in sleep, and then elsewhere in *The Interpretation of Dreams* offhandedly cites cases in which his need is actually indicated in a dream, one wonders if he may possibly have failed to report that in his dream, say, of cleaning the Augean Stables with his own urine stream (1900, 5:468–71), having concluded his Herculean dream-labors, he got out of bed and performed further cleansing in his own WC. Might he have been repressing this incentive in an effort to protect his master postulate that the manifest content of a dream is almost never—and always in a disguised form—the same as the latent content? In short, if you have to urinate in pure empirical terms and you dream you have to urinate, and the dream gets consumed by the "theme" of urination, however bathed in personal megalomania it may become in the process (and we all cleanse our stables or feel our shame in our own way), wouldn't one suspect that the latent/manifest theory was suffering from a slight case of exclusionary oversight? For if manifest and latent collapse into one and the same thing in this particular instance, what (on the principle of *Falsus in uno, falsus in omnibus*) of other instances—such as undisguised dreams of lust, power, paranoia, fears of the town bully, of drowning, of failing, of suffocating, of eating asparagus spears in a top hat, and so on? At the very least, surely sometimes, as in the urinary dream where the dream so clearly emanates from a simple physiological need, dramatizes the satisfaction (or frustration) of that need, then awakens the dreamer to make sure that the need gets carried out in actuality—as it were, all but leading the dreamer by the hand to the bathroom—surely here, if only by way of compromise, we can safely say, "Sometimes a pee is just a pee." [6]

In short, everything about the repression-"fixed" symbolic mechanism flies in the face of what we know about brain activity. Gerald Edelman puts the point succinctly: "Objects in the world are *not* labeled with dimensions or codes, and the way they are partitioned differs from person to person and from time to time. . . . Meaning simply refuses to be bound by a fixed set of terms in a specific coding system" (1992, 237). The proof that all these objects on Freud's (or any other) list are sexual symbols is that they recur in dreams that are found to have a sexual orientation. But the sexual orientation was most likely established in free associational analysis and, as Wittgenstein says, "no matter where you start from, the association will always lead finally and inevitably back to the [supposedly repressed] theme [of sex]" (1966, 118). Analysis, then, goes on to bear out that sex was on the analysand's mind in a particular

6. In the Count Thun dream, Freud actually discusses this question of the physiological need to urinate as "brought on" by the content of the dream itself: "One might, I think, be inclined to suppose that these [urinary] sensations were the actual provoking agent of the dream; but I would prefer to take another view, namely that the desire to micturate was only called up by the dream-thoughts" (1900, 4:218). Well, who is to say? There is ample evidence that the sound of water flowing in the waking world can bring on the urge to micturate, so perhaps we shouldn't rule it out in dreams. But the burden of proof here is really on Freud, who argues his case strictly from the evidence of his own nocturnal habits.

dream, having been detected outside the dream, and of course the usual subjects (hats, doors, suitcases, tables, neckties, relatives) are invariably found at the scene of the crime. But as a semantic or hermeneutic rule, this seems rather like blaming the mirror, as the Russian proverb goes, for your own ugly face—that is, attributing to the image what one has discovered by external proof. It is not that the analysis itself is wrong with respect to the patient's problem, but that almost any dream could be made to yield the same result. The symbol list is so broad and inclusive of reality that it would be difficult to imagine a dream that would not have one or more such sexually resemblant objects in it. So it's a matter, as Captain Renault says in *Casablanca,* of rounding up the usual suspects. And the suspects are always there to be rounded up because dream reality, like waking reality, is full of ordinary things that are either long or recessed in shape.

One arrives at the overall conclusion that fixed symbolism is a confusion of information and meaning. Comparatively speaking, information is a permanent classification (two plus two equals four, the day contains twenty-four hours). Meaning, on the other hand, is dynamic; it changes as new life experience widens the arena of possible application: I somehow overcame the childhood symbolism of the dental office (at least for emotional purposes); asparagus (for me) means my wife's quiche, the acanthus of Greek architecture, the lower farm at the Putney School in Vermont (where it grew profusely), Thanksgiving dinner, and so on. To treat the images conjured by the mind from its own experience as units of information, and especially as information categorically shared by all other minds, is to ignore the nature of memory itself, and with it the nature of meaning. If this is the way the human brain worked in other dimensions of thought, it would be as monolithically simple as the brain of a snake.

I recently composed an entire paragraph in a dream that consisted of an explanation of what happens when you omit a single negative (a "not") from a sentence. The dream has otherwise disappeared from memory, like the paragraph itself, but it probably had something to do with grading papers and working on this book at the same time. When I am writing I have an unusual number of composition dreams. The important thing, however, is that the paragraph was accompanied and abetted by an image of the negative as a wooden shim that slides under the sentence and lifts it to another semantic level. When the shim is removed the words of the sentence collapse onto the page, like cards falling rhythmically from a poker player's hand. Lo and behold, a negative!

The shim metaphor is even more impressive when you realize, as I instantly did, that it was inspired by a personal dental habit I had lately taken up and must relate here, albeit with some embarrassment. On the recommendation of my hygienist, I had begun the practice of cleaning my teeth "on the job"—meaning as I sit privately at my word processor writing things like this paragraph. The tool is a long thin plastic bar with a hole in the slanted end through which one slides the point of a toothpick, broken off just behind the hole and held in place by a screw-cinch. It is a wonderful device for prying loose hidden negatives (to continue the metaphor) that accumulate between the teeth, and I am happy to say that it has singlehandedly put an end to the problem of plaque.

I doubt very much if Shakespeare could have done more with such an image. But the thrill I feel is not that of poetic achievement; it is rather the thrill of experiencing firsthand how deftly the dreaming brain can shift thoughts from one sector to another on the strength of a secondary resemblance. Of course it makes no sense: the negative is not a shim. But in contrast, when you remove or insert a negative in a sentence you do, in a sense, fill it out or empty it. So there is my toothpick, stored over there somewhere in the dental hygiene section of my brain, and over here is my dream belaboring, for God knows what purpose, the problem of the negative, that slight, ubiquitous grammatical implement through which we empty sentences or fill them up without otherwise altering them. And, being the machine that it is, the dream insists on a visual equivalent; it calls for a backup, so to speak. And across the circuits a hemisphere away comes my tooth shim, fresh from success in the art of cleaning house; the two converge and fuse, as if a magnet had been set to the brain. Foolish, by the light of day, but not a bad effort considering that signals move along the neural axon at about the speed of light.

Yet I now see that I have involved myself in a cluster of sexually charged images and I wonder if this whole paragraph—including the one that I dreamed and forgot—may be motivated by the theme of masturbation. This is not meant as a cynical joke. Nor is it intended as a satiric comment on psychoanalytical dream interpretation. Writing, pure and simple, is (now that I think about it) a masturbatory activity. Writing is to masturbation what oral speech is to sexual intercourse. It is a strictly private affair and no true writer cares (at least while writing) whether the prose goes on to inseminate others with its charm or reason or persuasion. The thrill of writing exhausts itself pretty much in the doing. One makes love, as it were, to or with one's brain. I think all writers know this. Ask any French writer from Montaigne to the French post-Freudians. Ask Henry James, John Updike, or Nicholson Baker. Above all, ask Freud. He "strums," as Baker would say, on every page and comes very close to doing it with the door wide open in the Dora case and the report of his dream of Irma's injection when he peers into poor Irma's oral cavity—the word *trimethylamin* going through his brain like a hot poker—and sees "three curly structures" in her throat, but fails to see—or fails to report—what the dream was really about! Indeed, Freud's whole theory of dreams is masturbatory, based as it is on the cathectic release of mental energy in a harmless discharge. And by george, the record shows that Freud privately had a masturbation problem in the bargain.

There is one major difference, however, between my theory and any likely psychoanalytic variation. I would insist that writing, in or out of a dream, is no more a metaphor of masturbation than masturbation is of writing; moreover, that writing and masturbation belong to the same "family" only in the sense I have described (or in other similarities I've overlooked). That is to say, I found myself a few moments ago writing about sexual symbolism and I was suddenly reminded of a recent dream that had to do with writing, and inevitably with teeth. And behold, a

metaphor burgeoned. I have never before thought of writing as masturbation, but I now see that I have overlooked one of its many dimensions.
Indeed, it is faintly uncomfortable to be comparing writing to masturbation, but there it is: why hadn't I seen it before, after reading all that
French criticism on the sexual pleasures of the text. How dense can I
be? It is just as easy to be reminded of writing when you have sexual
themes on your mind as it is to be reminded of sex when you think
about writing. So too I might, in a dream, confront a male sex organ and
be instantly reminded of asparagus. The two are absolutely co-lateral,
and no more psychical privilege is extended to one or the other than
my ordering (or dreaming of ordering) asparagus soup one night and
alphabet soup the next. It all depends on all that is going on in the mind
at a given moment—again, the principle of natural selection in small.

In short, my comparison is a metaphoric, not a symbolic one; and
there are dozens of things one might compare writing to, just as there
are dozens of things to which "mounting" staircases can be compared.
If this were not the case, the brain would be an impoverished dwell-
ing place for consciousness, an autopathic nest of one-way streets, all
leading to the groin. Nevertheless, classical psychoanalysis tells us we
are driven by sexuality. The problem with this idea is that it conceives
sexuality as residing in the loins. It does not see that sexuality is itself
a metaphor. To consign the dream to the service of the libido is a
sad appropriation of imagination's resources—unless the libido is conceived widely as the vibrancy of creativity itself, that force that comes
so powerfully into play not only in thoughts of sexuality but in the
practice of joining, splicing, and impregnating words and images and
pigments and sounds to produce new images of the world. All thought
is metaphoric, I. A. Richards tells us, and by way of a wonderful sexual
metaphor he adds that metaphor is "the intercourse of thoughts" (1976,
94). Poets sit upon an inexhaustible mine of comparisons; the supply of
words and images is infinite. To be a poet is to be a consummate abuser
of categories, to be driven by resemblance, lured to extremes, utterly

promiscuous where possible meanings are concerned. For genital sexuality is only the biological end of the reproductive mechanism that also leads the brain to make new verbal progeny. The force that through the green fuse drives the flower is finally the same force that drove Dylan Thomas to coin that splendidly fecund metaphor.

7 ·

Remains of the Day

The general theory of day residue was active well before Freud, who claimed that all dreams can be related to a point of contact with the experiences of the previous day (1900, 4:165). Later psychologists have extended the period to several days (at which point it is referred to as the dream-lag effect), but most agree that in the majority of dreams there is a residue from very recent experience, and that the dream seems to use this residue either as a "node" around which the dream forms or as a subsidiary "helper" in the dream, in combination with long-term memory residue. In other words, a strip of today's experience typically gets spliced onto a strip of experience from the past; but of course in the dream these are usually inextricably confused, and there is rarely, if ever, anything in a dream one might call a singularity, or something that is itself and nothing else. This has led some theorists, among them Allan Hobson, to argue that this is the brain's way of converting short-term memory into long-term memory, but as yet we can't explain why the dream chooses one event from the day instead of another, or what mental gain there might be in a dream in which your brand-new Birkenstocks show up on your feet at a family reunion remembered from your childhood. In any case, it is possible that it isn't what images are being correlated that matters but the process of correlation itself, which may be accomplishing very different purposes of which the images are only indications.

Still, it is puzzling that the day residue should be such a persistent feature of dreams and that events within twenty-four hours prior to the dream should have a higher rate of appearance than events of two or more days earlier (for a review of the research, see Nielsen and Powell, 1992). This is another of those aspects of dreaming where we seem to be peering obscurely into the very mechanism of the dreamwork. Here is something the dream habitually (if not always) does; hence there must be some critical relationship between day residue and dream function. It is like the jewel thief who always leaves a Lincoln penny or a white rose at the scene of the crime; if one could only plumb the significance of that clue one would have the perfect avenue to the criminal's identity. And so it is that the day residue seems to harbor the whole secret of the dreamwork's way of going about making dreams.

On commonsensical grounds one could argue, with Freud, that the day residue is a fresh memory, therefore more likely to enter a dream; but, by the same token, one would further expect that the most important events of the day—the most dramatic, traumatic, shocking, unusual, rewarding, and so on—would therefore be first in line in the fresh events queue. But this is not true—unless, like Freud, one sees these "indifferent" events from the day as the censored carriers of the truly "significant" ones. In any case, the day residue must be performing some important work in relation to dreaming, had we the brains to figure it out.

Here is a simple example that will serve as a "node" for examining the problem: one morning my wife and I were emptying the dishwasher. I was specifically assigned to the knife-and-fork basket and I came upon the basting brush used for the previous night's pork chops. It was still wet and somewhat soggy and, squeezing it between my fingers, I wondered whether all the basting sauce had been rinsed out of it. I decided that it had, but then I didn't know where to put it. The most logical place seemed to be in the crock with the spatulas, soup ladles, and whisks. So that's where I put it, until my wife rerouted it to the drawer where the steak knives, the can openers, and the Chinese encyclopedia are kept. That night the brush popped into a dream in which I was using it to put shaving lather on my face in the bathroom. I have always used an electric shaver; but in summer months, when I'm usually at home all day, I sometimes don't shave for two or three days running and the penalty for this negligence is that electric shaving becomes difficult, protracted, and mildly irritating, and I often think about switching to a straight razor. This was the case on the day before my dream and I may have had similar thoughts. But even if I had had such thoughts, I would hardly have used a brush, basting or otherwise, as lather comes in a can and is applied, normally, with the fingers. But there I was lathering with the basting brush, and the most likely reason is that I had had this unexpected little adventure in the kitchen that morning. Maybe there is a common theme in waiting three days to shave and putting the basting brush in the wrong place, and they were drawn together, on the attraction of these impacted negative energies. But this seems a remote explanation at best. As for an emotional affect, I recall feeling nothing; it was what psychologists call a mundane dream: I was simply shaving with a basting brush as if this were a perfectly routine procedure.

I realize that this dream is boring, but then, as W. H. Auden once said, so is the unconscious. Still, it takes us to the bedrock of dream image formation. It isn't the dream itself that arouses my interest but the way the two pieces of it came together. Here are two unrelated things, an improperly stored basting brush and a three-day growth of beard, dropping out of waking experience into my memory and sticking together like snowflakes falling into dreamland. After the fact I can imagine all sorts of reasons for the attraction, but none of them accounts for the ingenuousness of my brain using one of these things (the baster) to accomplish the other (the act of shaving). Why not a regular shaving brush? Why not apply the lather with my open hand? Why dream of shaving in the first place? Yet somehow—I assume—the freshness of the baster incident and the texture and sogginess of the brush, plus my three-day beard, offered just enough tactile incentive to permit the union to occur, without the least consideration of more conventional means. In short, the dream, as always, was less interested in "realistic" concerns than in putting together these things that are sufficiently charged, for whatever incentive, to get into the dream and sufficiently willing to cooperate once they are there.

This, and countless similar fusions in my dream experience, leads me to suspect that some dream images might arise from "magnetically" induced collisions of events, feelings, and objects from recent day experience. The survivability of a day event into a dream image may in some cases depend on the energy it has stored from a gratuitous combination with another event from the day. Unfortunately, we have to use qualifying phrases like "*some* dream images" or "in *some* cases" in our speculations, but there is no reason to assume that dreams follow a single invariable practice. Perhaps it is the nature of dream images, hence dreams themselves, not only to be expressive of important psychic concerns but to be "born" as offspring of the union of two or more fresh experiences that are somehow attracted to each other or that somehow provoke a collaboration. Day residue, then, may work a little like electrical capacitors, which consist of two equally charged conducting surfaces separated by a dielectric. The charge need not be a significant psychical affect (anxiety, guilt, and the like) but any subliminal feeling produced by the conjunction, or perhaps no subliminal feeling at all. For instance, if you were to crack a tray of ice cubes, the sound might unconsciously remind you of rocks coming loose under your feet, and that night you might have a dream about scaling a glacier. The precariousness, fear, or whatever feeling was generated would not have brought on the image; it would work the other way round. The image entered innocently into the dream and served as the provocation of a familiar or relevant emotion. Moreover, there is no reason to limit the scope of possibilities or the number of operative elements. The point would be that certain day experiences combine metaphorically with still other networks of experience and that these might, like the capacitor, become "ticking" bombs in which potential dream plots are "stored."

This would seem to apply to Freud's own dream of the botanical monograph which was accompanied by "a dried specimen of the plant, as though it had been taken from a herbarium" (1900, 4:169). So we have a book "mating" with a plant specimen. Freud's own discussion of this dream has been much debated, and usually on the grounds of his own interpretation. But suppose that the possible range of meanings is posterior, rather than prior to the mating of the book and the plant which happened to be "traveling" down short-term memory lane together on this particular night as a consequence of belonging to the same day residue. That morning Freud had seen a monograph entitled *The Genus Cyclamen* in a bookstore window, and the day before Fliess had written Freud that he had envisioned Freud's dream-book "lying finished before me" (169, 172). Freud would call this a condensation (and we might

note that capacitors are also called condensers); the difference would
be that Freud maintains that the images were selected by the dream-
thoughts on the basis that "those elements [of the day residue] which
have the most numerous and strongest supports acquire the right of
entry into the dream content" (284). I wonder if the same result couldn't
be achieved if it happened the other way round: that the two images attracted the dream-thoughts (Freud's powerful professional ambition),
which after all had been on or in Freud's mind for some time. Notwithstanding Freud's anxieties about the dream-book, fresh thoughts don't
necessarily emanate in dreams. I'm simply suggesting that one of the
contributions made by day residue may be to "condense" thoughts into
dream form, as opposed to being the "indifferent" hosts to thoughts
looking, so to speak, for a place to condense. A literary parallel might
be the scene in *Hamlet* in which Polonius tells Ophelia how

> with devotion's visage
> And pious action we do sugar o'er
> The devil himself.

Claudius, overhearing this, recalls "aside" his deep guilt for his brother's
murder and says,

> O, 'tis too true.
> How smart a lash that speech doth give my conscience.

So, too, dreams might be provoked by the lash of *accidental* couplings,
like encountering a botanical monograph in the window of a book-
shop and receiving a letter from a friend the day before about an all-
important and unfinished book project. What I'm probing here is the
possibility that dreams are as behaviorally versatile as the memory formations of waking life. Sometimes an object or experience provokes an
emotion, as in Claudius's case; sometimes we project an emotion onto
an object or experience, as when Othello projects his entire frustration
onto the handkerchief he gave to Desdemona.

The interesting question to be asked, perhaps, is whether all the meanings Freud, or anyone else (Erich Fromm, for example), finds in the monograph dream are there, *in* it, in a causal and synchronic sense, or *behind* it, in a merely life-historical and diachronic sense. Or, to put it another way, to what extent does the fact that something precedes a dream in the dreamer's psychic history figure as the cause of it? I am putting aside here, for the purposes of understanding the nature of day residue, the familiar psychoanalytic notion that if something occurs in the discussion of a dream it must have been on the mind of the dreamer and becomes part of the analytical paraphernalia for interpreting the dream. It is not, after all, the dream that is being interpreted but the analysand's psychical situation, of which the dream was only a symptom. For diagnostic purposes, this may be a valid procedure, but its diagnostic validity does not prove that such reactions were part of the dream's cathectic charge—in short, that the dream combined the two images, as Freud assumed, for thematic purposes that were somehow in place in advance of the combination itself.

Freud's analysis of his dream leads him through an intricate chain of associations from his wife's fondness for cyclamen flowers, his experience with cocaine, recent conversations with certain colleagues, Fliess's letter, all the way back to his botany class in secondary school. These are pieced together—a full day after the dream, incidentally—by such constructions as "I recalled" or "It was not until I recalled this daydream that I realized . . ." or "My thoughts then went back to the occasion . . ." In short, the analysis consists in allowing memories to flow forth that might be associated with the elements of the dream. But it is not a foregone conclusion that all this recall belongs to the dream or informs the dream either directly or indirectly. In other words, it is not a given that all that is *in* the mind is also *on* the mind. What encourages such a conclusion in Freud's case, of course, is that the recall process occurs in the context of a theory that dreams are censored displacements, the true meanings of which are always latent and elsewhere. Therefore an image is only the tip of the iceberg, and what is available below it is the entire psychic history of the dreamer. One sorts one's way through this history

to the true kernels of the dream by a process of memory-matching—
that is, finding likely precedents that "resemble" the dream image. The
problem is that all recall of memory works on a similar principle of association; memory is like a sweater that can be unraveled on the snag
of a single instigating thought, if one goes far enough. With something
specific in mind—it can be anything—you can go almost anywhere in
the kingdom of memory by simply catching the right resemblant trains.

For example, to come back to my dream of the shaving brush: it
occurs to me, a year later (at this writing), that the original source of
my knowing much of what I know about shaving brushes is probably
my memory of my father's brush setting upright on the bathroom cabinet shelf of my boyhood home in Pennsylvania; in the army I used a
razor and shaving brush; moreover, my brother-in-law, who is a photog-
rapher, used a shaving brush to dust his camera lens; and so on. All of
these, and much more, constitute, in a certain sense, the history "behind" the dream. And there is doubtless a similar history "behind" the
basting brush that could be pursued through a lifetime of barbecues,
meats, smells, and cooking events. But would these memories have anything to do with the origin of the dream in some particular thematic
sense? I now recall that the dream was also concerned, on the periphery, with pork chops. It is true that pork chops did not appear in the
dream (being inappropriate, I suppose, to a shaving scene) but could
I not therefore pursue the possibility that the dream has something to
do with my father, who had a fondness for pork chops and other kinds
of "basted" meats, and that this is one of the causes of his comparatively early death and something I might look out for? So the dream
was a warning to beware of too much basting, the baster standing in, as
it were, for the pork chop I had consumed the previous night, and the
shaving for the fate of my father. In a manner of speaking, I was cutting
my own throat with my father's razor.

What an ingenious dream! Everything is right there—basting, pork
chops, my father, my own worries about weight, cholesterol, the brevity
of life, the works. It makes perfect sense. Except that none of this oc-

curred to me during or following the dream, and I've really stretched my memory in piecing it together. Of course this does not preclude the possibility that some such thoughts might have been *on* my mind in some remote way. But if the emotional tenor of a dream doesn't offer a key to a possible direction of meaning (apprehension, foreboding, concern), it seems arbitrary to assign it a meaning — however ingeniously the meaning connects "the facts" of the dream — for which the only evidence is that it was part of the dreamer's history. With a little effort, I could probably dip further into my history and find another interpretation that is equally ingenious. The truth is, I have a virtual library of memories to draw from, and as connections occur to me I can attach them to the dream as if they had been there all along.

This, of course, is the way metaphor and association work. A metaphor — "John is sharp as a tack" — doesn't lead us to a heretofore hidden aspect of something that has been there all along; it *persuades* us that if we view the object through its lens, a similar known aspect will come forth — something we knew about the object already, perhaps, but which was obscured in the gestalt of the whole. In other words, metaphor points a finger at something and in doing so causes you to overlook everything else. In this regard a metaphor is more like a used-car salesman than a sphygmomanometer or an EKG machine: it doesn't measure something, it ignores everything but what it wants you to see. And a dream interpretation works in much the same way except that it carries the added authority of being the causal factor behind the association; that is, the single truth of the dream. "That must what the image means," we say. Technically speaking, the best possible interpretation of a dream would allow for any number of possibilities — not very helpful for analysis, perhaps, but closer to the way images go about meaning anything. Even so, are all of these possibilities, as Pierre Macherey might put it, "the pillars of an explanation or the pretext for an interpretation" (1978, 82)? That is, are they causes, or are they effects of a cause?

The larger question is how are dream images caused? Are they, as Freud insisted, caused by psychic pressures, stresses, and so forth — the

things that become in turn the "meanings" unearthed in the dream interpretation—or do they give rise to the meanings in some other way? In
short, suppose, contra Freud, that dreams are not necessarily instigated
by significant psychical materials. I am not questioning the idea that
many dreams clearly are or that all dream images carry the dreamer's
personal history of such images. I'm simply opening the possibility that
memories from preceding day(s) provide the matter of dreams without being cathectically charged; rather, they may become cathectically
charged in the dream itself. Freud tells us that the day residue is notably
"indifferent" or trivial and that these unimportant experiences "take the
place of psychically significant ones" (1900, 4:176) through the process
of censorship. This is one way of accounting for an image's point of origin, but it requires that we accept the notion of censorship, which is the
linchpin of Freud's theory of dreams. If we put the idea of censorship
aside, how can we explain the triviality of so many dream images?

One possible explanation is that the triviality of the image is of
little interest to the dreamwork, or that what seems trivial to the waking
mind has a very different status in the dream. Maybe the rules governing the choice of dream images are similar to those of waking reality.
For example, a considerable part of waking mental experience and recall involves our perception of things that attract us because they possess particular qualities—among which might be beauty, ugliness, pitch,
shape, position, color, and distinctiveness of various sorts. Why should
such objects or experiences not stick in the mind and find their way into
dreams on the very grounds that they stood out from waking reality and
were bracketed or marked in a kind of mnemonic photograph?

One of the more recent theories maintains that day residue consists primarily of "subjective objects," or objects from the day that have
a special, and largely unconscious, meaning in our lives. This theory is
put forth by British psychoanalyst Christopher Bollas:

Freud's theory of the dream's day residue . . . strongly suggests that
during the day we nominate persons, objects, and events as psychically

significant so they will be residual to the day, already forming part of the potential dream furniture. In my view, to create a day's residue, the person projects a part of himself into the object, thus psychically signifying it. This gives the object meaning, converting it into a tool for possible thought: the thinking that is special to the dream state. To do this, however, the subject must "lose himself" in moments of experience when he projects meaning into objects, a type of erotic action that must be unconscious and one in which the person is not being, as it were, thoughtful. (1992, 22)

It is reasonable to think that a good many of the things that show up in our dreams (like my basting brush) have this sort of significance in our lives. The problem comes in determining whether it is the sole criterion for a day residue, or whether there may be others as well. Moreover, the nature of the "subjective object" is such that it is difficult to know if or when something falls into this category; by nature it is likely to be, as Bollas puts it, an "unthought known" (20). I suppose analysis would help to uncover its possible knownness, in any specific case, but more to the point, how would you go about proving that a particular day residue *had not* been thus "subjectivized" or that it didn't have an unconscious and possibly repressed meaning you knew nothing about? How, in short, could you prove that the Birkenstocks that showed up in your dream aren't somehow related to the memory of an old family reunion, even though you can find no similarity between the two things? Suppose at such a reunion, long ago, you had been treated to a game of horsie on the leg of a friendly uncle who was wearing an odd pair of sandals: the event had gone "unthought" about all these years, but you somehow bumped the event to the anteroom of your mind on the afternoon you bought the Birkenstocks, wagged your leg up and down in the shoe store, and the combination of energies given off by the two things brought on the dream, as in my basting brush dream.

My only reservation about Bollas's theory also has to do with whether one projects a part of oneself into the object or the object projects itself into one's consciousness. This topic (empathy, "objec-tivifed self-enjoyment," and so on) has been much debated in aesthetics for some time. Objects can't do any such thing in the literal sense, having no minds to project with. What I mean is that perceived objects "nomi-nate" themselves, so to speak, by virtue of a striking quality or circum-stance attending our perception of them; they have what Don Kuiken calls "felt presence"; and they "engage" our attention by virtue of pos-sessing a "perceptual tension" of some sort (1995, 142). As a result, they cling, like burrs to a sweater, and you may have no idea they're there, much less why. Take the case of a leftover potato cake languishing in my refrigerator for three days on top of a plate of leftover broccoli. On the third night I had a dream in which there was a party and I was passing a tray of snacks. A guest said, "May I have the potato cake?" I looked and there indeed was the single potato cake *on top of* whatever I was serving. This seems to me an excellent example of nomination—meaning simply that through repeated visits to the fridge I had developed a subtle "rela-tionship" with the potato cake without knowing it. It was an "unthought known," and it thus achieved, as they say in commerce, a "favored nation status," something utterly insignificant with just enough of an edge over other "leftovers" of the day to get into the dream when my hors d'oeuvre tray was being passed. You have to admire its persistence.

Of course, the potato cake had no "say" in all of this. Nor should we search for some sort of symbolism lurking behind potatoes. Dream imagery may be utterly meaningless; it need only be capable of adapta-tion to the dream occasion, and I take it that the principle of nomination would include any means through which a person, object, or event from the day becomes framed in our attention (or inattention). As countless experiments in subliminal perception from Poetzl (1917) forward have shown, there is a threshold at which perception, so to speak, doesn't know it is perceiving. A stimulus received in the waking state might sneak into the brain as a memory trace without arousing a picture. Owing to the limited channel capacity of the waking consciousness, in which thousands of pieces of information are assaulting consciousness simultaneously, it would be carried as a lower-order signal. But with the onset of sleep, which shuts out communication with the teeming outside world, available channel capacity is suddenly increased, thus permitting "room" for a conscious representation of subliminal perceptions in the form of an image (Dixon, 1971, 316). To a degree, this form of perception is what makes possible composite police sketches of a suspect. The witness can't picture the face directly from recall, but through the process of feature elimination and adjustment a likeness can be recreated as the witness matches or rejects the features, one by one, from the subvisually stored memory of the face. It is through this process, and heightened access to old and new memories through free association, that the dream populates its world with composites and images the brain didn't know it had stored. According to waking logic, one would think that such events from the day as a puncture wound suffered in a carpentry project, an unexpected check for a thousand dollars, or even news that you had a disease would go sailing through the gate like a flashing ambulance behind a police escort and find their way into dreams. But this is not the way perception works between the waking and sleeping states. What shows up—or what is identifiable as day residue in a dream—is typically a fragment of something from the day or a detail you recorded for no known reason. The temptation, as always, is to treat day residue as if it made sense, or as if there were a reason, however unconscious, for the dream selecting this detail instead of that detail. But it may not work that way. Maybe the mind remembers a detail because it fits into a sensory category of some kind, the sort of thing that happens in déjà vu episodes. Or maybe a peculiar asymmetry or symmetry (again, a "felt presence"), even a kind of beauty, nominates an object for recall. There is no limit to the possible kinds of causes for selecting a particular stimulus because selection would depend on the global holdings of the individual brain at a particular moment.

For example, say you have parked your car but you have trouble finding a coin to put into the meter. You search your pocket and come up with a dime, but as you try to insert it in the slot the dime falls to the sidewalk with a clink. Already this is becoming what we might call a marked, or framed, experience, something that gets pulled out of the smooth flow of routine and constitutes a departure, however slight, from a normal progress—a small glitch in the day. So the brain records it, not for the purpose of dreaming about it later, but simply because the experience has clinky edges, unusual lineaments—something that *hasn't* happened before—or perhaps has, in another time and place, like feeling a slippery basting brush and being subliminally reminded of shaving lather. Perhaps there is a category ("The Clinking Coin") of such incidents in your memory and this one subliminally alerts it that a new member is about to be added. As Hobson says, the brain/mind links it "in hyperassociative fashion to every network with which it shares formal features" (1994, 116). It might be little more than an infinitesimal piece of experience, the sound of metal on concrete, and yet its "size" or importance has little to do with its being recorded in one or more of your networks. And you go to sleep that night and in the course of a dream you are standing on a street, for reasons having nothing necessarily to do with the coin falling, and lo and behold there is a parking meter. And as you look at it, it seems oddly enhanced. But you get in your car and the dream moves on to something else and that's the last you see of the meter. And you wake up the next day and wonder about just what I'm wondering about here: how, or why, did the dream include the parking meter? Of all the things that happened to you yesterday, why this? And the reason is simply that you were getting in your car and the parking meter saw an appropriate chance to announce its presence because a parking meter is a close metonymic relative of parked cars.

Here is a personal example that will serve as a model for this process of happenstantial image formation. Recently I was reading an article written by a friend on the proliferation of the author (as creator of a "text") metaphor into legal matters of surrogate motherhood. One sentence runs as follows: "By today the flag of authorship has been raised over pictorial and graphic works of most kinds, including architectural plans, commercial advertisements, labels, and fabric designs" (Rose,

1996, 3). When I read this the image of a ship came forcefully to mind, owing principally to the close conjunction of *flag* and *-ship*. I doubt that *authorship* on its own would have spawned such an image because its suffix (*-ship*) is so conventionally buried in its task of denoting a state or condition (as in kinship, friendship, statesmanship). But *flag*, so to speak, flags, or brackets, the ship in authorship (only three syllables removed) and produces a seagoing vessel. Could this have been subliminally on my friend's mind? It certainly could (though he says it wasn't): the context is that of copyright (we read on the previous page) being "an expansive, imperial doctrine, forever conquering new territory in the name of the author" (2). So flag earns its right to be in the picture, whether the "imperialism" is occurring on land or sea. But I doubt if the image of a flagship would have occurred to me without the propinquity of *flag* and *-ship,* and I doubt that my friend was trying to be supersubtle and raise the sunken ship in authorship. In any case, I'm not trying to restrict connotations (indeed, both are possible in the "territorial" context), only to suggest how new and unplanned images might spring from accidental or inadvertently "leading" combinations. And in a dream, unlike a written article, once the ship has been squeezed out of authorship, it sails into the dream, flag flying, and the dream has to deal with it by giving it a role in the new context the ship has itself created by simply showing up. In short, this is a verbal variation of the process of genetic mutation constantly producing new and different individuals because something unanticipated has occurred.

A good deal of our day residue must be transacted at such ambiguously motivated levels. I cannot count the number of instances in which small shards from the day have come floating in and out of my dreams and on waking, either immediately or at the end of sleep, they seemed to me to have the strange stamp of having been rescued from extinction for some "reason" known only by the dreaming brain. The point, in any case, is that these images must have gotten into the dream for reasons that have nothing to do with my understanding them, nothing to do with symbolism, and nothing to do with waking expectations. They are day events which, because of the context in which they occurred, must be reincorporated, or reremembered—the memory retrofitted, so to speak, to keep its representations up to date. Thus when you encounter a familiar thing in a new and perhaps unusual context, though it didn't occur to you at the time, the thing must be re-processed by way of expanding its associational and evocative limits to suit your experience, and dreams would be one avenue, among others, by which this could be done.

But there is no good reason to assume that the day residue is a motivated ingredient in dreams in the sense that it is a displacement of something important. Surely there is no psychical rule that prohibits the appearance in dreams of objects, sights, sounds, and people that have left an impression for reasons that would be impossible to assess. We have to allow for a good deal of slack in dream construction if we are to avoid the troublesome notion that dreams are "thought out" somewhere else in the dreaming brain, an attitude that I suspect Bollas holds. It stands to reason that day residue always occurs in dreams (if we can be so bold) because it is fresh experience and therefore presumably more accessible. Moreover, if several things are retained from the day, it does not follow that they are retained because they relate to the same set of concerns, though it seems probable that they all spring from the same "species" of concern because they are offspring of a single consciousness. Hence, all products of a consciousness have something in common, and even if they are not related by immediate pressing concerns, there is an excellent chance that they are distantly related and can be seen as extensions, down the line, of such concerns. As Dixon has put it, "There are two opposing forces operating when a person is confronted with new information: one is to incorporate all new input, and the other is to maintain already existing information without modification" (1971, 101). There are no right or wrong "decisions" in this matter, and there is no reason to assume that the brain incorporates or rejects on the basis of a specific anxiety or theme. In fact, to come back to the woman's shower/snake dream from chapter 6, there is no categorical proof that it had anything to do with her problem.

At any rate, there is no pinning it down to the possibility I have advanced here. It is altogether conceivable that something from the day experience might actually induce a dream simply because it is strongly charged, something you can't get out of your mind (like a tune), and yet you don't even know it's in your mind. Or it may enter the dream on the coattails of something else. This wouldn't necessarily disprove Bollas's notion, which makes considerable sense insofar as almost any perception one has in the course of a day becomes unavoidably subjectivized. If I witness an accident, I will see it my way, and you will see it yours, but if we will dream about it, we will do so unavoidably in different ways because, having passed through the portals of two different memories, it has become two different accidents.

I have another private, and largely unexplored, theory about day residue. I call it the Galápagos theory because I once read that certain species of spiders arrived at the Galápagos Islands by being borne aloft on the wind. They had been swept into the air in Borneo or Australia or one of the land masses where they flourished, were carried thousands of miles, virtually weightless in the thrall of the wind stream, and when the time came were harmlessly dropped to earth at the Galápagos (or the luckier ones were). So they got there on the winds of chance, aided and abetted by certain characteristics of their own (heavier animals came no doubt on logs and floating parts of wrecked ships).

I suggest that this may be how certain kinds of day residue get into a dream—day residue that undergoes what you might call the luck of the draw. First, there must be millions of perceptions, sights, events, and so on, that occur in any given day, all potential candidates for that night's dream, but millions simply don't make it, just as millions of spiders and other insects didn't make it to the Galápagos Islands. The brain isn't interested in passing all its day experience into the dream anyway. The dream is probably just one of the things that can happen to a day experience en route to the permanent memory. But what enters the dream may do so, in some cases, because conditions are fortuitous for survival, irrespective of the importance of the content. Maybe certain perceptions attach themselves to the wind currents of thought and come to a certain prominence because they were in the right place at the right time, with the right characteristics and neuronal backing. Theoretically, almost anything could float into a dream and the dream would simply use it in some capacity, even as a wall hanging in a dream-room or a parking meter on a dream-sidewalk. All that would be necessary is that a perceptual experience be somehow marked off from the flow of perceptions that make up a day owing to some anomaly in its occurrence. To put it another way: things may slip into dreams by inadvertently becoming metonymical parasites on other experiences that serve as their hosts.

It so happens that reality bore out my theory on the very day I had concocted it. While I was writing these paragraphs about the Galápagos, my wife was vacuuming the living room because the cat had brought in the disorganized remains of a gopher from the backyard. It occurred to me, in a spasm of guilt, that my study carpet hadn't been vacuumed since I had installed the new computer furniture several weeks earlier. But the Galápagos was too pressing and the thought passed out of mind. However, that night I found myself vacuuming the floor in a dream. Here, it seems to me, is an example of day residue that had legitimate cause to survive and become a dream because the vacuuming had become directly affiliated, however mildly, with the sensation of guilt, and guilt, I've discovered, is one of the big dream incentives. But suddenly, while dream-vacuuming in the vicinity of the closet where I hang my trousers, I heard the clink of a coin being drawn into the vacuum, knocked about inside and then spit out on the carpet. I looked down to discover a quarter partially embedded in the pile of the carpet, which the dream had unaccountably turned from beige berber to a dark brown shag. And beside it another quarter, and beside that another, and another, and so on, until I had an overflowing sense of wealth that I can only compare to those boyhood dreams in which I discover hidden treasure in my backyard.

However, there is one more relevant detail: on the file cabinet next to the trouser closet there is a cup containing change emptied from my pockets. Moreover, it frequently happens that I forget to empty my change from the pockets before hanging up my trousers, and of course when I turn them upside down all the coins fall to the floor. Consequently, the coin density is particularly high in the vicinity of the file cabinet.

So the dream had changed the carpet from berber to shag, my parking meter dime (from the paragraph written that same day) to a cache of quarters, and (dare I speculate?) the parking meter (which consumes coins) to a vacuum cleaner. But it had the clink of the coin right. Or was it the vacuum cleaner that brought on the clinking coins? Maybe the parking meter had nothing to do with the coins? Or maybe the parking meter drew the vacuum to the coin-infested part of my carpet, providing as it were a secondhand magnetism. Or maybe the vacuum didn't need to be reminded, having a coin history of its own to rely on. Or was I killing two coins with one dream? And what have clinking coins to do with anything anyway? But no matter how I look at it, it seems to me that the coins got into the dream by hitching a ride on a sturdier vehicle. It was the clink that survived and came gloriously to a fruitful life in the dream, like the lucky spiders who fell to earth on the Galápagos.

I prefer, of course, to think that *all* of these explanations (including Bollas's) are correct, not to mention others I may have overlooked. Indeed, it is just the possibility of multiple origins that may have accounted for the coin's getting into the dream. It is said that learning (that is, memory) is increased by repetition, which is to say by reenforcement. So it seems reasonable that when something like a clinking coin occurs in two independent contexts it gets an additional "boost" of memory support. In short, there may be other kinds of systems and actuality than the ones we know about, yet we seem addicted to the idea that everything that takes place in the mind makes some sort of sense or occurs at some level of intentionality. If a thought occurs, in or out of a dream, it must have an explanation. But maybe the life of the brain is filled with accidents of juxtaposition that have little to do with making sense and more to do with innate attractiveness. Maybe there is a level at which thought occurs as pure symmetry or happenstantial resemblance, all thought perceptions sweeping down the axonal channels, like bumper cars at the carnival, and forming odd coalitions that attain the force of chained bullets.

Perhaps my Galápagos theory is too exotic. A homelier analogy occurs to me. In golf, as in all sports, there is a strong element of chance. The golfer may strike the ball perfectly, but once in the air the ball becomes subject to environmental whims and may land in the most unpropitious of places. The good golfer will know how to deal with such exigencies better than the amateur and will have a higher average of well-placed shots and rescues, but skill and strategy are always subject to Darwin's "conditions of existence." No hermeneut of the sport would confuse these roles of chance and skill. One might justifiably claim that X has an unfortunate hook in his swing or an uneven stance that leads to poor positions in the field, but no one, analyzing the play of a particular hole, would claim that X's ball landed directly behind a divot of grass *because* X had misplanned the shot or had an unconscious fear of divots, or that there was a direct cause-effect relationship between the skill of X's swing and the ball coming to rest behind the divot. The unlucky lie is simply one of the vagaries that makes golf a challenging sport. Golf, in this sense, is rather like all play activity, and finally like life itself—part chance and part plan. It is my contention here that dreaming resembles golf as it resembles play and life: all are processes that occur in a dynamic field of play in which there is always an unpredictable element that necessitates continual adaptation. Golf may begin on the first hole and proceed in order to the eighteenth. But the dream never ever knows where it goes for the simple reason that there are hazards of every known sort that constantly affect the life of every image.

8 ·

Involuntary Poetry

In 1835, the German dramatist Georg Büchner gave his character Robespierre (in *Danton's Death*) the following thought: "And isn't our waking a more lucid dream, aren't we sleepwalkers, aren't our conscious actions dreamlike, only clearer, more precise, more complete?" (1977, 40). More than a century and a half later, two physiologists from New York University, Rodolfo Llinás and D. Paré, wrote in the journal *Neuroscience:* "Let us formally propose then that *wakefulness is nothing other than a dreamlike state modulated by the constraints produced by specific sensory inputs.* Findings in support of this rather outrageous statement come from morphological and electrophysiological studies" (1991, 525).

The first of these statements is not expected to be taken as anything more than the opinion of a character in a fiction, though Büchner himself may have believed it, and he was not only a poet but also a professor of medicine at Zurich. Indeed, it is an opinion that can be traced back to antiquity through Shakespeare and Calderón (who wrote a play entitled *Life Is a Dream*). The second statement comes from the world of hard science and is backed by graphs, statistics, EEG charts, and more than one hundred bibliographical references from similarly erudite journals, most of which are beyond my reach. I bring them together, in part, because they represent what we might call the bookends of dream study and its relation to waking life: one based on feeling and intuition, one on experimental evidence. These two approaches, I might add, are rarely found in each other's company. Moreover, the two quotations also illustrate how one can arrive at similar conclusions by almost opposite means. Of course, I am not sure that the two statements are referring to the same thing, in the purely technical sense. But I wonder if Llinás and Paré haven't offered the "morphological" proof for what Büchner was expressing as a personal feeling: that waking experience is simply a "more precise, more complete" extension of the dream state, the preciseness coming from the constraints that "modulate" waking life—the constant need to look where you're going, to be attentive to what you say and to whom you say it, and in general to watch your p's and q's in order to survive.

Another interesting question is, what might be the implications of this "outrageous" idea for the relationship of dreams to the waking fictions we write and tell one another? The two most obvious links between dreams and fictions are that both are processes for connecting previously unconnected aspects of experience and that both recreate human experience in story form, using what I have called here chain thinking. Moreover, they differ from the writing of history and autobiography, their near neighbors in this latter regard, in that they deal only with hypothetical or imaginary events. Dreams, Jean Paul Richter once said, are "involuntary poetry" (1973, 151n). How far in a morphological direction, then, can one press the idea that poetry is *voluntary* dreaming?

Like Büchner I am proceeding intuitively, more or less as a student of my own dream life. One of my continuing interests is the problem of how dreams manage to achieve a narrative structure. That is, how does a dream plot a sequence of events that never occurred but is simultaneously experienced as reality? What is intriguing about any dream is how the brain can design and maintain an environment, a series of events, and a cast of people, about half of whom you've never seen before, but who came to you so vividly, right down to the pores on their faces, their manner of speaking and moving, that you might recognize them on the street the next day. Moreover, how do these events, no matter how incredible by waking standards, unfold according to a causal logic that is as unimpeachable to the dreamer as the logic of waking causality? To me this is one of the deepest enigmas of dreaming: how is it that one can be within a dream, as one is within waking reality, and simultaneously produce the world one is in—rather like the mollusk that secretes its own shell and then lives in it. In short: how in the world does the dream know how to dream? We have looked at this problem from the standpoint of the image, but there are other aspects of dream authorship to examine that will take us beyond using the tri-temporal understanding of images developed in chapter 4.

The same problem of pinning down the author occurs when we

look at fictions written by authors while wide awake. At first glance, fictions don't seem as enigmatic as dreams in this respect. An author sits at a desk thinking up imaginary events that form a story, revising here, adding there, until it is coherent and complete with beginning, middle and end. Some people (called writers or poets) are better at this than others, but it's all as natural and unremarkable as telling a bedtime story. What I find encouraging about Llinás and Paré's theory is that they add scientific support to my purely intuitive feeling that storytelling—as we all know it in the waking state—springs from the same "skill" that allows us to dream, and vice versa. Moreover, waking storytelling is simply "modulated by different constraints" on the imagination (including responsibility to a reader who expects coherence, tension, and crisis in a story), and while creating the story the storyteller is, in a manner of speaking, actually dreaming under different, if more leisurely, constraints.

This is easy enough to say, in a weak metaphorical sense (poets, after all, have always been called dreamers). But what if it were true in a more physiological sense? Perhaps we have too quickly drawn a distinction between the waking and sleeping states on the basis of physical differences. Waking, to come back to Büchner, may be like "a more lucid dream" (*ein hellerer Traum*) than we tend to think, and nowhere more dreamlike than when one engages in the mental production called storytelling—the mode in which Büchner wrote Robespierre's speech. Storytelling, then, might be thought of as an altered state of waking consciousness. It is to waking consciousness, perhaps, what lucid dreaming (as I understand what that term implies) is to normal dreaming. In both cases, there is a certain sense of out-of-bodiness or transcendence, and a certain godlike power to be both inside and outside the fiction at the same time. Writers commonly report two things that occur in the composition process: first, that the story, when it is going well, "writes itself"—meaning, I gather, that the writer becomes more like a secretary than an author. In this happy state, the story unfolds as fast as one can write it down, and the awareness of being the author of these events is mixed with a sense of watching them *taking place* while creating them: writing and experiencing interpenetrate each other, as in a dream.

The second thing that writers often say (and this would apply as well to painters, composers, daydreamers, and scientists) is that in this bracketed state of focused attentiveness, or "once-upon-a-time-ness," one's consciousness of immediate time and space is dramatically altered. In short, one is isolated in a zone of consciousness that is very like the state that dream psychologists refer to as "single-mindedness" (see Rechtschaffen, 1978). It is all a matter of the degree of fusion of the imaginative and the empirical modes, of authoring and experiencing. I make the analogy with the lucid dreamer as a kind of intermediary position because, just as the lucid dreamer is slightly awake, or slightly *outside* the dream while being largely *inside* it, so the waking author is slightly asleep, or slightly *inside* the fiction while being largely *outside* it. And I take this hybrid zone of lucidity as being a kind of "sliding" common denominator binding the two operations on a continuum that works much like a rheostat. Among other things, it produces interesting hybridizations in literary quality as well. For example, one would think that waking fictions produced while the story is "writing itself" in this state of involuntary lucidity would be better than those produced in the more voluntary or deliberate phase of creation, and this is true some of the time.

But not always: in this wonderful mesmeric mood, I have sometimes written what I thought were brilliant scenes, until I looked at them next day and found they were poor in motivations, character consistency, or narrative probability. What happened, I think, is that I had fallen into a mode of thought in which I had emotionally written the story but had failed to provide what T. S. Eliot would call its objective correlative— that is, a reader-oriented text that becomes the equivalent of my emotional logic. What this suggests is that one can go "over the line" and lose contact with the requirements of waking fiction. In other words, the constraints of waking life are momentarily invaded by the associational liberties most readily available in the dream state, even though one is certifiably awake during the process. In descriptions of how they work, some writers say they write best when they allow their imagination to dictate the flow, but that the results must often be edited, or retrofitted, to waking standards of intelligibility. In this regard, we might recall here the old argument that dreams inadvertently undergo such revision when they are written down or reported to other people. In other words, they are submitted to the constraints of grammar, public speech, and understanding, and in the process become bizarre, like my brilliant scenes.

But one might still ask: how does a dream "write itself"? We are immediately caught in a Scylla-Charybdis situation between whose extremes it is difficult to steer a straight course. If we assume that a dream is, on one hand, made by an agency exterior to the dream itself in some other part of the neuronal works, we inherit the Little Author, a real Scylla of a solution that simply evades the problem by blaming the dream on something prior to or simultaneous with it. If, on the other hand, we say that the dream dreams itself, our craft is shipwrecked on the Charybdis of tautology. Still, despite the risks, I think it is safer to steer a course on the Charybdis side of the channel. I suggest that the dreamer does compose the dream as it unfolds. I am not implying any conscious composition process, but rather this somewhat quirky postulate: *the dream happens to me but I also happen to the dream.* This means, simply, that in one sense I experience the dream in roughly the way I experience the waking world. I am *in* it, but not *of* it. I am awake and conscious during the dream; I can think, assess what is happening, make intelligent (or not so intelligent) decisions, even solve (or think I solve) problems. In short, the dream happens to me. Yet beneath this "everyday" awareness the same brain/mind is evolving the dream events at an unconscious level. This is the level of "mindlessness" discussed in chapter 2 (the level at which we connect Uncle Harry and the meerschaum pipe without thinking about it). But this mindless process does not occur independent of my everyday consciousness during the dream; hence the second part of my postulate—*I also happen to the dream*—that is, I unconsciously influence the course of the dream. And here we arrive at something like Freud's notion of wish-fulfillment, the difference being that the wishes the dream fulfills are not only those of desire but also those relating to one's worst fears. An illustration will show how this works.

In a recent dream I found myself locked in a small room (which was perhaps the size of an elevator) by a menacing man who was clearly not above killing me. Then suddenly he was in the room and the door was shut and locked. Now we were in the same situation. Strangely enough, he immediately lost his menacing aspect, perhaps because we were both trapped. He asked me, "Is there a way out?" I thought, "Maybe there's an exit in the ceiling," and, lo and behold, in the ceiling I saw a re-movable panel almost exactly like the panel in my own hallway ceiling that leads to the attic. The problem was that I couldn't lift my body through the hole because I had no ladder. Immediately I saw on the wall of the room an exposed two-by-four joist which served as a rung, and presently I was able to lift the panel and climb through the hole into what turned out to be a near replica of my own attic.

I have observed this phenomenon of the dream coming true or obeying my thoughts hundreds of times, and I believe that it must be something of a paradigm of dream composition. It does not imply a conscious intentionality on the part of the dreamer, that the dream did what I, as participant-dreamer, *wanted* it to do, that dream composi-tion is a simple matter of wish-and-ye-shall-receive. Rather, it suggests that when a possibility occurs to the dreamer it does so in a field of associations evolving in the dream itself—room, exit, ceiling, and lad-der all forming a common set—again, a metonymic network of things that "belong" together. These are the plot tools the dream has to work with. Indeed, the size of the room probably reminded me of an eleva-tor, though the analogy did not occur to me until this present moment. But elevators, like my attic, have ceiling exits; in fact, Hannibal Lecter, in one of my favorite terror movies, escaped the police in *The Silence of the Lambs* through just such an exit, and it is quite likely that Han-nibal Lecter was wandering in the same field as the menacing killer in my dream. Moreover, Hannibal Lecter is also a killer toward whom the audience has an ambivalent feeling (for example, he kills the right people and he befriends the heroine, Clarisse). I'm not building my explanation of the dream on this idea because I've already cast suspicion on this business of reading things into dreams after the fact; I'm only illustrating the possible depth of any given metonymic field, which is never exhausted by what the dreamer may have consciously in mind. In other words, if this isn't the right explanation, there are plenty of others available, given the complex holdings of an average memory.

So my locked room comes to have an exit, not because I had willed a happy ending to the dream, but because conditions within the dream in progress allowed that possibility. In another dream, guided by different emotional incentives, it is equally possible that no exit would be available and that I would suffer the consequences. There is clearly no way to account for a particular emotional incentive in a dream; that would be like trying to account for why one feels happy, depressed, elated, or gloomy during any particular waking moment. A dream incentive, which is tantamount to dream intentionality, is a global state of mind; that is as much as one can say except that there is good neurological evidence that the brain's limbic system, thought to be the seat of emotional experience, seems to have a strong influence on memory recall and dream construction (Rosenfield, 1988, 164–65; Winson, 1985, 31–32). At any rate, a dream "writes itself" through the collaboration of the dreaming consciousness (normally a participant or observer in the dream) and the emerging materials at hand. There is, in other words, a subliminal collusion between dreamer and dreamwork. It all depends not upon what the dreamer wanted or upon any long-range goal established in advance of the dream, but upon what the interaction of emotional incentive, an emergent field of objects, people, and events (possibly drawn from the day residue) dictated in terms of "wave" probability. Further, the conduct of the dream is also subject to collisions of imagery (clang effects, and the like) and such outside influences as room temperature, household noises, leg cramps, kneading cats, and far-off sirens. So, between collision and collusion, there is no telling what will happen in a dream.

I don't believe this explanation poses a split between the mind of the dreamer and a "mind" in the dreamwork itself. The dreamer "writes" the dream as it comes within a field of limited possibilities but does not realize that he or she is doing the writing. Indeed, in his exploration of hallucinations, Daniel Dennett refers to such narratives as "stories without authors," a "process that weaves back and forth between centrally generated expectations, on the one hand, and confirmations (and disconfirmations) rising from the periphery on the other hand" (1991, 12). The story develops in a sort of systolic-diastolic rhythm whereby a certain level of emotional expectation in the dreaming "victim" is converted into confirmations—or disconfirmations—as *next* events. One never knows what these events may be, but they arrive by virtue of the constant "generate-and-test" behavior of the perceptual system.[1] The dream is a cumulative process whose developments are not controlled by the dreamer but originate in the dreamer's thought about the experience in progress. It is a matter of thought, occurring at any level, being converted to imagery and thereupon constituting a point of "ori-

1. To be more scientific about this matter, the same point has been made by biologists Skarda and Freeman, who offer a new view of the perceptual process. Perception is not "the sum of responses to stimuli . . . like a reflex, in which whatever hits the receptors is registered inside the brain." Rather, "it begins within the organism with internally generated (self-organized) neural activity that, by re-afference, lays the ground for processing of future receptor input. . . . It is the brain itself that creates the conditions for perceptual processing by generating activity patterns that determine what receptor activity will be accepted and processed. Perception is a self-organized dynamic process of interchange inaugurated by the brain in which the brain fails to respond to irrelevant input, opens itself to the input it accepts, reorganizes itself, and then reaches out to change its input. . . . Perception does not just 'copy' objects, it creates their meaning for the organism" (1990, 279–80). Skarda and Freeman are dealing strictly with the visual perception of environmental stimuli. In the dream there is no such thing, only the mistaken sensation that one is experiencing an environment. I don't know how relevant a consideration this is, but it seems unlikely that the perceptual apparatus would undergo a radical change during the conditions of sleep.

entation" from which future possibilities must be drawn—again, natural selection. Thus the dreamer dreams the dream without suspecting that he or she is the efficient cause of what is going on. In the waking world, one might say to oneself in a similar situation, "Is there an exit here?" and there would or would not be an exit, as conditions empirically indicated. In a dream, to ask if there is an exit is already to posit the possibility of an exit. In the very naming of the word, an exit already "hovers" eidetically. Whether it will become a true exit will depend on the nature of the emotional incentive to which the dream is in thrall.

For example, I suspect that the change in the menacing man's attitude toward me when he was accidentally forced to share my "cell" might have paved the way for our fortuitous escape through the ceiling. Why he changed his attitude is impossible to say, because of course dream characters don't have motivations—we infer them (Blagrove, 1992a). But the fact that he did suggests that a "softer" kind of fear might have been lubricating the dreamwork, and having lowered the stakes, he cleared the way for my discovery of an exit. So the logic of the dream events is dependent on the overriding emotion. How do I know, after all, what incentive leads me to select this rather than that, or to go here rather than there, when I make my choices in daily life? The fact is, I "feel" like making the choice, meaning that a certain emotional incentive has biased my decision ("No, I'd rather not walk on the beach today."). And so it is that the events of dreams are guided by our feelings without our having the slightest clue that we are collusive partners in the process.[2]

2. Imagine living in a waking world that obeyed your private thoughts to the letter. Everything would "come true," or come about, as soon as your mind thought it. This might happen in a dream, depending on the weight of the probabilities at play at the moment. In waking reality, of course, you would catch on very quickly that *you* were somehow the cause of these events and you would think twice about thinking at all. In a dream, our single-mindedness deprives us of any such awareness, and we unknowingly create the experience that we seem to be only experiencing.

The word *feelings,* as I am using it, is not as vague as it may sound—as in our term *gut feeling,* which scarcely pins things down to a clear point of ori-

I suspect that much the same process occurs in the writing of fictions. To come back to Llinás and Paré, however, I should point out that they are not favoring the dream state over the waking state; they are suggesting that cognitive abilities are the same in dream and waking states and that differences in the two kinds of experience have to do with the nature of the input and how the brain processes it. In the waking state this input would be our sensory experience coming from without; in the dream state it would be the experience already stored in memory. Attention is presumably equal in both directions; attentiveness is simply a matter of adaptation to what is being allowed to pass through the gate. And I suppose we could hypothesize that intense imaginative activity (such as we find in waking artistic composition, daydreaming, children's play, or deep meditation) could be considered as a modified attentive state of a similar kind, and that perhaps one would find a comparable degree of *intrinsically* generated brain activity in such states. This isn't my territory, by any means, but it might be interesting to see the electrophysiological results if you wired up John Updike's or Doris Lessing's brain while they were writing. What kinds of correlations might there be with their REM thought? And would measurements be different when

---

gin—at least in normal usage. It turns out, however, that *gut feeling* may be the best term after all—if one uses it, as I do, in Antonio Damasio's sense of feelings being "the sensors for the match or lack thereof between nature and circumstance," or between one's genetic makeup and social interaction, on one hand, and one's situation, on the other. Feelings "serve as internal guides. . . . They are neither intangible nor elusive [but] are just as cognitive as other percepts. They are the result of a most curious physiological arrangement that has turned the brain into the body's captive audience" (1994, xv). Feelings, then, are our means of allowing us to sense "body states" (pleasure, pain, terror, etc.), and Damasio argues that one cannot separate the body systems from the brain's cognitive systems or think of the body as the brain's "house." It is the body—the "gut," if you will—that "provides a basic topic for brain representations" (xvii), including those of our dreams.

I also concur with Paul Hernadi's notion of feeling having an "objective" as well as a "subjective" dimension: that is, feeling, in contradistinction to knowing (cognition) and willing (volition), "objectivizes—rivets to a single target of attention—the organism's initially inchoate response to its environment" (1995, 118).

the writing was going well—when the story was "writing itself"—than those that would occur when it was going poorly and John and Doris were looking out the window or sharpening pencils, waiting for their Muses—that is, for dreamlike single-mindedness—to return.

My aim is to suggest how dream and story authorship might be something the brain does without thinking about it—that is to say, without help from a separate creative agency that "thinks" for the brain. To come back to Traherne's poem (chapter 3), "It doth not by another engine work,/But by itself; which in the act doth lurk" (1958, 50). In short, a dream moves at the speed and dictates of its own "found" images; there is nothing outside the dream operating it, like a puppeteer pulling strings. The dream is simply the full operation of the dreaming brain in which lurks all the resources of memory that compose it.

We can say somewhat the same thing about the waking narrative as well, except that the waking state is more susceptible to interruption and multiple trains of thought caused by life in the empirical fast lane. That is, a writer will probably answer a ringing phone, thus breaking off the composition process; a dream, in contrast, will convert the ring into a sound that can be incorporated into the dream itself. The central consideration about narrative structure is that it presumes an ability to arrange events not only in a causal sequence, which is a simple achievement ("Mary went outside. There she saw a cat. She followed it into the woods," and so on), but also in a thematic direction, which is not a simple achievement (in fact, it is what amateur storytellers have the most difficulty with). I suspect that authorship of both kinds is better defined, in the long run, as a way of remembering than as a way of creating something. This isn't a new idea; it goes back to Plato's *Meno* and comes up through Freud's belief that the creative imagination is incapable of inventing anything; all it can do is arrange things it already knows in new relationships.

Let us take a simple case of creativity and see where it leads. How can we see the faces of people in the foliage of trees and the billows of clouds when they are so obviously not there? Moreover, it is almost a dead certainty that a fellow looker can't see the same face but may be perfectly able to find a face you can't see. The explanation is that the face grid is an elementary construction consisting of three or four marks or dark spots (eyes, nose, mouth), and depending on the angle (frontal, profile, uplifted) even these don't have to be in a normal arrangement. Remarkably little in the way of visual configuration is needed to create a face. All you have to do, then, is to employ your eye as a sort of face-seeking missile and it will find a face somewhere in the infinity of facial possibilities in the tree. I've found that there is a special way of doing this, however. It isn't so much a matter of looking for faces, as if they were already there to be found, like the faces that have deliberately been put into drawings in children's books. You have to let your vision fall into a glazed or abstract "scanning" mode, and then think of noses, or eyes, or chins. And, finding a nose-like shape, you concentrate intensely on it and think, "That's its nose," and with luck you will subliminally edit out inappropriate or nonfacial shapes and a face will appear. It's very much like birders calling warblers out of trees with the "pishing" sound. They don't find the birds; they ask the birds to find them. In any event, having "built" such a face you can find other faces with which it can be made to overlap. Moreover, the face seems to be filled with character and nuance. You can even endow it with an attitude and, with a little imagination, a history. And if there's a little breeze the face will even laugh or cry or the jaw will move and it will talk to you. And if you're really successful you can hear what it is saying.

But the most miraculous thing of all is that, having found a face of some sort, you can "think" it into resembling specific faces you already know. In my experiments with this exercise, I have said to myself, "This is the face of Clint Eastwood," and Clint appears, or a reasonable facsimile of Clint; then I think, "Now do Bill Clinton," or Barbra Streisand or Herman Sherk (my high school chemistry teacher). And they all appear on command—half of the time, anyway. What can be going on here that this accidental combination of shadow and shape can be so versatile? It has to do, I suspect, with the Rorschach quality of the configuration. I'm not looking at a face, but a meaningless shape that allows me to ignore some parts of it and emphasize others, depending on what my eye is looking for. You could probably just as easily look for feet or animals or foot-long hot dogs. On the other hand, if you looked at an actual photo of Clint Eastwood you would have no luck getting him to become Barbra Streisand or your chemistry teacher because his facial features would be too finely resolved. But foliage, like a Rorschach blot, will become whatever you want to see in it—within reasonable limits. There has to be just enough "facial" information there from which your memory of faces can draw. And then you fill in the blanks by a process neuroscientists call *vector completion,* which means just that: filling in the blanks of a degraded (or incomplete) vector according to a known prototype (see Churchland, 1995, 280–86).

I should confess that this exercise isn't always successful. Sometimes it is hard to project a specific face onto the foliage or to move from Clint Eastwood to, say, Ted Kennedy, and there are probably various reasons that might account for such failure. But it happens often enough to prove the point that the only face that is there, in the thicket, is the one you've put there from your memory's storehouse, and that's why your friend can't see the face you see (and why you can't easily communicate to a fellow-birder where the bird you see is located in the tree). As an overall rule, I would say that all perception is strongly influenced by expectation. If you go looking deliberately for Clint Eastwood in a tree or a cloud, you are more likely to find him than John Wayne or Julius Caesar, whom you weren't looking for.

And this, I presume, is more or less the frame of mind in which artists paint pictures and writers write stories. Creativity, according to Paul Churchland, may be defined as "the capacity to see or interpret a problematic phenomenon as an unexpected or unusual instance of a prototypical pattern already in one's conceptual repertoire" (1995, 278). If this is too austerely stated, try the art historian E. H. Gombrich's version, that the artist is someone who doesn't paint what he sees but what he already knows how to paint (1965, 86–90). In any case, one thing leads automatically to another; or, more correctly, what is already there leads to the kinds of next things that are most likely to continue the pattern of likeness the artist has in mind. Moreover, there is no reason to think that this same process of visual deception doesn't operate in the dream state, where there is even less constraint on the power of imagination to realize its prodigies. In a dream, if something in a face should remind you of Clint Eastwood, the complete Clint is likely to show up, even though he may be wearing Indiana Jones's hat.

So the brain obviously has the capacity to call forth its pictorial holdings — its memories — in reaction to slim structures of resemblance it finds in reality. And these holdings seem to be attached to, or at least to summon, still larger frames of reference that follow them like a comet's tail. Thus the brain seems categorically unable to consider any of its productions in pure isolation, as a figure without a ground, or an object without a history; almost automatically the brain is drawn to narrative structures which may be thought of as ways of motivating the image, or giving it some sort of context ("This face has just experienced something painful. Perhaps someone it loved has died."). But note also that this act of perception is as much a form of reading as it is a form of authorship; for the tree or cloud is, in this instance, an unintentional text which calls forth, in my reading of it, the "message" of a face. It doesn't make any difference whether the text is intentional (a novel or poem) or unintentional (a tree or a cloud); the act of interpretation is the same whether you're reading Updike's *Rabbit, Run,* an X ray, or a Rorschach blot: we always bring to the text a set of signs — or what in this connection I prefer to call memories — even if the "text" happens to be a chaos of leaves and branches. We call this creativity, but as a mental process it is better called an act of involuntary memory, wherein something new is brought forth from something old through an act of revision that completes the imaginative or creative act. That is why we can say that creation is an act of remembering — or, to put it another way, an act of recombining memories. Moreover, it is an act of *involuntary* remembering. Indeed, if you go looking for a metaphor in an analytical or conceptual mode of thinking, you are likely to come up dry. You can't go to the metaphor; it must come to you via a memory circuit you have inadvertently opened.

A good empirical analogy might be that of an electrical storm building to the point of discharge in the form of lightning, which takes the path of least resistance to the earth. The ground, in the case of the dream, would be the topography of memory in which certain associations might stand out like tall trees in relation to the charge. This excitation or feeling thus becomes itself the cause of an imaginary cause and by this means the cause-effect sequence, as we normally understand it, is inverted. The formation of a dream image, which is always dynamically changing, requires nothing more than the impetus of an association—call it cause or effect—that is imponderably complex and therefore requires a story of its own. And at some point along the line, when the charge becomes strong enough perhaps, the process begins to accumulate the lineaments of a story. That is, it accumulates a quotient of emotional energy, a feeling, so to speak, in search of a conceptual framework, or a kind of prognosis as to what kinds of things can happen to such an energy in its further evolution, on the basis of our personal memory of the waking world. All in all, a narrative would be an exercise in a force following the line of least resistance, somewhat like a slow bolt of lightning—or, once again, like natural selection.

As we all know, dreams cannot be explained this simply. Sometimes dream images seem jammed together, producing bizarre constructions, and sometimes not. Sometimes the plots don't seem all that relevant in their continuations, though who can say what is or isn't relevant in a dream? Perhaps there are purely physiological reasons for this (such as a rush of acetylcholine, in Allan Hobson's theory, or a fever, or a strong Hungarian goulash), but there are good poetic reasons as well, or at least these image productions can be explained on the same grounds that we explain the images of waking authors. For example, William Empson, in *Seven Types of Ambiguity* (1949), discusses images that move from simple ambiguities to highly complex ones. There are images in poetry that seem to be the result of meanings that don't agree with each other (type 4), or images that lie halfway between one aspect of an idea and another—as it were, an image in transition, not yet clear in the author's mind (type 5), and finally (type 7) images that express a fundamental division in the author's mind when the author is "of two minds." And the consequent image, Empson says, "is at once an indecision and a structure" (192). Such an image, I gather, would be tantamount to what in psychiatric terms would be called ambivalence, in which one might hold opposing attitudes toward someone at the same time (like love and hate). At any rate, I see no reason why Empson's poetic categories would not figure in the dreamwork as well as they do in poetry, as dreams have even less time to resolve any ambiguities they cast up as a consequence of "indecision," multiple associations, or ambivalent feelings.

Coming back to Llinás and Paré, if both the waking and the dream states share common cognitive processes, there is no reason to assume that the dreaming brain is any more sure of where it is going than the waking brain is. And in dreams, of course, ambiguity would assert itself primarily as visual bizarreness, or a jamming of images that on empirical grounds don't quite form a unity. One could argue for dreams what we commonly assume about literary works: they aren't in the business of resolving ambiguities but of simply *displaying* them. No one has ever definitively explained what makes Hamlet tick, and that's primarily because no single thing makes him tick: he is structured like a contradiction, though a very coherent one to be sure. He is, as Empson would say, at once an indecision and a structure. Anyway, there seems to be no reason for claiming that dreams can't dream about doubts and indecisions as much as they dream about outright fears or desires. We spend a good deal of our time in doubt and indecision, and the dream's job is to cast up images that imitate these states of mind, not to make sense where none is to be found.

Let me apply the principle to a recent dream. Bigelow, a friend of mine from New York City, was visiting me in a dream that took place in a field where carnival or theater apparatus was being set up. He appeared rather suddenly in the plot. In the dream I looked at him and was suddenly reminded of my colleague Peter, who now struck me as being about the same height as Bigelow and having the same general facial structure. I noticed this, even remarked it to myself in the dream, and

Bigelow suddenly became Peter, and the two kept changing places as it occurred to me that one had somehow become the other. While I had no control over the process, it was later clear to me that it was I who was provoking the shifts, not the dreamwork willing something erratic on the Peter/Bigelow figure. In other words, I thought, "Bigelow looks like Peter," and the dream would echo my thought by producing Peter, and then I'd think, "Peter and Bigelow do look alike," and Bigelow would reappear, or there would be a composite figure that would pass as both. Of course these changes didn't occur quite so abruptly, but they did occur and it seems inescapable that the changes corresponded to my thoughts about who reminded me of whom. It's very much like the parapsychical principle of influencing objects at a distance through strong mental concentration, though of course it happens automatically in the dream. The only difference was that in this dream I was experiencing the power of changing identities in an unusually aware state, as though my thoughts were a magic wand that could bestow new identities on the figures of the dream. I'm not sure how it finally turned out (you rarely are, in these transformations), but it seemed to me pretty clear evidence that the dream works co-responsively with the thoughts you are having about it, and that the dream, in a manner of speaking, is a visualization of your thought, most of which is occurring beneath awareness.

To make this the single rule of dreaming would be going much too far. If this were always the case, imagine what dangers you would expose yourself to when you even thought about danger; or, on the brighter side, imagine what sexual success you could have in dreams at the very sight of an attractive woman or man coming your way. But it doesn't work like this. The most you can say is that sometimes, where dream characters or animals or things like houses, cars, and machinery are concerned, the dream begins to follow mysterious codes of resemblance in which identities become unstable and things oscillate with their similarity to other such things. My own interim explanation for all this is that plot-lines in dreams, as in waking fictions, are already unstable; whereas characters, places, and objects are, as in daily life, generally more stable. But stability, in any form, is antithetical to dreaming. Dreams are not paintings, least of all still lifes. They are in continual motion. Thus all identity is subject to instant revision and expansion in a dream. You just don't notice it because that is a condition of dream perception that is as normal as room temperature. This is the best in the way of a rule that I have been able to find.

However, there is more to be said about the Peter-Bigelow dream. When I thought about this dream the next morning, I decided that Peter and Bigelow *don't* really look alike, after all. The dream was wrong, or at least proceeding on very slim circumstantial evidence. I suspect that anyone seeing them side by side would find no resemblance. It certainly had never occurred to me, but then I never had cause to think of them in the same thought frame. Now that it comes to my attention, there is a slight categorical resemblance in the sense that they do have angular, squarish faces and high cheekbones and are roughly the same height, but this seems a remote basis for a correlation (surely I know other people who look *more* like Bigelow than Peter: for instance, I've always thought Bigelow looks like Richard Dreyfus). I think the match required a second-level correlation that has to do with what was happening in the dream at the moment. I recall that there was some sort of series of high platforms being set up in a field that may have indicated a theater performance about to be held, and I had some part in it. I was apparently a stagehand, just doing what I was told. And it happens that both Peter and Bigelow are associated with the theater, Bigelow in my past at Yale Drama School, Peter in my present department. So there was a double association at work. Physical resemblance, by itself, would not be sufficient, but if it is abetted by the accident of a theater event in the offing and the need for me to have instructions on what to do, whatever it may have been, Peter and Bigelow begin to resemble each other. Thus one line of connection bleeds over into another. So a refinement of the rule might read: *a weak resemblance of type A* (facial structure) *may be strengthened by a secondary common denominator of type B* (occupation, environment, etc.). Or, in another variation: *given*

an additional incentive to see resemblance, a dream will modify its quali-
fications for resemblance. An instant's thought will tell you how this rule
applies to waking life, as when A hires B for a position over C, D, and
E (who are better qualified) because B is also A's brother-in-law.

So, to come back to my dream, Bigelow and Peter looked alike
(were interchangeable) primarily because of the theater context. Had
the dream put me in, say, an athletic context (tennis), Bigelow probably
would not have been in the dream and my tennis partner Paul would
have. And now, wide awake and squinting out the details, I can even see
a resemblance between Paul and my old roommate Bob, with whom I
played tennis on a recent visit.

All in all, with regard to choices of this sort, dreaming is similar to
drawing a doodle on a napkin. You begin by making a circle, to which
you append a second interlocking circle or a square, then you put a
small circle inside the square, a triangle inside that, shade the area outside the triangle to the circular border; then you notice the whole thing
is getting lop-sided, or unpleasantly asymmetrical, so you add a window
looking past the whole affair into an abstract landscape, and before long
your original circle is buried in whimsical geometry. You have a pleasing
structure, perhaps, because the whole process has been brought about
by the spatial "needs" of the drawing at each point (balance, symmetry,
interest), but you couldn't have guessed it would turn out as it does, nor
could you tell (unless by memory) which figure had been the parent of
all the others. And so a dream is a kind of time-space doodle that uses
the remembered forms of waking experience as its circles, squares, and
triangles. The function of any single element in a dream, one might say,
is to *belong* to what is already there, and to this end anything that appears in a dream cashes in its discrete identity at the gate in exchange
for a provisional identity that becomes the toy of an evolving contextual
environment.

Thus what we commonly call plots (in literary fiction) are nothing
more or less than continually evolving patterns of imagery and events.
As a simple example: I am driving a car at high speed on a two-way

country road. At the top of a hill I see ahead of me a hay rake traveling extremely slowly. These are two events, one caused by the other (it is likely that one might see hay rakes on country roads). The next event, in all likelihood, will have something to do with the oncoming closure of my car and the hay rake: I try to pass, yet a car is coming from the other direction; I can't slow down in time; I barely avoid the hay rake by driving off the road. And so it is with images and characters in a dream. Each episode, each "frame" of the dream narrows the possibilities of the ensuing episodes within certain limits of expectation. I shall return to this theme in my discussion of scripts and dream plots in the next chapter. Here, I need say only that it is no great miracle of compositional skill that dreams stick to the point as well as they do; for the most part, they follow a logic of resemblance drawn directly from the dreamer's complete fund of experience in the waking world. But this overall reliability is what gives us the erroneous idea that when dreams "fail" to make sense something is wrong with them. It isn't a matter of failure or making sense at all; the term *failure* can be applied only to something with a deliberate or intentional origin and purpose. The explanation lies, rather, in the nature of dreaming, which is not to make sense but to make images that belong to each other at some level of personal association, usually beneath the scrutiny of the dreamer.

In this regard, I am puzzled by Allan Hobson's discussion of the incoherence of dreams in *The Chemistry of Conscious States* (1994). Hobson argues that "One of the most precious myths about dreams . . . is that, in spite of their microscopic chaos, their overall plot design is unified" (122). Not so, he says, and as proof he offers an exercise conducted in his dream seminar called dream splicing. He took twenty random dream reports, each of which contained one scene shift. Then he cut ten of the reports in half with a scissors at the point where the scene shifted. Finally, the pieces were transposed, "heads on tails, heads on heads, tails on heads, tails on tails." Then all twenty dreams were passed out to the seminar and each person was asked to distinguish the spliced dreams from the unspliced. No one had more than "better than chance" success. From this Hobson reports that "Dream coherence may be in the eye of the beholder, but it is *not* in the text of the reports" (123). Thus dream plots, he concludes, are not unified.

It strikes me there is something self-fulfilling about this experiment, and I suspect it has to do with the standard of coherence being tested. "The significance of [the exercise]," Hobson says, "is that, although each subplot may be a storylike unit, there is no story line connecting one subplot to the next" (123). First, much the same thing might be said, within limits, of certain novels and plays that explore the vicissitudes of several families (Tolstoy and Shakespeare come to mind). It is true that in the end coherence is usually established in such cases, and that the various subplots in some way usually, but not always, intertwine (Jacobean subplots are notoriously unintegrated into the main plot). So if you spliced scenes in a different order from, say, different Shakespearean history plays, you couldn't tell if something was unusual until it became clear that two different stories were being told. I mention this only to establish that shifts and re-beginnings are common technical features of waking fictions and that the relation of one plot to another has very little to do with causal logic. However, this aside, there is another problem with the integrity test.

What disappears from all dream reports is something that couldn't possibly survive the dream, and that is what we might call a psychical coherence, or a coherence established by likeness of affect. A recall of dream events, in other words, couldn't capture the subliminal ways in which one dream sequence might bring on another, even though the new dream sequence involved an entirely new set of characters and a new locale. But who is to say that segment A didn't contain the seeds of segment B, or that both A and B weren't variations on a theme that had no particular identifying marks from the waking standpoint. Who is to say that some overall quality—like aggression, fear, joy, frustration, or even something less definable like Empson's self-contradicting ambiguities—isn't coming into play? I'm not arguing for the coherence of dreams, at least not in all cases. But I wonder whether one can judge the coherence or incoherence of something as relentlessly hyperassociative as a dream, or a dream series, from the waking standpoint, and apart from the psychic environment in which it was born.[3] Hobson might find these remarks an example of what he refers to as the predisposition of "the integrated brain-mind . . . to discern integrity, unity, and singleness of purpose in any text that appears to be integral. And when integrity does not reside in the text, we impute it" (1994, 124). But I'm not imputing integrity; far from it, I'm questioning whether integrity, as we know and admire it, has anything to do with dreaming. I'm also suggesting that it is possible to impute nonintegrity on the same unjustified grounds. This is our old verificationist problem from chapter 3, and we will confront it again in the next chapter. Its primary limitation is that it sees everything through analytic glasses, and there are certain kinds of experience that cannot be seen by the analytical eye.

No, there is a lot of "incoherence" in dreams. It's just that we have no way of making sure where it begins and ends or what causes it. Much of the commentary on dreams assumes that all dream events are intentional at some level: that is, if you dream of playing cards with a dog, the dog can be explained as a symbol standing for something else, since it makes no sense in the realm of coherence. But such a theory ignores the

---

3. Melvin Lansky, in his essay on the dream as an investigative tool, mentions a number of studies that have failed to distinguish dreams of schizophrenics from the dreams of nonschizophrenics on the basis of "manifest contents alone" (1992, 486). One of the explanations might be that the quality of "schizophrenia" does not manifest itself at the manifest level. Except for odd descriptive qualifiers ("the room was foreboding and eerie") dream reports virtually leave behind the real dream, not only in its overall atmosphere but in the inseparable coalition of feeling and image that characterizes dream events. It is one thing to say "the room was foreboding and eerie," quite another to be in the room suffering, say, the terror of self-dissolution. In one way, dream events and people are already schizophrenically inclined in a nonpathological sense. That is, everything in a dream is part of what R. D. Laing would call a false-self system, in which the dreamer is parceled out to the images he or she imagines in the dream. At the very least, all dream characters and objects are bathed in the peculiar aura of the dreamer's consciousness, much as the characters in a Shakespeare play are all little Shakespeares pretending to be Rosalinds, Mercutios, and Hamlets.

possibility that the connection between dog and card playing is simply submerged in the dreamer's experience. The connection may not involve meaning at all but simply metonymic propinquity, whereby dogs and cards belong in the same category for a particular dreamer. Or, to refine the idea a bit further: dog and cards might, in this particular instance, be part of a double metaphor in which both refer to a common tenor. I'm thinking of cases, some personal, in which an author might be tinkering with two different ways of saying the same thing and arrive finally at a mixed metaphor or a catachresis—that is, a combination that seems incoherent because the common denominator is missing—something like Milton's "blind mouths" or Hamlet's "to take arms against a sea of troubles."

I can illustrate this point by turning to one of my most indelible memories of youthful embarrassment. In 1947 at the DuBois Undergraduate Center in Pennsylvania, as a freshman reporter on the school magazine, I was assigned to interview a town dowager about the town's early lumbering industry. The interview was conducted in an elegant sitting room in her house, just off campus. In the course of the interview she mentioned that one of the pioneers in DuBois lumbering had been the Post family. Wanting to show some knowledge of the world (at seventeen), and being journalistically aggressive, I interrupted politely and asked if they were related to the Saturday Evening Posts. With a graciousness for which I am forever thankful, my hostess overlooked the blunder (perhaps even taking it as a joke) and with a gentle smile said, "No, not those Posts." On the level of waking logic I had committed the terrible mistake of confusing basic categories. But on another level, my thinking (thinking now more coherently about it) had been quite astute. Poor perhaps by practical standards and purposes, but aesthetically speaking I was in the right mode: it is thanks to such false connections that poets produce rhymes and punsters puns, and (dare I try again?) that dreams, like running fences, are inclined to take the shortest distance between two posts.

9 ·

The Möbius Script

In chapter 3, we murdered the verificationist who insisted that we had prematurely called dreams real experiences, and we threw his corpse into an abandoned mine shaft deep in the desert. Whereupon we proceeded to treat dreams as bona fide experiences undergone in sleep, on the assumption that if you *seem* to have an experience then you must be having it (whatever the experience is). Or—as we need all the support we can get—as Allan Hobson crisply puts it: "Here's the simplest test: Are we aware of what happens in our dreams? Of course. Therefore, dreaming is a conscious experience" (1994, 209). If you read Tolstoy's account of Prince Andrey's fall in the battle of Borodino, you aren't experiencing a real battle; you are experiencing a fictional account of battle, which may be the next best thing to being there, but it isn't the real thing. And you know it isn't the real thing, but it's an experience all the same. So, too, are dreams. Whether you call them illusions or false or delusive memories, or seeming experiences, or night fictions, or whatever, dreams aren't occurring as real veridical events but as experiences of a virtual sort.

The problem in making comparisons of this kind is that in the dream state, unlike the state in which you read books, you are deprived of any means of telling the difference between real and virtual experience (again, lucid dreams excepted). So you think you're experiencing the real thing during the dream ("I'm falling off my horse!"), and only when you wake up does the veridical give way to the virtual. So, in a way, you have two experiences for the price of one: the real experience tucked into what will turn out to have been a virtual experience and the recall experience in which you go back over the events from an empirical perspective, awed that something that seemed so real could have happened only virtually in your head. And there is still a third experience: the experience of confusion and mystery that is perhaps best summed up in the parent's assurance to the child who has just awakened in terror: "There, it's only a dream." At any rate, it hardly seems appropriate to use the same standard of verification to make judgments about both real and virtual experiences. Saying that dreams aren't experiences is a little like saying that the people in China are speaking the wrong language because you don't understand it.

In any case, verificationists don't give up the ghost so easily, especially when their deaths have not been verified. So we are about to confront them again, this time as a way of solving the problem of how dreams learn how to "tell" stories. For dreams are not like blood pressure or pulse, or the digestive system (to return to my earlier analogy): they tell true falsehoods about our real experience.

One of the more curious debates in the history of dream theory occurred with the publication of the archverificationist Norman Malcolm's famous work *Dreaming* (1959), which virtually denies any experiential status for dreams. We seem to have dreamed, Malcolm argues, but we have only a waking impression of having dreamed, and all we know is the dreamer's report of the dream. Malcolm's thesis is so audacious, so contrary to all that has been thought and said about dreams, and so ambiguously argued, that respondents have been puzzled about just what he is and isn't claiming. There are such things as dreams, but they are not genuine experiences (thoughts, emotions, feelings, and the like). Many philosophers have risen to the bait of his bold frontal attack on the "received" theory of dreaming, and for the most part refuting Malcolm has been something of a duck shoot. Here I want to center on the response of Daniel Dennett, one of the foremost duck-shootists in philosophy, whose essay "Are Dreams Experiences?" (1977) takes up the argument (without siding with Malcolm) by asking whether we actually experience a dream "presentation" or come by the dream memory from some more indirect route. As usual with Dennett, we are treated to a highly inventive argument, but it is hard to know how seriously to take his discussion of the infamous cassette theory of dreaming, which occupies a good deal of the essay. I bring it up here as an approach to the problem of the composition process of dreaming: either dreams are composed during the dream (as I believe), or, as the cassette theory maintains, they were composed unconsciously at a prior time in waking or sleeping life or even REM sleep. The cassette theory, then, maintains that dreams are not dreamed, they are only composed and stored, like recordings.[1]

Like Malcolm, Dennett entertains the notion that dreams are not real experiences but illusions that strike us on waking as having been dreamed. They are false recollections. But what is being recollected and how did it get into mind? Dennett begins by considering those rare dreams in which an external noise or action (an alarm clock ringing, a car backfiring) is incorporated into the dream as if the dream had anticipated the sound that becomes its climactic event. The example Dennett offers (the "one remotely well-documented case"), that of a dreaming man in a sleep laboratory who was awakened by cold water dripped onto his neck. He immediately reported a dream in which he was singing in an opera and suddenly "he *heard and saw* that the soprano had been struck by water falling from above; he ran to her and as he bent over her, felt water dripping on his back" (1977, 235). The question is, how could the dream have known in advance that the water was going to fall and have prepared its narrative in such a way as to resolve itself when the sound finally arrived?

Dennett wisely rules out any possibility of precognition in such dreams and postulates that the dream might have (1) occurred at extraordinary speed or (2) composed itself *backward* after the sound and is then "remembered front to back" (235). These he abandons as being farfetched explanations for the phenomenon, and he suggests that (3) the cassette theory, which maintains that dreams are inserted directly, and unexperienced, into memory banks by an unconscious composition process during either waking or sleeping time and stored, like cassettes, "available to waking recollection depend[ing] on various factors" (237). Thus, after hearing the backfire of a car on the street outside, the sleeper would awaken and recall a pre-recorded cassette dream in which he

1. This is also a question raised by Wittgenstein. Is it nonsense, he asks, "ever to raise the question whether dreams really take place during sleep, or are a memory phenomenon of the awakened?" (1968, 184).

was shot, or shot at, by an assailant. No dreaming takes place: it is "an unexperienced process" (239) until the sleeper is awake and reports the "dream" or thinks about it. All in all, it is very much like hearing a song and being reminded of a forgotten experience of many years ago—except that in the case of the cassette dream the experience never really happened to you but was "dreamed up" without your awareness and stored until the sound provoked it to life.

I have never met anyone who endorses the cassette theory (which probably originates with Freud, who allows it only as a possibility [1900, 5:495–97]), and I suspect that Dennett doesn't endorse it as much more than a philosophical prod for "undermin[ing] the authority of the received view of dreams" (1977, 227–28), his avowed aim in the essay. He says he selected it because, of all "rival theories, [it] runs most strongly against our pretheoretical convictions" (236). In fact, he keeps the theory at arm's length by referring to "the cassette theorist," as if the theory were held by someone else and he himself were a lawyer hired to present the best possible defense. And as with any good defense lawyer, there are so many questions Dennett doesn't bother asking that it is hard to think of him taking it as anything more than a hypothesis. If it proves fruitless, or silly, one can always discard it in the way philosophers often entertain and discard unlikely hypotheses ("Do oranges have feelings?") in order to understand the rules and limits of knowing. Moreover, one of Dennett's favorite philosophical tactics is to lead you down the path of a false hypothesis to the point where you are ready to buy it and then he points out its absurdity. So, as Dennett puts it in another essay, "Where Am I?" (1988), you never know where Dennett is until he gets there. He escapes behind the scenery of a profusion of examples, like the phantom of the Cartesian opera. Unfortunately, Dennett doesn't really arrive anywhere in the cassette theory, he leaves it "an *open* and *theoretical* question" (249), but one is left with the nagging impression that the question is about as open as the question of Brutus's honor after Marc Antony has finished him off in the forum speech. At any rate, Dennett's argument has led still other theorists (Globus,

1987, 72–77) to conclude that he is dead serious in denying any kind of experiential status to dreams. But we find no mention of the cassette theory in Dennett's later book, *Consciousness Explained* (1991), where he speaks of dreaming "a dream that [is] so shocking that it wakes you up" and asks whether the pains one sometimes feels in dreams are real pains (61) — questions scarcely forthcoming from a cassette theorist. In another passage, he notes, "The volatility of metamorphosis of objects in dreams and hallucinations is one of the most striking features of those narratives" (14), and if dreams came only in cassette form there could be no experience of metamorphosis at all, as the dreams would be "canned." Anyway, my aim here is not to imply that Dennett is even a closet cassette theorist himself, but simply to undermine the theory with which *he* hoped to undermine the received view. That is, I want to partly undermine it, for I also believe there is something very cassette-like about the way dreams shape their narratives.

Let us devise an experiment that might bring this all into better focus. Suppose it were technologically possible to wire a dreamer with a micro-subtle trembler switch so that when the emotional affect of a dream reached a significant physiological intensity a switch would be tripped and a bell would ring. Let us refine it even further and say that only when the emotion of fright occurred in sleep would the circuit be completed. In other words, lust or joy or embarrassment or an urgent need to urinate wouldn't ring the bell — only fright, which has, let us say, its own distinctive sine wave. Imagine that our technology is foolproof and has been tested on thirty-eight philosophy majors, who wore the apparatus for a full month, waking and sleeping, and that when any of them experienced fright it invariably caused a bell to ring. Now the device is ready to be tried out just at night on an innocent sleeping subject.

A week passes and our subject rings no bell and has no report of a frightful dream. On the eighth night, at 12:34 A.M. the bell rings and the subject awakens suddenly and reports that he had a dream about being mercilessly pummelled in a boxing ring by a huge creature resembling Sylvester Stallone. Here we have produced a physical result in the empirical world that was caused by a dream taking place in an imaginary world at exactly 12:34 A.M. (EST: Empirical Standard Time). Surely we cannot deny that the emotion has caused the bell to ring (given the sophistication of our technology) and that a dream has produced the emotion that caused it to ring precisely at 12:34 A.M. And on waking the dreamer immediately reports having the experience of pure fright. Surely the linkage between dream and bell now seems unassailable. Moreover, the cassette theory of dreams would now be defunct, or at least imperiled, because we have established that dreams do produce real, experienced affects and the dream could not have occurred after the bell rang. The ring could only have been produced by the dream, or, if you want to get technical, by a sudden surge of fright on the part of the subject for which there is no explanation. Either way, dream or no, the subject has had an experience during sleep that is verified in the waking world, and there seems to be no real reason to deny that it was the consequence of a dream because he reports dreaming it upon awakening.

Of course, we have no such technology (that I know of), and therefore I've proven nothing except that all of this might be the case if the technology were available. But then it might not. All I have tried to do is clarify the situation. If, on the one hand, the experiment would turn out my way we could say that dreams are experiences undergone during sleep, as there would no longer be a case for concluding that dreamers don't *experience* their dreams but are having real emotions on the spot during a dream. If, on the other hand, the bell were caused to ring by a duplicitous lab assistant secretly working for the cassette-theory mafia, and if the sleeper would *only then* awake and report a frightful boxing dream, the cassette theory would still be alive and viable and we would be tempted to invoke it in order to explain the bizarre coincidence of our sleeping subject being so fortuitously and literally saved by the bell. But even then there is no cause to conclude that *all* dreams were explained by the cassette theory because our conclusion could extend only to those dreams that seem to anticipate externally produced endings.

Actually, my experiment was inspired by much more mundane

dream experience. Technology aside, people regularly "ring bells" during their dreams—that is to say, they wake up during dreams with all sorts of emotions and physical affects, and all that is lacking is the technology to validate them. People who keep dream journals soon learn the knack of waking up and recording their dreams as soon as they occur, and it is hard to see how they might be having cassette dreams. Urination dreams occur, so to speak, in waves of increasing urgency (see the French nurse dream discussed by Freud, 1900, 5:367–68) until the dreamer is forced to abandon sleep and go to the bathroom. But the most telling case is, again, probably that of Michel Jouvet's famous cats. When the muscle atonia of the cats was surgically short-circuited, they physically rose in their sleep and performed disorganized predation routines during REM sleep. This does not prove that they were having experiences, in Dennett's sense of the word ("Can animals *recall* events? If not, they cannot have experiences" [1977, 247]), but it does suggest that the cats were having dreams *during* REM sleep and that they were experiencing in the dream what they were carrying out in their somnambulistic behavior.

Of course animals are not human beings. But the connections seem substantial enough to allow the "received" conclusion that what is going on in a dream is a real dream and not a false memory of a prerecorded dream. At least the cat experiments have convinced no less a neuroscientist than Allan Hobson: "Through Jouvet's work," Hobson writes, "we now know that we would act out our dreams were it not for this inhibitory suppression of motor output" (1988, 150). And if we did act them out, then there seems no cause to say that dreams are not experiences simply because our motor output is suppressed. There is of course an outside possibility that a pre-stored cassette dream of predation behavior could be triggered in REM sleep and produce a dreamed dream, but we would still be back with the received notion that dreams are experiences we have in sleep, and we would have added one more step to the process, and a highly exotic one at that.

Finally, another difficulty with the cassette theory is that it isn't clear why the brain would go to the trouble of creating unexperienced cassettes of dreams, as if it were running a community library, without telling the community the books were available. Why would a brain capable of experiencing daydreams in the certifiable waking state resort to a devious unconscious process for recording nocturnal dreams (or whatever they would be called), circumventing a dream presentation, and storing them against the possibility of future use in, for example, these external stimuli experiences? As for how to explain the sort of dream that actually anticipates the arrival of an accidental external stimulus, Gordon Globus argues persuasively that such dreams might be accounted for by the difference between dream time and clock time (1987, 74–77). And indeed, along this line Dennett himself offers a possibility in his later discussion of the Phi phenomenon in *Consciousness Explained.* There is "no privileged finish line [in mind-events], so the temporal order of discriminations cannot be what fixes the subjective order in experience" (1991, 119); or, more simply, just as "the representation of space in the brain does not always use space-in-the-brain, [so] the representation of time . . . does not always use time-in-the-brain" (131). This is not the place to work out the particulars, but I can see how Dennett's concept of "multiple drafts," or parallel and multitracking processes of sensory inputs, could be adapted to cover these dreams that gave rise in his 1977 essay to the cassette discussion. Moreover, the phenomenon of false familiarity (my chapter 4) might explain the anticipatory dream: that is, if one can recall within dreams episodes that didn't take place (the recall of the greenhouse conversation), perhaps one can *seem* to recall episodes that are triggered by a sudden noise. Finally, there is good evidence that dreams don't end precisely upon waking. During the period of hypnopompic emergence from the dream the affect and plot of the dream continue for a brief time in a sort of afterglow, and it is perhaps in this zone of "recall" that one can invent responses to external noise and stimulus, especially if one takes into account Globus's differential between dream and clock time.

Given these considerations, I might mention the principle known in aesthetics as consistent continuation, whereby the viewer of a painting tends to see the painting as a "sample" of a world and to extend the scene hypothetically beyond its frame. This does not involve the actual visualization of images, only an extension of quality, so that a Van Gogh painting wouldn't really stop at its borders but continue Van Gogh-esquely in all directions, just as reality does (Sparshott, 1983, 142). In principle, a variation of consistent continuation might work as well in anticipatory dreams in the sense that an outside stimulus (dripping water) would orient the dreaming brain to move swiftly in a watery direction. And it would probably take less dream time or clock time to douse a soprano, run to her aid, and get doused oneself than it would to report it—assuming that the opera motif was in progress before the dripping began. Anyway, the main problem is that we have so few documented cases of this phenomenon, and it seems extravagant to discredit the received theory that dreams are experiences we have during sleep on the grounds of a few scattered and casual reports. And it is possible that something *like* a cassette memory, or what Freud calls a "ready-made phantasy" (1900, 5:495) is the valid explanation for such dreams.

Why waste time with the cassette theory at all, then, if it turns out to be so silly? In an odd way the notion of a cassette experience—or non-experience, as Dennett might put it—has a good deal to be said for it if we think of the cassette not as the composition *process* or as a "stored" and as-yet-undreamed dream, but as a ready-made model or schema on which dreams tend to organize their contents. Suppose we assume, then, that the brain doesn't store dreams in cassette form but that it stores structural *instructions* for making dreams that are automatically brought into play when the dream process begins. The cassette theorist's argument becomes somewhat more provocative in this light. For example, in the following passage from his essay Dennett observes:

Although the dream cassettes would have to be filled at some time by a composition process, that process might well occur during our waking hours, and spread over months (it takes a long time to write a good story). The composition might even occur aeons before our birth; we might have an *innate* library of undreamed dream cassettes ready for appropriate insertion in the playback mechanism. Stranger things have been claimed. Even on the received view the composition process is an unconscious or subconscious process, of which we normally have no more *experience* than of the processes regulating our metabolism; otherwise dreams could not be suspenseful. (1977, 237)

In short, if the cassette theory is wrong in its particulars, there are undoubtedly levels on which the brain/mind does have an innate library of undreamed "dream cassettes," though it would be more accurate to refer to them as memory structures. What is innate, or imprinted in memory, is not specific experience itself (in dream form), much less undreamed dreams, but narrative capability, which is to say the capacity to arrange imagined events into structures of feeling based on accumulated patterns of experience and emotion. In general, it is a *learned* sense of what goes with what under what conditions. This is the sense in which the rules of composition, the instructions for making stories, "might even occur aeons before our birth"—indeed as far back as the first dreamer. I'm not suggesting a genetic transmission or the operation of a racial memory, simply that the possibilities for narrative structure are finite and conterminous with the structures of human experience. This brings us back to the discussion of Dawkins's memes in chapter 2.

One thing that can be said about dreams is that they are like stories in not being new formations of experience but variations on old stories; old stories persist and are put into new "cassettes" because the possibilities of human experience don't change that much. After fifty thousand years we are still killing and making love and satisfying ambitions and revenges; or, as Robert Ornstein wittily puts it, we are still driven by the four Fs of survival: feeding, fighting, fleeing, and sex (1991, 198). I have read that there are essentially fourteen basic kinds of stories. Another estimate might claim that there are really only twelve, or ten, or even three. It all depends on how close you stand to experience itself and whether you tend to lump things together or split things into smaller and smaller groups. From a great distance all stories might be seen as variations on the *Odyssey* (as good an ur-story as any), which is the original "It's hard to go home again" story; viewed up close, however, the *Odyssey* itself might be seen as a collection of many kinds of odysseys (it's hard to do *anything*).

It follows that the situations out of which good (and bad) stories are made are never invented by writers; they are simply borrowed from the meme pool of human experience. Story situations—sometimes called archetypes, sometimes master plots—are self-replicating, meaning that they are told over and over, surviving all cultural change, and quite often the tellers are under the illusion that they have created the situation, as opposed to the language in which the situation is reified. There are, simply, no new situations, primarily for the same reason that there are no new geometric structures that haven't been named (triangle, trapezoid, square), or no new human relationships (mother, father, sibling, lover, friend, grocer). Some situations are better self-replicators than others, if only because they have more "depth." For example, the adultery situation seems to be a far better self-replicator than the situation we might title "Robbing from one's uncle or aunt," at least by my informal survey of world fiction. On the same grounds, the "X is jealous of Y" situation is better than the "X supports Y's candidacy for mayor" situation. The reason is that adultery and jealousy are permanent human situations bearing on central human relationships, one reason (among others) that the Othello story, which Shakespeare cribbed from an Italian novelist named Cinthio, is one of the world's best. Not only does *Othello* combine the adultery and the jealousy themes; it adds a third as piquant as either, the theme of the malevolent friend. And even this is a gross reduction of the story-appeal of *Othello* because there are also the memes/motives of interracial marriage, the "exotic" warrior in a civilized land, the fatal temptations of alcohol, among others. In short, story situations spring naturally from the realm of problem-putting and problem-solving and, as such, are impossible to avoid in both literary fiction and dreams, having much the same inevitability as the curve, the straight line, and the angle in painting and architecture.

Dreams, of course, are not known for their facility in telling stories. For all their bizarreness, dreams tend to be rather plodding by fictional standards. We tend to be either seeking something or avoiding something, which is pretty much what we do on a simple shopping trip or a car ride home during rush hour. And we remain substantially ourselves, whatever we're doing. We take our habits and attitudes into our dreams, and our dreams comply by putting us in probable situations in which we undergo the typical tensions of daily experience, even though the scene might be a monastery in Tibet. It has been said that great writers write about their personal handicaps, and usually without knowing what the handicap is. Someone has discovered that an "asthmatic" style runs through Proust, who had asthma, a "blind" style in Milton, and one could probably find a theme of deafness at the base of Beethoven's music. Without making such simplistic claims, we might make a similar case for dreams: we put ourselves in the situations we "deserve" as a result of having particular fears and needs, or certain traits like aggressiveness, paranoia, or high-threshold guilt. It's probably a good thing that most of the time our dreams are boring enough to put us to sleep. The point is that dreams do something to these boring experiences, in sleep, that consumes the consciousness with interest.

Let us look at two examples from opposite ends of the spectrum, common dreams based on a more or less universal structure of feeling. They occur often enough in the literature of dream reports to suggest that they are "archetypal" dreams. They are examples of the blank scripts, or cassettes, on which our past dreams, and dreams as yet undreamed, are written.

I frequently dream of the sea, even before I moved to a coastal town. For the most part these are pleasant dreams, even though deep water is one of my greatest fears. In these dreams, it always occurs to me that the sea is very powerful and ominous, which is hardly an original thought. As if to oblige me, the sea begins to realize this potential

in strong waves assaulting the shore, and in some cases I am even in-
undated by the waves, never with any serious consequences, somehow
never getting wet. What I take to be the subject of these dreams is the
same desire that I feel while watching the sea from the beach in waking
life. Like most people, I am fascinated by powerful waves, by the great
humpbacked tubes of rolling water and the flash and breaking of surf
on rocks. The bigger the waves, the better. Indeed, I keep betting that
the coming wave will be even more spectacular than the last. I simply
pick a wave that seems to have more dark shadow in front of the curl
than the last few waves and I put my money on it. And I can wait for
long intervals in the hope of the "big one," the so-called Ninth wave,
arriving while I am there. This is, of course, the lure of the sublime, and
it must be a powerful and profound attraction for most people. Among
other things, dreams realize the potential of such experiences; they release nature from the restrictions and probabilities that usually contain
it in reality. And I cannot help but think that this is a deep-seated desire:
to see reality now and then break its rules.

Southern California recently experienced severe fire and earth-
quake damage. No one, except the arsonist, would wish such disaster
on people. But when you are watching fire rage out of control from the
safe vantage point of a television viewer, you experience something like
a thrill of satisfaction as the rampage runs higher. I say this with some
hesitation, thinking it may be misinterpreted, and I probably wouldn't
say it had I not so often observed the "look" in people's eyes when catas-
trophes strike. I think this has less than nothing to do with a lack of
fellow-feeling for the victims. It is not a form of morbidity, or something
one desires at the expense of others, but what I take to be a craving for
full-bore astonishment. I cite it here as the source and pattern of many
of our dreams, including fantastic vistas, "emerald" cities, Turneresque
landscapes and seascapes, and some Titanic dreams which inspire the
"oceanic" feeling of all-in-oneness. It rises, as Kant would say of the
terrible sublime, from the absence of risk to the beholder and the possibility of experiencing what is so absent from daily life: a participation in

the overwhelming spectacle of nature gone wild. More personally, while sitting on my back deck I sometimes look at the ridge line of the Santa Inez Mountains directly behind my house and I imagine the gigantic oval of a gray spaceship appearing, in a slow silent progress, gradually blanketing the sky; and all its splendid ventral details (hatches, ladders, tubular ducts, struts, windows, catwalks, weaponry, stabilizers, the bubbles of communication ports, sensor systems) unfolding before my eyes, all the things that made the movie *2001* such a feast for the eye. I hope that the spaceship will be friendly, of course. But friendly or no, the extremity of such an event is what I crave. Beneath such fascination is what we may call the lure of apocalypse, a vision of which terminates what is perhaps the world's greatest book of stories. All stories strive for their own version of apocalypse, which is to say, for the most extreme, all-encompassing event on which to end, and to this end the movie version will invariably enlist a two-hundred-piece orchestra to help the audience over the emotional summit of the experience.

On the other, unsublime (or ridiculous) end of the scale, let us take the relatively common indoor dream in which you find yourself in your underwear (if that) at a party. What sort of "generic" experience is this dream made of? I take it as a commonplace that parties, like sublime landscapes, present certain potential dangers: for example, the possibility that no one will want to talk to you and you will feel "naked" in your isolation. Parties bristle with opportunities to make a fool of oneself. For example, consider the anxiety you feel in arriving at a party and discovering that you are inappropriately dressed: all the men seem to be wearing ties except you. What I do in such cases is to look around frantically hoping to find other men who are tieless as well, then join them, or stand near them so that attention will be deflected away from me. Here are at least two more behavioral "cassettes" which we might express as proverbs: "Misery loves company" and "There is safety in numbers."

Proverbs aren't really plots or narratives in themselves, but they are closely linked to plots. Proverbs, as Kenneth Burke has put it, are strategies for dealing with social situations, and situations are the basis of literary fictions. Literary works, Burke says, are therefore "proverbs writ large" (1957, 256). To put it another way, literary works, like dreams, are made of plots, and every plot attracts a school of proverbs, like pilotfish attending a shark. So proverbs are really attitudinal structures referring to the dangers and rewards of scripted life and, as such, there are hosts of proverbs for every conceivable situation. If you look at the headings under which books of proverbs arrange their contents, you will find proverbs for regret, grief, success, quarreling, forgiveness, fear, envy, danger, cruelty, evil, lust, courage, ambition. If we do it, feel it, or think it, there is a proverb for it; in fact, there is even an old proverb that supports the point—"Proverbs are the children of experience"—and one might easily amend it to read, "Dreams are the children of experience." As such, a proverb is a thematic category, not an action in itself but a direct presentation of an attitude toward action. A proverb, one might say, is at once an attitude and an incipient story structure.

Of course, I don't mean that proverbs themselves figure in dreams. I mean that the attitudes out of which proverbs arise, as a genre of waking literature, are the same attitudes that form the spine of dreams and fictions. So dreams are dramatizations of attitudes, or children of experience, and this is the sense in which the structures on which dreams play themselves out are "stored" in memory, *like* cassettes but *not as* cassettes. I should add that I am referring here to purely descriptive proverbs rather than to admonitory or moralistic ones, or the kind that are embroidered and hung on walls. That is, I speak of proverbs that describe the world as it is, rather than as it should or should not be. Dreams, for the most part, have little to do with recommending or criticizing forms of behavior; they simply display the behavior, whatever it may be, without editorial comment, just as good fiction does. A theme, in short, is not a thesis. I'm not suggesting that a dream couldn't urge you to do one thing instead of another, but there is no guarantee that it is the right thing or that it won't strike you as stupid when you wake up and think about it.

To come back to the party dream, it is unlikely that anyone would ever get caught wearing only underwear or, even worse, being completely in the nude at a party, but nakedness in dreams can be accounted for by a common syndrome sometimes called catastrophic expectancy, or the merciless aptitude of the dream to take your dream-plight as far as possible—a milder form of apocalypse. This is also our old friend MM, or maximization of magnitude (see chapter 6). In short, we create a worst-case scenario—or worst-case script—for every situation with a potential loss or danger because, as Murphy's proverb runs, "If anything can go wrong, it will." So the high incidence of nudity at dream-parties can be explained, in part at least, as the classic worst-case scenario, or the maximal form of paranoiac exposure (unless, of course, you happen to be a nudist). Indeed, what is paranoia but the maximization of a psychic magnitude called insecurity?

Anyway, dreams seem to have a knack for perfecting the negative possibilities of a situation. Trying to back up a car in a dream is almost guaranteed to bring on defective brakes or paralyzed feet; looking for a bathroom is either futile or will produce one located at the end of a narrow, steamy, low-ceilinged hall awash with contamination, the toilet already in use, unusable, out of order, or piled high with a "museum of human excrement" (Freud, 1900, 5:469). Then there is a whole class of dreams we might refer to as enigma variations, which are masterpieces of the MM principle. These are existential dreams in the sense of being *de trop.* They are dreams of the body, of the habits of being, of frustration and confinement to helpless repetition, and the stubbornness and materiality of the things that surround us and refuse to behave as we would like. They are what Francis Bacon spent his life painting, and God help him if he dreamed the experience as often as he painted it. There is no getting out of the rhythm of such a dream, whose musical equivalents are Ravel's *Bolero* and *The Little Drummer Boy.* The reason for the rigidity of the enigma dream, of course, is that the rhythm, or the structure, is what is really on the dreamer's mind—that is, the *impossibility* of the thing getting done, whatever it may be.

In short, dreams, like fictions, are made out of universal concerns and situations, which is to say that they rely on scripts and subscripts for their structure. However bizarre dreams may become, their logic and believability, the very fabric of their probability, has to do with their being modeled on standard structures one doesn't need to remember because they are all we know how to do, rather like riding a bicycle — or, to come back to my lightning analogy, they are the line of least resistance between an attitude, or a feeling, and a behavioral embodiment of that attitude. What makes our nakedness completely believable in a dream is not some failure of a proper sense of waking probability that comes with the dream state but rather that nudity coincides perfectly with a certain emotional probability, or what feelings go with what sorts of experience. Because the content of dreams is clearly related to the mood of the dreamer, particularly on the unhappy or disturbing end of the scale, it would seem plausible that it is this emotional probability that the dream remembers, rather than, say, physical or causal probabilities. In short, if I feel like flying in a dream, I can fly. So our paranoia, which is a powerful global feeling, needs a host, an experience to feast on, and it isn't particular about plausibility. This is why it is possible to fall passionately in love with a donkey in a dream: it isn't the object that is the source of believability but the structure of an emotion attaching itself to the nearest object at hand.

Do our dreams, then, follow scripts borrowed from waking life? My response to the question is yes, but that dreams are not obliged to stay with a script that brought them to the party, as we tend to do in waking life. Indeed, one might hypothesize that *most* of our dreams are concerned with *the friction caused by having to follow scripts so rigidly in daily life.* It is not a question of a restaurant dream following the restaurant script in which you come in, sit down, order, eat, pay, and leave, in that sequence. It is hard to see what could be the point of having such a dream, unless you happened to get hungry in your dream and just popped into a restaurant. In any case, anything can happen in a restaurant, but whatever happens will be based on a script of some sort. And this is true of the dream as well. For example, David Foulkes offers a hypothetical dream of someone being served rocks in a restaurant as an illustration of how dreams violate scripts (1985, 169). The waiter puts a plate in front of you and there they are, broiled rocks, hardly what you ordered. This makes perfect dream-sense, but note what happens next in Foulkes's hypothetical dream: the dreamer and the waiter immediately go off into the mountains to look for more rocks, and they end up in an old cave where they find a small child with a dog. Why this sequence? Well, here are two more scripts, spinning directly off the broiled rocks script: the old prospector script, followed by the lost child script (which goes all the way back to baby Moses in the bullrushes). How do we get from one to the other?

We can never know the answer to that question because it lies in the reaches of private associational memory. In fact, we might ask why Foulkes thought of being served rocks as opposed to, say, slices of bass fiddle with string spaghetti, in which case the waiter and the dreamer might have gone off to a concert. One possibility is that there are salient metaphorical connections between rocks and chunks of meat, not to mention baked potatoes which look (and sometimes taste) like rocks. I don't know if that's what brought on Foulkes's rocks, but one can explain such a shift as arising because one thought pattern has been replaced by a stronger one. Anyway, I can't conceive of a shift from one narrative to another that wouldn't be aroused by some incipient desire or ambivalence, and the resultant sequence of events would derive from a script that would serve as host to that desire.

So scripts compete with scripts, just as they do in literature, and in life. Just as every proverb has its antithesis ("Repentance comes too late" versus "Never too late to mend"), so for every script there is an antiscript or a deviant script. And what would happen if you, as dreamer, couldn't make up your mind in a dream whether you wanted to follow a certain script from life or rebel against it? Here we are back to the problem of ambivalence, and of course the dream would get all confused and be at war with itself, temporarily, until the strongest script won. The dream would be like Hamlet—tossed between at least two scripts (vengeance versus hesitations about vengeance) and unable to make up its mind which one to follow, so it follows both (in a devious way). And so it is with all literary works, each of which is based on an interplay of scripts, a conflict of scripts, or a violation of scripts. Even violations of scripts are themselves scripted because although it is true that "there are many ways to skin a cat," there is also "nothing new under the sun": there is no form of rebellion that hasn't already been worn into a cowpath by script violators from Adam and Eve to Madonna. The sad truth is that you can't walk into a room without being scripted for behavior of some sort, simply because the self is, in great part, a product of the social process.

I once suggested this idea in a classroom and aroused considerable skepticism from students who resented the idea that there was no room for human freedom of thought and action in my theory. The students were right to complain because I hadn't made sufficiently clear that scripts, as Roger Schank has said, are also "capable of self-modification" (1986, 11). That is, even though we have learned everything we know and do through social practice, each of us does it somewhat differently, and as we mature or meet frustration and impasses we change our scripts to adapt to our psychic needs. The point stands, however, that we are still following a script: though individuals, societies, and species (DNA being the master script) modify their behavioral scripts to accommodate a changing world, they remain scripts even so, and if this were not the case the life of the species—any species—would quickly degenerate into chaos.

One might ask why, if we can allow such things as "cassette" dream instructions, there can be no undreamed cassette dreams. In neuronal terms, is one more difficult or more elaborate than the other? If one, why not the other? My answer is that the cassette theory has not yet established the specific usefulness of a collection of dreams, as yet unexperienced by the dreamer, much less the purpose of avoiding dream presentation, which has strong precedents in the daydream and in the mentation that occurs in reading fiction, where images are continually cast up from the words. Moreover, it isn't clear how feeling and emotion could play a part in undreamed dreams, as they do in dreamed dreams. Most of all, it is hard to imagine what the brain might be up to in storing undreamed dreams, whereas scripts are simply another form of mapping and categorizing experience, which is the brain's constant project. There is also the problem of the inflow of new concerns and preoccupations that outdate the old stored cassette dreams (are the cassettes then revised?), and so on. What we know about imaginative compositions, if not all thought processes, is that they are "transformational rather than replicative" (Edelman, 1987 265); it is a self-reactionary and self-repairing process that "weaves back and forth," as Dennett writes in *Consciousness Explained,* "between centrally generated expectations, on the one hand, and confirmations (and disconfirmations) arising from the periphery on the other hand" (1991, 12). In my own terms it is a weaving back and forth between socially given scripts, on one hand, and the unique materials cast up moment by moment in the dream images, on the other.

All of this comes perilously close to a tautology, rather like saying that the source of experience is experience itself. But we tend to neglect the relationship between dreams and social experience, just as it is said that fish will be the last to think about the water they live in. I doubt if anyone wonders how it is that you are able to ride a bicycle in a dream — you just get on and ride, but riding a bicycle in a dream is only an elementary variation of the dream script in which you ride it to your own funeral. Scripts, one might say, are the algebra or grammar of narrative organization: the stored "cassettes" from which all dreams necessarily derive. If this is true, we might take a step toward demystifying the creative process by seeing it as a complex act of *remembrance of things learned.* Since French physician Nicholas Vaschide in the nineteenth century, it has been a commonplace to say that the dreamer plays all the roles in a dream: prisoner, judge, lawyer, jury, and executioner. In a certain sense, this is true. But notice that even Vaschide's metaphor constitutes a script we might call the crime-and-punishment script, which precedes whatever personal drama the dreamer eventually puts into it.

To put it more specifically, behind Kafka's *Trial,* which is based partially on Kafka's dreams, is the waking world of social and parental accusation and judgment that gave Kafka his bad dreams in the first place— a vicious hermeneutic circle in which we pass from waking experience to dreams to art without any fundamental change in structure. So what I'm trying to describe is not simply a tautology but what we might call a psychic Möbius strip in which the same structures provide the vitality for life in the waking and the dream worlds, primarily because they are the only structures available to the order-prone mind.

The Death of the Finch

I shall proceed to choose out one of my own dreams and demonstrate upon it my method of interpretation. In the case of every such dream some remarks by way of preamble will be necessary.—And now I must ask the reader to make my interests his own for quite a while, and to plunge, along with me, into the minutest details of my life; for a transference of this kind is preemptorily demanded by our interest in the hidden meaning of dreams.

—Freud, *The Interpretation of Dreams* (1900, 4:105–06)

h o p e   t h a t   t h e reader will take my invocation of one of Freud's most famous passages as intending no similarity to my own business in this chapter beyond the procedural one. What follows is an attempt to conclude my discussion, as Freud begins his, through the example of a personal "specimen" dream that involves, if not "the minutest details of my life," at least some of my deepest feelings. The meaning of my dream, however, is not "hidden" but very clear, at least emotionally, though I am well aware that others, holding different views about such things as symbolism, meaning, censorship, and interpretation, might find other meanings of other kinds, or contest my own from other points of view. But, in my belief, meaning is not something arrived at or produced, and above all it is not something that is translatable into terms other than those of the original experience. You can't extract the meaning of Hamlet's "To be or not to be, that is the question" by saying that Hamlet is tossed between the alternatives of life and death. You can say that, obviously, and be perfectly right within certain semantic limits, but I doubt that anyone would be moved, or fixed, by a Hamlet who said, "I've been thinking about suicide of late. It's a big question." Nor, to take a still deeper "plunge" into the subtext, can you exhaust Hamlet by saying that he is tossed between killing his uncle and symbolically killing his father who stands between him and his mother—one possible meaning of Hamlet, among several million. It is precisely the *tossing* that has meaning, that fixes us, and to a great extent what is being tossed about in the line is a certain sonorous embodiment of indecision, the very music of indecision, or what Yeats called the thinking of the body. Meaning is something undergone *in* experience and therefore something that is invariably diminished by the conversions of conceptual interpretation, which invariably cause one to see a particular tree in a forest at the cost of losing the forest itself (see Macherey, 1978; Gendlin, 1982; States, 1993, 140-85). Richard Jones makes this point nicely: "Interpretations of the product (the work of art) are often used to analyze the processes assumed to have been involved in its creation. Whatever the usefulness of such interpretations, the result is often to prevent one from really experiencing the work of art in terms of its own system of meanings" (1974, 156-57). This is broadly the sense of Rudolf Arnheim's belief that "The work of art does not ask for meaning; it contains it" (1974, 55). Speaking conservatively, this is doubly true of dreams, if only because of the inevitable obscurity of personal "systems of meaning" that are based on a unique lifetime of experience. In any case, meaning—or at least conceptual meaning—has not been my preoccupation in this book, however appropriate it is to the psychoanalytic endeavor. My concern, rather—to return to my opening—is "the transit of waking experience into dreams, and secondarily . . . the relationship between dreams and fictions"—considering fictions, as always, as dreams in street clothing, or dreams as naked fictions, and considering both not as systems of signification but as systems of involuntary expressiveness.

By way of preamble, I begin with a boyhood memory. One afternoon, when I was eight or nine and living in the village of Albion just outside Punxsutawney, Pennsylvania, it came to pass (and not for the first time) that I threw a large rock at a robin foraging too busily in my backyard. To my utter shock the rock struck the bird squarely on the back, and in a quivering instant the robin was dead. What I remember of the feeling produced by this event is a sense of shame, terrible immediate guilt, confusion, and possibly, just possibly, a rudimentary tincture of the most profound of all emotions—grief—which I could not yet have known at first hand. I would guess that that part of the feeling, unless I am misremembering it, could be best described as the emotional foundation out of which grief arises, something necessary to know in order to feel grief, but not grief itself. To me grief is the strangest of the so-called base-level emotions, primarily because it runs the scale from violence to torpor. The precondition for it is love or a strong affectional value placed on something or someone, and this was certainly not the case with the robin. Simply put, grief is the overwhelming awareness of loss, but more complexly it is the result of one's discovery that time flows in one direction only, a truth that is normally masked by the animation with which everything living continues to remain itself. For everything that is valued is valued as a sort of instant history of itself: Mother is always dependably Mother, summer is always a time when there is no school, the robin dependably hops in furious bursts over the lawn (and is therefore very hard to hit with a rock or a slingshot), and so on. All things continue to be themselves, and thanks to this wonderful persistence there is a fair amount of security in life. The cancer of grief finds its natural host in this all too vulnerable zone of comfort, and at the highest possible stake. For once life is out of a living thing it cannot be called back, and in that realization the tranquility of a lifetime of safety is temporarily shattered and permanently put on notice. I threw the rock, thoughtlessly, at a creature I neither resented nor understood and had my first exquisite awareness of how the value of all things rides on the current of an indifferent causal order.

During the seven weeks in April and May 1994 when my sister, Lois was dying in Monterey, I had no dreams about her or about anything I can construe as being related to the likelihood of losing her. I don't know why this was the case, but it leads to an interesting speculation, made in fact by Freud (1900, 4:18), that dreams do not haul coal to Newcastle; that is, they are somehow guided by a principle of clemency or, more realistically, redundancy: the sponge stops absorbing water when it is full, too much is too much, there is no need to dream about grief in the midst of grief, and so on. There is a good deal of research to the contrary, suggesting that dreams are either direct or displaced reflections of our problems and moods, and my own dreams bear this out on a regular basis. However, I am referring mainly to situations of what we may call higher magnitude, and the period of my sister's long coma and death was one of the highest magnitude I have ever endured. Such situations, in my experience, find their way into dreams only gradually, if at all, and it may be that the magnitude of the situation insulates us from the additional pain of a dream, somewhat as shock temporarily insulates the body against pain following an extreme insult. There is probably no dependable theory one can sort out, but for the most part dreams seem to concentrate on more common sorts of frustration or desire, like getting lost in the city or solving a problem left dangling from the day. This was a fact noticed by psychologists even before Freud, who made it into the most famous and enduring theory of dreams: that these trivial images were only the censored displacements of the real problems.

Despite all this, however, I couldn't help wondering about the absence of dreams of my sister during this period, and in an odd way, being a student of dreams, I was more than curious about the first dream in which she would appear. What would it be about? How would my dreamwork deal with her illness, and at length (when in the fifth week we learned it was inevitable) her death? To put it another way, how would I handle the occasion in this other reality that I inhabit nightly with such anticipation? As it turns out I didn't have long to wait. Two nights after her death, when I had returned to Santa Barbara from Monterey, I had a dream in which I was running along a path toward a house where some friends were having an afternoon gathering. All I remember about the foregoing part of the dream is that it was pleasantly social: people, activity, houses, open country, and so on, and I was joining the group with very positive expectations. Then suddenly, on a path parallel to my own, slightly below it, I saw a finch speeding along on the ground in the opposite direction, much like the Roadrunner in the cartoon. The finch was a brilliant green-yellow color, as delicate as a Christmas ornament, and it seemed mechanically propelled. Inexplicably, I found a large pebble in my hand and I tossed it back over my head, almost aimlessly, in the bird's direction. No sooner was the pebble in flight than I conceived the consequence, and I shouted, "No!" But the bird was already squeaking aloud in pain; the pebble had cleanly severed one of its wings and it was vainly flapping the other wing in a pathetic effort to right itself. I now saw that the bird was made of flesh and that there was no undoing the damage I had done. It was an unbearable moment. I began to howl, and I felt precisely what I had felt two days earlier at the hospital during the final twenty minutes of Lois's life.

Before this dream, I had not thought about the robin incident for many years, but it came back to me the instant I woke up, almost before the dream had run its course. There, suddenly, was the dead robin, exhumed from memory intact, as if it had been waiting all this time for the occasion to reappear. If I held any beliefs of the sort, I would say it was taking its revenge. In any case, it took only a moment more to relate the dream to my sister's death. Here, then, was the first dream. She hadn't appeared in it, but beyond any doubt the three things were inescapably fused—the robin, the finch, and my sister (wreathed in birds), all condensed into a dream whose actual "plot" bore no similarity to my experience at the hospital. But, as Freud often said, the only trustworthy things about our dreams, beyond the dreaming itself, are what we think and say about them when we wake up. I'm not sure I believe this, but I am also not sure that the dream is over when you wake up. So we have here a kind of classic dream problem: Why the "displacement"? What was the finch doing in my dream? Why should I not have dreamed directly of my sister? Or of a robin? And what has the death of my sister—if all this is plausible—to do with both bird incidents provoking all this guilt and shame?

To look at the latter question first (because it interests me the least): I think the element of guilt has rather conventional origins in this case. I felt no guilt for my sister's death in the sense of the direct responsibility I plainly bore in the case of the robin incident and the finch dream. Lois has been one of the strongest forces in my life; we have had a kind of "siamese" intimacy ever since I was born—the date happened to be her tenth birthday—and proceeding through scores of long letters written during periods of separation. This culminated in her gift of a photo album of my "Life and Times" in 1989, in which the opening sentence of her introduction reads: "When you came into my life on my very own tenth birthday, it was required that I keep track of you." Still, even in such positive cases, guilt—survivor guilt it is called—finds its natural place in the death vigil. One of the feelings I steadily experienced during my time at the hospital arose from the simple truth that *my sister* was doing the dying, not I, and in the presence of such a devastating event, one feels a kind of dumb shame at being free to come and go, to breathe unfrantically, to pass the time by talking, pacing, reading a book, or taking a lunch break in the cafeteria, and even the luxury of boredom. Add to this the obvious sense of helplessness, which expresses itself in continual efforts to make the dying one more comfortable, to fluff the pillow, cool the brow, sponge the lips, or to spend long hours in the attitude of vigil, beyond any practical use (other than "being there"), and to bring one's thoughts always, always, back to the grim business of dying, following, say, an interval of family levity (a curious feature of the death vigil is the number of jokes that are told). In short, it seems wrong to carry on normally, though the wrongness has nothing to do with responsibility. It has rather to do with the luck of the draw. And then there is probably an overlay of personal regret at all the past insufficiencies (the disagreements, neglects, things promised but left undone) and the feeling that things could always have been better between us, or that I might have appreciated her more, had there been time when I wasn't so busy, and of course now the time has run out. So: guilt feeds on guilt. Anyway, all of these thoughts, fleeting or otherwise, are there in different ways and different proportions, I suppose, in each watcher. They are coaxed out of us by the extremity of the event itself which of course allows generous time for retrospection, none for alteration. And over all else there is the unanswerable authority visible only in the damage being done before our eyes: death, being our only true experience of apocalypse, sweeps everything (including jokes) into its process, as into the funnel of a maelstrom. If there is any connection between the finch dream and the hospital scene, beyond the emotional consequence, it probably lies along some such lines. If there is more, I don't want to know about it.

Thinking about all this now from some emotional distance, I find other questions more interesting: why the displacement in the dream from my sister to the green finch? Why did I not simply dream of my sister (as my niece Leslie had the night before her mother's death)? Had the dream repressed its true content and offered a "compromise formation"? I don't know that psychoanalysis would suggest this as the cause of the displacement. But it is the logical place to begin: if one assumes that something should otherwise have appeared, is there not reason to suspect it has been repressed?

This idea seems to me completely wrong, as my reader will have gathered by now. I have never put much stock in the notion that dreams are repressive mechanisms. My own experience suggests that dreams are more likely to undo the tapestries of repression that we weave so successfully during the day. Or to put it in a more neutral light: dreams are indifferent to barriers we erect around unpleasant or fearful thoughts. Of course, psychiatrists would probably want to know what business I had in saying what I have and haven't repressed. But, more specifically, I am unable to see that much has been repressed, assuming we think of repression as the censorship of unpleasant or violent *feelings,* as opposed to unpleasant images. In a certain sense, one might say that the actual image of my sister had been repressed, but this assumes that the dream was about my sister rather than about something else. The feeling of grief was certainly not repressed, and if not the feeling, why its object? How could dreaming of the object (my sister) have made the feeling even more painful, or dreaming about the finch less painful than it might otherwise have been? Pain is pain. So if I hadn't dreamed of my sister I certainly experienced, or *re*-experienced, the full emotional effect of her death, and what can be the difference, as I immediately made the connection upon waking? Indeed, so clear was the connection to me, on emerging from the dream into the hypnopompic state, that it seems academic to separate the dream from the waking realization.

Why, then, the finch? To trace this image to a possible source, one would have to know more about thinking and consciousness than we are likely to know for a long time. What is missing from most dream interpretation, in my view, is a sense of the complexity of mind environment, the inexhaustibility of the sources of mental imagery, and the very good possibility that a dream is a confluence of energies far more diverse than any analysis could possibly determine—indeed, as complicated as consciousness itself. I suspect that dreams are more like telephone trunk lines, over which many messages are passing simultaneously, than a simple telephone conversation. Overall, I suppose one might claim that the image of the finch, like the flying birds in one of the dreams Freud treats, captures a certain quality of the death experience, the flight of life from the body metaphorically equated with the loss of the finch's wing and its certain death. But this seems suspiciously like "poetic" thinking which attributes to the dream an interest in nuance of the sort that delights us in art, as if dreams had the time or inclination to conjure effective metaphors to please the waking. As I have suggested in the foregoing pages, I can see no evidence for dreams indulging in such elegant symbolism. For one thing, there is no need for symbols of this sort in dreams: dreams deal in equivalencies and resemblances, not in disguises, and if these turn out to be amenable to symbolic analysis in the literary or psychoanalytic sense of the term, that is something the dream could not care less about.

I think the finch got into the dream on very different grounds. For one thing, the finch was a small section in a series of more or less pleasant dreams of the same night that had to do with a number of people and interconnected places. I have forgotten the other particulars (and this in itself removes any hope of a clear explanation), but the finch came into the dream only as I was running along the path. It, too, was running (not flying) along the path, but in the opposite direction. However, it turns out that there is something like a smoking gun that might more directly account for the finch: within the very week of the dream one of our cats had brought a freshly killed bird into the living room. If this sounds like solid evidence for the finch's presence on the scene, I must add that this is an all too frequent occurrence, it being our fate to enjoy both birds and cats who do not enjoy one another. Still, it is one possibility. But finding a dead finch from a recent day residue doesn't solve the problem of the relation of the finch to my sister's death. I think the problem comes in treating the finch as a displacement, rather than as an image in its own right.

My own guess is that the dream was no more about my sister's death than it was about the death of the finch. This argument has nothing to do with a priority of values but with what I take to be the conditions under which dreams select and combine images and thoughts. If there is a latent content beneath the dream it is the total emotional history I have only partially outlined here, though in the interest of simplicity it does seem plausible that the finch, having arrived on the scene through whatever provocation, then served as the trip-switch and conductor of an emotional excess that had charged my life in recent weeks. It is very likely that this "excess" had no place to cathect itself (as Freud would say) in this particular dream prior to the finch's appearance. But once it entered the dream the finch must somehow have revived a memory of the robin episode, and suddenly from the finch came the pebble, from the pebble the disaster, and from the disaster the reprise of my grief.[1]

---

1. The finch dream has an unusual and rather puzzling sequel. Three days after the first anniversary of my sister's death, approximately the same interval as the finch dream, I had a dream—again, a fragment—in which I was crossing a large parking lot to join some relatives and friends. On the asphalt I saw a rabbit, lying face upward with its paws in the air. Its mouth was open wide and it was gasping for air, clearly suffering the late stages of dying. I stopped and looked more closely into its mouth, whereupon I realized that its internal organs were being slowly liquified. The back of its throat was yellow and hard and resembled the inside of a segmented lobster tail. Feeling a powerful urge to put it out of its misery, I looked around for a rock or a board, but found nothing. Then I realized with a shudder that I was incapable of killing it. I felt shame at my cowardice and I stood there, unable to move in either direction, until I awoke.

The day residue behind this dream, as nearly as I can make out, is as follows. I had telephoned my relatives in Monterey on the anniversary of my sister's

The one certainty about dreams is that the feelings always get through cleanly, though they may be attached to objects and creatures that have little connection, symbolic or otherwise, to the feeling's probable sources. This is even the case with ambivalent feelings: however complex or self-contradictory, they are finally clean feelings, since the confusion of contradiction is a feeling in its own right. So what we have is seeming distortion and confusion on the level of the image, and absolute clarity on the level of the emotion—insofar as emotions can be

---

death; a few days earlier my wife and I were commenting on a *Newsweek* article on the Ebola virus raging in Zaire. What struck us was that the virus literally liquifies the internal organs of its victim. The day before the dream I had talked with a landscape architect about my gopher problem, and he told me of a case in which the trap had not succeeded in killing a gopher and he found it necessary to "put it out of its misery." This story recalled a recent episode in which one of the cats brought a live gopher into the house; I forced it into a shoebox we keep on hand for visiting lizards and birds, took it into the backyard, and released it. It then occurred to me then that I had added one more gopher to the ever-growing community that was slowly devastating our garden.

All of these things come together in the rabbit dream. Once again, my sister does not appear in the dream except in the powerful impression of death-in-progress and its most striking feature, the gradual deoxygenization of the body and the hardening of the throat cavity and tongue—all of which was so painful to watch in my sister's case. I had no thoughts of my sister during the dream, but on waking (again) I immediately made the connection.

Such a thing has never happened in my dream life and I have thought that it may, after all, have been pure coincidence. On balance, what are the odds of having a second dream about a dying animal, with attendant details and affects that duplicate each other, virtually one year to the day after the first? What has probably happened here is a case of "fearful symmetry" of the two situations. The anniversary of my sister's death, the telephone call, and my personal recollection of the hospital scene precisely one year later at 11:20 A.M., May 27, 1995, must have set in motion a reprise of the finch dream under altered circumstances. In a manner of speaking it was the same dream, revised to include "updated" day residue from recent experience. And there is a small marvel: dreams, apparently, have work to do, like the grass in Carl Sandburg's poem, and the work must have something to do with bringing the past into the present.

I should add that during the year following her death I had only two dreams in which my sister appears. In both she was alive and well.

called clear. All of which leads me to suspect that my finch was not a surrogate or a displacement of my sister, but a *variation,* and that her death, crass as it may seem to say it, was a variation of the robin incident in the backyard fifty-five years earlier. What I mean is that dreams are not about things, events, or people; they are, to the best of our knowledge, about emotions and attitudes, which have a certain structure and portability. Emotions are timeless: they survive their occurrence in specific events and they are subject to re-arousal.

Yes, you might say, but our emotions are never free-floating; they are always fused with things, events, and people. One does finally care more about one's sister than about a finch. This argument misses a possibility that seems to me borne out of the finch dream. It was not necessary that I dream of my sister in order to express what her death meant to me emotionally. There is a sense in which dreaming of a green finch or dreaming of my sister comes to the same end. But what her death meant to me, the terrible grief of the event, was inextricably mixed with the death of the robin, the deaths (in due course) of my grandfather and my father and mother, various aunts and uncles, my boyhood friend John at the age of forty-five, several colleagues and friends over the years, the deaths of a series of spoiled and much-loved cats, the death of a nine-year-old boy I had never met who was killed while playing on a neighboring street, and so on. To put all these griefs together, irrespective of species or closeness of relationship, is not to devalue any of them in the least. Among many other things, I am a history of grieving, and no single grief can be isolated or finally distinguished from other griefs, though some griefs are easier to bear and more short-lived than others. In short, to embody the affect of grief in an image is to open the whole box of one's accumulated grief. What emerges, then, is not grief only for this or that, but Grief incarnate in a single image—grief that death is the terminus of all experience.

I would like to examine this idea somewhat less analytically by looking briefly at the relationship of dreams and art as two things the human mind does with its stored experience. The common denominator is that in our encounter with both art and dreams we are often moved to powerful emotions. Emotions aroused by art are often called fictional emotions, a woefully misleading term. It doesn't mean that the emotions are false, or partial, or illusory in the sense that they don't genuinely affect the nervous system to the point of real tears, laughter, or anger. It means only that the characters, events, or images that provoke them are themselves unreal, and therefore that beyond the emotion there is always the awareness that the stakes are also unreal. This is what makes it possible to enjoy painful emotions aroused by works of art, though the same emotion caused by an event in daily life might be unbearable. So art offers a built-in circuit regulator whereby the quality of the emotion is purely felt but its empirical grounding is shunted off onto impersonal soil and compromised, a little as our concern for aerialists is compromised by their performing over a net. The emotions aroused by dreams are obviously not of this kind, as there is no dream awareness that what is happening isn't really happening. The episode of the finch was as real and emotionally intense as the death of my sister, though hardly as prolonged. For dreams contain still another kind of circuit regulator or, more properly, a circuit breaker: when the emotion becomes unmanageable, the dream awakens us and we realize that "it was all a dream"—in short, a self-created fiction.

As an illustration, for me one of the most moving passages in poetry is the line King Lear speaks over the body of his daughter Cordelia at the end of the play. It doesn't evoke its proper feeling out of the flow of the play, but for the record it reads: "Thou'lt come no more,/Never, never, never, never, never." It is probably not an accident that I should choose a passage that was an expression of grief, grief being the most moving emotion in real life and therefore one of the most moving emotions that can be produced by art. The truth is, for decades I've recited this line aloud while driving or pacing the floor in a frustrated effort to see how such simplicity can bear so much emotional weight. It has much to do with the weak quality of the verb *come,* which works in the line much as *be* works in Hamlet's "To be or not to be," as opposed to some firmer or more edgy verb like *live* or *exist.* It carries the weight of all the ways in which a loved person or thing *comes* to us. Finally, there is the incomparable redundancy of the *nevers,* the five coffin nails, as I call them, about which I will say no more, except that they are an unpassable trap for bad actors.

All of this is so much lit crit, and I go into it here with some reservation and hope that it won't be taken in that vein. I don't know what makes the line so clean and unimprovable, but over the years it has become an important part of the history of grief I've been speaking about here. And it was these words I spoke to myself in a barely audible voice at my sister's bedside just before the end. My God, you may think, don't critics ever stop? My only defense is that I am not a religious person and it was the best in the way of prayer I could manage; it came to me as naturally in the hospital as the Twenty-third Psalm came to my brother-in-law, Mel, who was standing next to me, and as easily as I believe the finch came to me in my dream. The experiences are different in many ways, but I think that all of them illustrate a deep creatural need to put any strong experience into its broadest possible dimensions (another variation of the maximization of magnitude principle.) For instance, it is quite noticeable that a death vigil is imbued with the kind of economy that you find in poetry. There is (dare I say it?) a certain beauty in the spareness of the proceedings, in the mannerisms of people, their movements, voice patterns and levels, all owing perhaps to the profound inappropriateness of excess, noise, and the random, and especially to the unrelieved focus of the occasion. Is this simply respect for Death? Or has it to do with the need to throw against Death what equivalence one can muster? In the face of death, as Shakespeare's Count in *Measure for Measure* tells us, we must be absolute, free from relativity and specification; we must be, for the moment, conditionless. Language is the opposite of these things, except for the language of poetry, which is sprung free somehow of the business of fussing about *things.* Moreover, I suspect that the prayers people speak in the presence of death belong as much to the province of poetry as to religion. To put it another way, prayer has as much to do with the metrical qualities of poetry ("The Lord is my shepherd . . .") as it does with the respect for the deity. And the chief service that poetry and prayer perform is to put some order, balance, and beauty on an otherwise unmanageable experience.

Finally, to return to my finch and *King Lear,* what to make, if anything, of the fact that at the head of this same scene, as they are being led off to prison, Lear compares Cordelia and himself to two birds in a cage? I don't know what possible connection this remote image has with the finch of my dream. It sounds to me ingenious and I'm not trying to sneak it in under the cover of my own skepticism. But is it any more remote than my robin episode? It stands to reason that there is an order and priority in the selection process whereby the possible next image of the dream (or a poem) is brought forth from the deep well of associated memories. It stands to reason, too, that the dreaming brain discovers its images, unearths them suddenly, as opposed to having them all together beforehand, like pigments set out on a palette. For the peculiarity of the dream, as we have seen, is that it has no time to look for its images. In any case, I have no interest in interpreting my dream, or in pinning down its sources, only in understanding what may forever be beyond understanding: how that astonishing sequence of images came about, out of what close and distant grace notes of recall, how something of such magnitude as this grief can ride on the flow of such fragile connections. Is it possible that if the line "We two alone will sing like birds i' th' cage" were not in *King Lear,* or in my memory of *King Lear,* my dream might have been different—there might have been no finch?

There is one other example that seems to fit into this discussion by way of summary, and it enters this meditation for reasons that will be immediately apparent. One of my favorite poems is Richard Wilbur's "Death of a Toad," which reads as follows:

> A toad the power mower caught,
> Chewed and clipped of a leg, with a hobbling hop has got
> To the garden verge, and sanctuaried him

Under the cineraria leaves, in the shade
　　Of the ashen heartshaped leaves, in a dim,
　　　　Low, and a final glade.

The rare original heartsblood goes,
Spends on the earthen hide, in the folds and wizenings, flows
　　In the gutters of the banked and staring eyes. He lies
　　As still as if he would return to stone,
　　　　And soundlessly attending, dies
　　　　　　Toward some deep monotone,

Toward misted and ebullient seas
And cooling shores, toward lost Amphibia's emperies.
　　Day dwindles, drowning, and at length is gone
　　In the wide and antique eyes, which still appear
　　　　To watch, across the castrate lawn,
　　　　　　The haggard daylight steer. (1950, 40)

I have no idea what inspired Wilbur to write this poem, but we can be sure that he didn't record all this by objectively observing the behavior of a real dying toad. Like all poetry, it is infused with the poet's own soul; it is humanized, like the cloud in Shelley's poem. To my certain knowledge, I saw no such thing in the eye of the robin fifty-five years ago, lying "as still as if he would return to stone." But I see it now in my mind's eye, thanks to poems like Wilbur's and a considerable experience with death. So in a certain respect, one might say that the emotion is there, in the object before us, which we see through the eyes of the poet. But what I find so moving in the poem is not the humanization of the toad, Wilbur's seeing the toad as having "human" qualities, or our translation of the toad into a symbol of human death, but how much sympathy the poem arouses for something that is not of our kind. In short, the toad is not a metaphor; it is a toad, a creature with which we can have no vocal or emotional commerce, a lost amphibian eternally beyond our understanding. There is no way to know the toad. Yet the toad dies, *too*. The blood is spent, the breath comes in dwindling jerks, the same recognizable process of perdition. The feat of the poem is to allow us, in the only language humans can understand, to see in the toad the ontological kinship of all dying things. This is the point at which species becomes an unnecessary category, or perhaps the point where all species come together as part of the same predictable journey of the protoplasm. The emotion Wilbur evokes from this brief death in the grass could not have been stronger had it been the death of a son, a daughter, or (to come to my point) a sister. All poets know that the "object of imitation" is utterly beside the point. It is what is seen in the object and got out of it that matters. And though there are many other differences between poems and dreams, this much holds true for both. The "trivial" images of dreams are no less expressive than the trivial images of art. The difference between art and dream is that art requires a true poet who has the skill to put "the best words in the best order," in Coleridge's phrase, in order to release the feeling to a person who listens; the dream, having no business in pleasing anyone, has only to find an image into which the emotional life of the dreamer can settle its inexhaustible density. The image is finally a place where the many converge in the one, an object, as it were, without boundaries that extends inevitably to the very edge of memory. It seems to me, then, that we should not drive a wedge between the image and its emotional import by trying to make it more like us than it is like itself, or de-trivialize it by making it a symbol for something more important. This is why I believe that my dream is finally a dream about the death of a finch provoked by the fresh and as yet unsettled, undreamed memory of my sister's death. The two become confused, as well they should, for they are variations of the same loss, and loss is finally what it is all about.

Works Cited

Alquié, F. (1965). *The Philosophy of Surrealism.* Ann Arbor: University of Michigan Press.

Ammons, A. R. (1970). *Uplands.* New York: Norton.

Arcaya, Jose M. (1992). "Why Is Time Not Included in Modern Theories of Memory?" *Time and Society* 1 (no. 2), 301-14.

Aristotle. (1967). *Poetics.* Trans. Gerald F. Else. Ann Arbor: University of Michigan Press.

Arnheim, R. (1969). *Visual Thinking.* Berkeley and Los Angeles: University of California Press.

———. (1974) *Entropy and Art: An Essay on Disorder and Order.* Berkeley and Los Angeles: University of California Press.

Barrett, Deirdre. (1992). "Just How Lucid Are Lucid Dreams?" *Dreaming* 2 (no. 4), 221-28.

Blagrove, Mark. (1992a). "Scripts and the Structuralist Analysis of Dreams," *Dreaming* 2 (no. 1), 23-37.

———. (1992b). "Dreams as the Reflection of Our Waking Concerns and Abilities: A Critique of the Problem-Solving Paradigm in Dream Research," *Dreaming* 2 (no. 4), 205-20.

Bollas, Christopher. (1992). *Being a Character: Psychoanalysis and Self Experience.* New York: Hill and Wang.

Boss, M. (1977). *I Dreamt Last Night.* Trans. Steven Conway. New York: Gardner Press.

Boyd, Richard. (1986). "Metaphor and Theory Change: What Is 'Metaphor' a Metaphor For?" in *Metaphor and Thought.* Ed. Andrew Ortony. New York: Cambridge University Press, 356-408.

Büchner, Georg. (1977). *The Complete Collected Works.* Trans. and ed. Henry J. Schmidt. New York: Avon.

Burke, Kenneth. (1957). *The Philosophy of Literary Form: Studies in Symbolic Action.* Rev. ed. New York: Random House.

———. (1962). *A Grammar of Motives and a Rhetoric of Motives.* Cleveland and New York: World.

———. (1964). *Perspectives by Incongruity.* Ed. Stanley Edgar Hyman. Bloomington: Indiana University Press.

Carlson, Marvin. (1984). *Theories of the Theatre: A Historical and Critical Survey from the Greeks to the Present.* Ithaca and London: Cornell University Press.

Chuang-Tzu. (1974). *Chuang-Tzu: Inner Chapters.* Trans. Gia-Fu Feng and Jane English. New York: Random House.

Churchland, Paul M. (1995). *The Engine of Reason, the Seat of the Soul: A Philosophical Journey into the Brain.* Cambridge: MIT Press.

Crick, F., and G. Mitchison. (1986). "REM Sleep and Neural Nets," *Journal of Mind and Behavior* 7 (Spring-Summer), 229-49.

Damasio, Antonio R. (1994). *Descartes' Error: Emotion, Reason, and the Human Brain*. New York: Putnam.

Davies, Paul, and J. R. Brown, eds. (1993). *The Ghost in the Atom*. Cambridge and New York: Cambridge University Press.

Davies, Paul, and John Gribbin. (1992). *The Matter Myth: Dramatic Discoveries That Challenge Our Understanding of Physical Reality*. New York: Simon & Schuster.

Dawkins, Richard. (1989). *The Selfish Gene*. New edition. Oxford and New York: Oxford University Press.

———. (1992). *The Extended Phenotype: The Long Reach of the Gene*. Oxford and New York: Oxford University Press.

Dennett, Daniel C. (1977). "Are Dreams Experiences?" in *Philosophical Essays on Dreaming*. Ed. Charles E. M. Dunlop. Reprinted from *Philosophical Review* 85 (1976), 151-71.

———. (1988). "Where Am I?" in *The Mind's I: Fantasies and Reflections on Self and Soul*. Composed and arranged by Douglas R. Hofstadter and Daniel C. Dennett. New York: Bantam, 217-29.

———. (1991). *Consciousness Explained*. Boston: Little, Brown.

———. (1995). *Darwin's Dangerous Idea: Evolution and the Meanings of Life*. New York: Simon & Schuster.

Dixon, N. F. (1971). *Subliminal Perception: The Nature of a Controversy*. London: McGraw-Hill.

Eco, Umberto. (1984). *The Role of the Reader: Explorations in the Semiotics of Texts*. Bloomington: Indiana University Press.

———. (1994). *Six Walks in the Fictional Woods*. Cambridge: Harvard University Press.

Edelman, Gerald M. (1987). *Neural Darwinism: The Theory of Neuronal Group Selection*. New York: Basic Books.

———. (1989). *The Remembered Present: A Biological Theory of Consciousness*. New York: Basic Books.

———. (1992). *Bright Air, Brilliant Fire*. New York: Basic Books.

Edelson, Marshall. (1984). *Hypothesis and Evidence in Psychoanalysis*. Chicago and London: University of Chicago Press.

Emerson, Ralph Waldo. (1989). *The Critical Tradition: Classic Texts and Contemporary Trends*. Ed. David H. Richter. New York: St. Martin's Press.

Empson, William. (1949). *Seven Types of Ambiguity*. N.p.: New Directions.

Fosshage, James L. (1992). "The Psychological Function of Dreams: A Revised Psychoanalytic Perspective," in *Essential Papers in Dreams*. Ed. Melvin R. Lansky. New York and London: New York University Press, 249-71.

Foucault, Michel. (1973). *The Order of Things: An Archeology of the Human Sciences.* New York: Random House.

Foulkes, David. (1985). *Dreaming: A Cognitive-Psychological Analysis.* Hillsdale, N.J.: Erlbaum.

Fraser, J. T. (1990). *Of Time, Passion, and Knowledge: Reflections on the Strategy of Existence.* Princeton, N.J.: Princeton University Press.

Freud, Sigmund. (1900). *The Interpretation of Dreams. Standard Edition,* vols. 4 and 5. Ed. James Strachey. London: Hogarth.

Gackenbach, Jayne. (1991). "Frameworks for Understanding Lucid Dreaming: A Review," *Dreaming* 1 (no. 2), 109–28.

Gell-Mann, Murray. (1994). *The Quark and the Jaguar: Adventures in the Simple and the Complex.* New York: W. H. Freeman.

Gendlin, Eugene T. (1982). "Two Phenomenologists Do Not Disagree," in *Phenomenology: Dialogues and Bridges.* Ed. Ronald Bruzina and Bruce Wilshire. Albany: State University of New York Press, 321–35.

Globus, Gordon. (1987). *Dream Life, Wake Life: The Human Condition Through Dreams.* Albany: State University of New York Press.

Goffman, Erving. (1959). *The Presentation of Self in Everyday Life.* New York: Doubleday.

Gombrich, E. H. (1965). *Art and Illusion: A Study in the Psychology of Pictorial Representation.* New York: Pantheon.

Goodman, Nelson. (1978). *Ways of Worldmaking.* Indianapolis and Cambridge: Hackett.

Hall, Calvin. (1966). *The Meaning of Dreams.* New York: McGraw-Hill.

Hartmann, Ernest. (1984). *The Nightmare: The Psychology and Biology of Terrifying Dreams.* New York: Basic Books.

———. (1995). "Making Connections in a Safe Place: Is Dreaming Psychotherapy?" *Dreaming* 5 (no. 4), 213–28.

———. (1996). "An Outline for a Theory on the Nature and Functions of Dreaming," *Dreaming* 6 (no. 2), 149–72.

Heidegger, Martin. (1975). *Poetry, Language, Thought.* Trans. Albert Hofstadter. New York: Harper & Row.

Hernadi, Paul. (1972). *Beyond Genre: New Directions in Literary Classification.* Ithaca and London: Cornell University Press.

———. (1995). *Cultural Transactions: Nature, Self, Society.* Ithaca and London: Cornell University Press.

Hersh, Thomas R. (1995). "How Might We Explain the Parallels Between Freud's 1895 Irma Dream and His 1923 Cancer?" *Dreaming* 4 (no. 4), 267–87.

Hobson, J. Allan. (1988). *The Dreaming Brain.* New York: Basic Books.

———. (1994). *The Chemistry of Conscious States: How the Brain Changes Its Mind.* New York: Little, Brown.

Hobson, J. Allan, and David Kahn. (1993). "Self-Organization Theory of Dreaming," *Dreaming* 3 (no. 3), 151–78.

Hofstadter, Douglas R. (1980). *Gödel, Escher, Bach: An Eternal Golden Braid.* New York: Vintage Books.

Hubbard, Timothy L. (1994). "Random Cognitive Activation in Dreaming Does Not Require a Cartesian Theater," *Dreaming* 4 (no. 1), 255–66.

Humphrey, Nicholas. (1992). *A History of the Mind.* New York: HarperCollins.

Hunt, H. (1989). *The Multiplicity of Dreams: Memory, Imagination, and Consciousness.* New Haven and London: Yale University Press.

Jones, Richard M. (1974). *The New Psychology of Dreaming.* New York: Viking Press.

Jung, Carl G. (1974). *Dreams.* Trans. R. F. C. Hull. Princeton: Princeton University Press.

Koestler, Arthur. (1969). *The Act of Creation.* London: Macmillan.

Kramer, Milton. (1993). "The Selected Mood Regulatory Function of Dreaming: An Update and Revision," in *The Function of Dreaming.* Ed. A. Moffitt, M. Kramer, and R. Hoffmann. Albany: State University of New York Press, 139–95.

Kuiken, Don. (1995). "Dreams and Feeling Realization," *Dreaming* 5 (no. 3), 129–57.

LaBerge, Stephen, and Lynne Levitan. (1995). "Validity Established of Dream-Light Cues for Eliciting Lucid Dreaming," *Dreaming* 5 (no. 3), 159–68.

Laing, R. D. (1970). *The Divided Self: An Existential Study in Sanity and Madness.* London: Penguin.

Lansky, Melvin R. (1992). "Emerging Perspectives on the Dream as an Investigative Tool," in *Essential Papers on Dreams.* Ed. Melvin R. Lansky. New York and London: New York University Press, 477–96.

———. (1996). "Instigation in Freud's Dreams: Implications for the Understanding of Conflict." Unpublished manuscript.

Leiris, Michel. (1987). *Nights as Day, Days as Night.* Trans. Richard Sieburth. Hygiene, Colo.: Eridanos Press.

Lévi-Strauss, Claude. (1966). *The Savage Mind.* Chicago: University of Chicago Press.

Llinás, R. R., and D. Paré. (1991). "Of Dreaming and Wakefulness," *Neuroscience* 44 (no. 3), 521–35.

Llinás, R. R., and U. Ribary. (1993). "Coherent 40-Hz Oscillation Characterizes Dream State in Humans," *Proceedings of the National Academy of Sciences* 90.

Loewald, Hans W. (1988). *Sublimation: Inquiries into Theoretical Psychoanalysis.* New Haven and London: Yale University Press.

Macherey, Pierre. (1978). *A Theory of Literary Production.* Trans. Geoffrey Wall. London: Routledge & Kegan Paul.

Mahony, Patrick J. (1987). *Freud as a Writer*. New Haven and London: Yale University Press.

Malcolm, Norman. (1959). *Dreaming*. London: Routledge & Kegan Paul.

Matte Blanco, Ignacio. (1975). *The Unconscious as Infinite Sets: An Essay in Bi-Logic*. London: Duckworth.

McGinn, Colin. (1995). "Left-over Life to Live," a review of Daniel Dennett's *Darwin's Dangerous Idea*. *Times Literary Supplement* (Nov. 24), 3-4.

Merleau-Ponty, Maurice. (1963). *The Structure of Behavior*. Trans. Alden L. Fisher. Boston: Beacon Press.

———. (1964). *The Primacy of Perception and Other Essays on Phenomenological Psychology, the Philosophy of Art, History and Politics*. Trans. Carleton Dallery. Ed. James M. Edie. Evanston, Ill.: Northwestern University Press.

———. (1978). *The Phenomenology of Perception*. Trans. Colin Smith. London: Routledge & Kegan Paul.

Minsky, Marvin. (1988). *The Society of Mind*. New York: Simon & Schuster.

Nagel, Thomas. (1974). "What Is It Like to Be a Bat?" *Philosophical Review* 83 (October), 435-50.

Natanson, Maurice. (1974). "Solipsism and Sociality," *New Literary History* 5, 237-44.

Nielsen, Tore A., and Russell A. Powell. (1992). "The Day-Residue and Dream-Lag Effects: A Literature Review and Limited Replication of Two Temporal Effects in Dream Formation," *Dreaming* 2 (no. 2), 67-77.

Ornstein, Robert. (1991). *The Evolution of Consciousness: Of Darwin, Freud, and Cranial Fire: The Origins of the Way We Think*. New York: Prentice-Hall.

Overstreet, David. (1980). "Oxymoronic Language and Logic in Quantum Mechanics and James Joyce," *Sub-Stance* 28, 37-59.

Penrose, Roger. (1991). *The Emperor's New Mind: Concerning Computers, Minds, and the Laws of Physics*. New York and London: Penguin.

Peyser, Herbert. (1994). "The Unknown Freud: An Exchange." *New York Review of Books* (Feb. 3), 35.

Plato. (1937). *The Dialogues of Plato*. Vol. 2. Trans. B. Jowett. New York: Random House.

Poetzl, O. (1917). "The Relationship Between Experimentally Induced Dream Images and Indirect Vision." Monograph no. 7, *Psychological Issues* 2, 41-120, 1960.

Rechtschaffen, Allan. (1978). "The Single-Mindedness and Isolation of Dreams," *Sleep* 1, 97-109.

Richards, I. A. (1976). *The Philosophy of Rhetoric*. Oxford: Oxford University Press.

Richardson, Maurice. (1972). *The Fascination of Reptiles*. New York: Hill and Wang.

Richter, Jean Paul. (1973). *Horn of Oberon: Jean Paul Richter's* School for Aesthetics. Trans. Margaret R. Hale. Detroit: Wayne State University Press.

Roffenstein, Gaston. (1951). "Experiments on Symbolization in Dreams," in *Organization and Psychology of Thought: Selected Sources.* Trans. and ed. David Rapaport. New York: Columbia University Press, 249–56.

Rose, Mark. (1996). "Mothers and Authors: *Johnson v. Calvert* and the New Children of Our Imaginations," in press.

Rose, Steven. (1993). *The Making of Memory, from Molecules to Mind.* New York: Doubleday.

Rosenfield, Israel. (1988). *The Invention of Memory: A New View of the Brain.* New York: Basic Books.

Rycroft, Charles. (1979). *The Innocence of Dreams.* New York: Pantheon.

Sartre, Jean-Paul. (1966). *Being and Nothingness: A Phenomenological Essay on Ontology.* Trans. Hazel E. Barnes. New York: Washington Square Press.

———. (1968). *The Psychology of Imagination.* Trans. Bernard Frechtman. New York: Washington Square Press.

Schank, Roger C. (1986). *Dynamic Memory: A Theory of Reminding and Learning in Computers and People.* Cambridge: Cambridge University Press.

Schroetter, Karl. (1951). "Experimental Dreams," in *Organization and Psychology of Thought: Selected Sources.* Trans. and ed. David Rapaport. New York: Columbia University Press, 234–48.

Searle, J. R. (1986). "Metaphor," in *Metaphor and Thought.* Ed. Andrew Ortony. Cambridge: Cambridge University Press, 92–123.

Segal, Hanna. (1992). "The Function of Dreams," in *Essential Papers on Dreams.* Ed. Melvin R. Lansky. New York and London: New York University Press, 239–48.

Shelley, Percy Bysshe. (1890). *A Defense of Poetry.* Ed. Albert S. Cook. Boston: Ginn and Company.

Shklovsky, Victor. (1965). "Art as Technique," in *Russian Formalist Criticism: Four Essays.* Trans. Lee T. Lemon and Marion J. Reis. Lincoln and London: University of Nebraska Press.

Silberer, Herbert. (1951). "On Symbol-Formation," in *Organization and Psychology of Thought: Selected Sources.* Trans. and ed. David Rapaport. New York: Columbia University Press, 208–33.

Skarda, Christine A., and Walter J. Freeman. (1990). "Chaos and the New Science of the Brain," *Concepts in Neuroscience* 1 (2), 275–85.

Sparshott, Francis. (1983). "Preservation, Projection, and Presence: Preliminaries to a Consideration of Pictorial Representation," in *Essays in Aesthetics: Perspectives on the Work of Monroe C. Beardsley.* Ed. John Fisher. Philadelphia: Temple University Press, 131–46.

States, Bert O. (1985). *Great Reckonings in Little Rooms: On the Phenomenology of Theater.* Berkeley and Los Angeles: University of California Press.

———. (1988). *The Rhetoric of Dreams.* Ithaca: Cornell University Press.

———. (1992). "Tragedy and Tragic Vision: A Darwinian Supplement to Thomas Van Laan," *Journal of Dramatic Theory and Criticism* 6, 5-22.

———. (1993). *Dreaming and Storytelling.* Ithaca and London: Cornell University Press.

———. (1994). *The Pleasure of the Play.* Ithaca and London: Cornell University Press.

Steiner, George. (1983). "The Historicity of Dreams (Two Questions to Freud)," *Salmagundi* (Fall), 6-21.

Stekel, Wilhelm. (1967). *The Interpretation of Dreams: New Developments and Technique.* Trans. Eden and Cedar Paul. New York: Washington Square Press.

Stolorow, Robert D., and George E. Atwood. (1992). "Dreams and the Subjective World," in *Essential Papers on Dreams.* Ed. Melvin R. Lansky. New York and London: New York University Press, 272-84.

Strunz, Franz. (1993). "Preconscious Mental Activity and Scientific Problem-Solving: A Critique of the Kekulé Dream Controversy," *Dreaming* 3 (no. 4), 281-94.

Sylvester, David. (1975). *Interviews with Francis Bacon.* London: Thames and Hudson.

Tallis, Raymond. (1991). *The Explicit Animal: A Defence of Human Consciousness.* New York: Macmillan.

Thomas, Lewis. (1975). *The Lives of a Cell.* New York: Bantam.

Thurston, Mark. (1988). *Dreams: Tonight's Answers for Tomorrow's Questions.* San Francisco: Harper & Row.

Traherne, Thomas. (1958). *Centuries, Poems, and Thanksgivings, II.* Ed. H. M. Margoliouth. Oxford: Clarendon Press.

Ullman, Montague. (1995a). "Book Review: *Crisis Dreaming* by Rosalind Cartwright and Lynne Lamberg," *Dreaming* 5 (no. 1), 57-60.

———. (1995b). "Dreams as Exceptional Human Experiences," *Dream Network* 14 (no. 4), 28-45.

Weiss, Joseph. (1992). "Dreams and Their Various Purposes," in *Essential Papers on Dreams.* Ed. Melvin R. Lansky. New York and London: New York University Press, 213-35.

Whitmont, Edward C., and Sylvia B. Perera. (1989). *Dreams, a Portal to the Source.* London and New York: Routledge.

Wilbur, Richard. (1950). *Ceremony and Other Poems.* New York: Harcourt, Brace.

Wilshire, Bruce. (1982). *Role Playing and Identity: The Limits of Theatre as Metaphor.* Bloomington: Indiana University Press.

Winson, Jonathan. (1985). *Brain and Psyche: The Biology of the Unconscious.* Garden City, N.Y.: Doubleday.

Wittgenstein, Ludwig. (1966). *Lectures and Conversations on Aesthetics, Psychology, and Religious Beliefs.* Ed. Cyril Barrett. Oxford: Blackwell.

———. (1968). *Philosophical Investigations.* Trans. G. E. M. Anscombe. New York: Macmillan.

Zadra, Antonio L., D. C. Donderi, and Robert O. Pihl. (1992). "Efficacy of Lucid Dream Induction for Lucid and Non-Lucid Dreamers," *Dreaming* 2 (no. 2), 85–97.

Index

Adaptive theory of dreams (Weiss), 21–22

Agnosia, visual, 95

Alquié, F., on surrealism, 128

Ambiguity: of dream image, 203–04; Empson on, 203–04

Ambivalence, 230–31, 244; and ambiguity, 204

Ammons, A. R., 34–35

Animal dreams, 2; Jouvet's cat experiments, 20–21, 219

Arcaya, Jose M., on memory, 101–02

Archetypal dreams, 224–26

Aristotle, on Greek tragedy, 44–45

Arnheim, Rudolf: on role of context in perception, 126; on meaning, 236; on the symbol, 151

Art, purpose of (Horace), 1–2

Associative memory, 16, 29, 52–54

Associative thinking, 9, 26–27, 34–35, 102–09 passim, 117–31 passim, 154, 157, 175, 176, 180, 181, 192. *See also* Metaphor; Metonymy

Atwood, George E., 14–15*n,* 23*n,* 135*n,* 147*n*

Augustine, St., on time, 8–9

Authorship: in dreams, 4, 90; in dreams and fictions, 92–93, 190–211; and reading, 202; in waking state, 199

Bacon, Francis (painter), 124–25

Barrett, Deirdre, 71–72*n*

Binocular rivalry (Humphrey), 121

Biological aspect of dreams, 1–4, 10. *See also* Dawkins

Bizarreness in dreams, 103, 122, 125–28 passim, 203–04, 224. *See also*

Associative thinking; Metaphor; Metonymic deflection

Blagrove, Mark, on problem solving in dreams, 56–57, 60

Blanchot, Maurice, on sleep, 19

Bollas, Christopher, on day residue, 177–78

Borges, Jorge Luis, and Chinese encyclopedia, 29–30, 118

Boss, Medard, on dream experience, 80–81

Boyd, Richard, 152

Brain-mind problem, 38, 75–76; Churchland on, 76; Dennett on, 76

Büchner, Georg, *Danton's Death,* 189, 191

Burke, Kenneth: on "associational clusters," 46; on "cooperative competition," 39–40; as Darwinist, 39–41; on metaphor, 153; on Shakespeare, 40

Burton, Maurice, 59

Calderón de la Barca, 189

Carlson, Marvin, 29*n*

Cassette theory of dreams (Dennett), 214–22

Catastrophic expectancy, 228. *See also* Maximization of Magnitude

Cathartic function of dreams, 29*n*

Censorship and dreams, 5, 15–16, 135, 142–67 passim, 241; Freud on, 50–51, 63, 174–75, 177; Sartre's critique of, 16, 50; unfalsifiability of theory of, 51

Cézanne, Paul, 7, 9

Chain thinking, 190; Minsky on, 34. *See also* Metaphor; Metonymy